A-Z
ACCOUNTING

A-Z ACCOUNTING

Sandeep Sharma

CENTRUM PRESS
NEW DELHI-110002 (INDIA)

CENTRUM PRESS
H.O.: 4360/4, Ansari Road, Daryaganj,
New Delhi-110 002 (India)
Ph.: 23278000, 23261597
B.O.: No. 1015, Ist Main Road, BSK IIIrd Stage
IIIrd Phase, IIIrd Block,
Bangalore - 560 085 (India)
Tel.: 080-41723429
Visit us at: www.centrumpress.com

A-Z Accounting

First Edition, 2009
ISBN 978-93-80106-45-8

PRINTED IN INDIA

Printed at Salasar Imaging Systems, Delhi-110035 (India)

Contents

Preface

A-Z Accounting is designed to supply information to internal decision makers of a given organization, to facilitate their decision making, to motivate their actions and behaviour in a desirable direction, and to promote the efficiency of the organization. It is accounting based and individual, organization, strategy, problem, and decision-centered. An understanding of each of these foundations may allow the management accountant to design a management accounting system more responsive to the diverse needs and demands emanating from within and without the organization. Each of these chapters is that a failure to grasp any of these conceptual foundations of management accounting may result in deficiencies in the management accounting systems and inadequacies in the provision of the diverse services required by both the small and the complex organizations of today.

This book should be of interest to a variety of reader groups, including researchers in the management accounting area and accounting practitioners interested in the careful design of a management accounting system. This book can also be useful as additional material for a typical undergraduate or graduate course in management accounting. The student in management accounting should be aware not only of the new multidimensional scope of the field but also of the conceptual foundations that justify this extended scope. Most management accounting texts do not introduce and integrate all these foundations and are generally restricted to an exposition of cost accounting techniques.

Author

Chapter 1

Managerial Accounting

The set of techniques and thought to which devoted is usually referred to as *managerial accounting*. Managerial accounting is that branch of accounting thought and practice concerned with providing information that is useful to decision makers within the enterprise in making decisions related to the deployment of resources and exploitation of enterprise opportunities.

It should be emphasized that the boundaries of managerial accounting are not rigid. Managerial accounting has in common with financial accounting a focus on the enterprise and its activities. It differs in the sense that it serves a class of decision makers whose decision interests are generally different from those of the decision makers served by financial accounting. In addition, many of the decision models that have evolved for management use and for which accountants supply the necessary information inputs have been developed within the disciplines of managerial economics and managerial finance.

These decision models are often described as part of managerial accounting because it is necessary to understand management decision models in order to supply decision-relevant information.

Finally, it is becoming more and more widely recognized that business organizations operate through the coordinated efforts of human beings. Hence, success of most management decisions hinges on motivating the individuals involved to conduct their activities in a manner most consistent with the objective of the decision. The study of the interactions of individuals within organizations has for some time been important to the design of management accounting systems. Since the tools for such study have been developed in the behavioural sciences, the accounting discipline has increasingly embraced the behavioural sciences as a source for improved research and practice.

MANAGERIAL AND SOCIAL ACCOUNTING

INFORMATION FOR MANAGEMENT DECISIONS

Most introductory accounting texts examine questions of *what, why, how,* and *for whom* of financial accounting information. The intellectual, practical, institutional, and other considerations surrounding accounting information about business enterprises that is provided to external decision makers. Against this background we undertake a brief excursion into the realm of enterprise-related accounting information for use by a different set of decision makers-the management of the enterprise. Our purpose is to introduce the reader to several important classes of management decisions and to illustrate the kinds of accounting information that support each.

The Role of the Accountant in the Business Enterprise

When we refer to the accountant's role in a business enterprise, we are not thinking of all those individuals engaged in the management of the enterprise who, by virtue of their training or experience, can properly call themselves accountants. Rather we are referring to those relatively few who, at the moment, are actually engaged in producing accounting information for the use of others. It is this specialized role or function, not the individual who performs it, that we can usefully circumscribe.

In a functional sense, the accountant's role in supplying information for internal decision makers is much like the accountant's role in providing information to external parties. He does not engage in the decision choice itself. Instead, he participates in the earlier stages of the decision-making process, usually by providing information about alternatives for the consideration of decision makers. To the extent possible, the accountant maintains a detached attitude so as to avoid biasing the information provided in favour of any particular alternative. Otherwise he preempts the decision maker's role to some extent.

But this does not mean that the accountant cannot perform part of the evaluation stage of the decision process in addition to supplying basic information or alternatives. When he participates in the internal decision-making process, the accountant enjoys a closer relationship with the decision maker than is the case in financial accounting. Hence, the decision maker and the accountant can engage in a two-way "give-and-take" process until the accountant has a better understanding of the decision maker's decision model and information wants. As a result, the information provided in managerial accounting is often in fairly adequate final form for making choices between alternatives. This is less feasible in financial accounting.

LONG-RUN MANAGEMENT DECISIONS

To pursue our purpose of describing distinguishable classes of management decisions and related types of accounting information, it is useful to discuss first the objectives and constraints faced by management. The value of this approach is that, in general, different classes of management decisions can be identified with specific types of objectives and constraints.

The key to differences in types of objectives and constraints characterizing particular decision situations is, in turn, often explainable in relation to the time span of enterprise activities that will be influenced by the decision choice. One usually finds it helpful to separate management activities and decisions into long-run and short-run categories.

Long-run decisions: Long-run decisions are defined as those decisions whose outcomes commit the enterprise or directly influence its activities for many future periods. The long run is thought of as a span of time sufficiently long that a significant project or programme of the enterprise can be planned, implemented, and run its course. Short-run Short-run decisions are defined as decisions whose outcomes commit the enterprise or directly influence its actions for perhaps only one year at most. The latitude available in selecting alternatives in the short run is restricted considerably by the commitments made by the enterprise in past long-run decisions.

Long-run Objectives. From an accounting perspective, a business enterprise in a market economy is best seen in terms of a sequence of economic operations. Usually, the enterprise starts with an endowment of cash, its money capital, constituting a claim against resources, products, and services available in the economy. The enterprise expends a portion of that cash to acquire resources and uses those resources in the production of products or services. The products or services, in turn, are sold to other economic units that at some point remit cash to the enterprise in exchange. The new cash flows renew the enterprise's ability to acquire the same or different resources for employment in further production of products and services.

In this process there is usually a division of the enabling economic function, the enterprise function. Owners and creditors supply the necessary capital. Management identifies the most promising opportunities to provide products and services; it acquires, organizes, and directs the necessary resources to exploit identified opportunities. The contribution of suppliers of capital and the contribution of management complement each other.

Each group identified presumably provides a unique opportunity for the other through the organizational unit, the business enterprise. Each group will presumably wish to withdraw its resources from the relationship if other opportunities appear more attractive. The implication of this possibility for management is significant.

Profit Maximization. If it is expected that the enterprise will fail to earn returns for the suppliers of money capital that are at least equal to what they can earn in other opportunities of comparable risk, the enterprise will not attract the necessary money capital to function. If the enterprise consistently fails to produce products and services whose values exceed the costs of resources used, it will actually dissipate its money capital and jeopardize its ability to survive.

In either case, the opportunity for management to use its talents to the fullest is dimished by the faltering supply of money capital at the disposal of the enterprise. The best insurance against such a situation is for management to pursue a long-run objective of maximizing the value of the excess of the cash flows received for products and services provided to customers over the cash expended for resources used. Only in this way can management ensure that sufficient money capital will be available to maximize its own opportunities to employ its talents. This basic goal of management is often referred to as the profit maximization goal.

Profit Maximization and Other Goals. Long-run profit maximization is the preeminent goal of business enterprises in a market economy. But note the emphasis on "long-run." The statement would be shortsighted without that emphasis and would be contrary to the current stated policies of most significant business organizations. Those policies often include such goals as

- Betterment of employee morale,
- Employee education and training,
- Protection of the environment,
- Improved product quality,
- Community service, or
- Contribution to basic research in a particular field.

In the short run, one would expect such goals to conflict frequently with the pursuit of maximum profits. But clearly all are related, or rather *necessary,* to achieve maximum profits in the long run. So, if a very broad view of long-run profitability is taken, then the single goal of long-run profit maximization generally embraces all so-called *other* goals.

Constraints on Long-run Decisions. In the long run, management can conceivably alter virtually every aspect of a business, including its own (management's) composition. A distinguishing feature of long-run decisions is that they are relatively free from internally imposed constraints. Nevertheless, because long-run decisions (commitments) must be made as of a point in time, certain externally imposed constraints apply-at least in part.

Among the largely externally imposed constraints on long-run decisions are the laws and customs of society, the state of technology, the size of the population and labour force, worldwide and local supplies of natural resources, and so forth, which exist at the time of decision. Of course, some of these constraints can be influenced to some degree by an individual enterprise; for example, the passage of a new law may be the result of lobbying efforts on the part of business, or changes in the customs of society may be influenced by advertising campaigns. But in general, as of the time of any given long-run decision, external constraints impose some limitation on the enterprise.

Although externally imposed constraints affect each enterprise to varying degrees, there are two specific constraints on long-run decisions that are usually unique to each individual enterprise. First, at a given point in time, each enterprise faces a limited number of long-run opportunities that it can effectively exploit because of its location, its prior activities, and the composition of its management.

Second, each enterprise faces a limited supply of money capital with which to embark on alternative long-run courses of action. Although, as with the constraints mentioned above, management can alter these two restrictions in the long run, the alterations themselves may require the immediate commitment of scarce money capital and take some time to effect. Hence, at any given decision point, long-run alternatives are restricted by these two limitations.

Long-run Management Decisions and Related Accounting Information

Given the long-run profit maximization objective, the long-run success of the enterprise (management) hinges on management's ability to identify and implement the most promising product lines, projects, and programs within the enterprise's capabilities and its environmental and money-capital limitations. The first requisite to success is active seeking of opportunities, either to provide new and better products or services or to develop new and better means of production.

The former requires involvement, at least at some minimal level, in research into present markets and consumer (or industrial) preferences, plus product development research. The latter requires at least some involvement with industrial engineering as well as organizational, institutional, and behavioural research. All of these are essentially information-seeking activities contributed by specialists other than accountants. The contribution of accountants comes into play in another important requisite to long-run success of the enterprise-the selection of the most promising set from among the identified alternatives.

Capital-Budgeting Decisions. The essential feature of long-run opportunities (alternatives) is that they usually require considerable initial outlays of the enterprise's limited money capital for implementation. Initial outlays include expenditures for such things as long-lived assets to be employed in the programme, legal fees, and further costs of developmental and organizational research.

Over many future periods, related additional outlays are required to produce benefits in the form of cash inflows or lower total outlays than the programs they replace. Since long-run programs generally require outlays of scarce money capital, the process of selecting the best set of alternatives is usually referred to as capital budgeting.

Capital budgeting: Capital budgeting is the process of choosing the best set from among the available long-run opportunities requiring significant outlays of money capital.

The Accounting Role in Capital Budgeting

Choosing the best set from available long-run opportunities requires that each opportunity be evaluated with respect to the long-run objective of the enterprise. We have already noted that the objective of management in the long run is to maximize the excess of cash receipts for products and services over cash outlays for resources used in production. We have also noted, however, that most long-run programs involve initial outlays of cash to get started, followed by many periods of additional outflows and inflows.

Thus it is clear that in order to evaluate the desirability of long-run alternatives, some model is necessary that permits the decision maker to compare cash inflows and outflows of many future periods. One such model is the present value model, which converts cash flows of disparate time periods into their equivalent values in cash as of the time of decision.

The attractiveness to management of a long-run programme, project, or product line ultimately hinges on its real economic features, that is, the physical capabilities, quality, and demand for a product; the kinds and quantities of resources required to carry out a programme; and the kind of organization structure and production techniques required for implementation. Such information, as noted earlier, comes from nonaccounting sources such as marketing personnel, industrial engineers, and organization development specialists. The role of the accountant in bringing these relevant economic attributes of an alternative into focus for management is to translate them into the cash inflows and outflows that they imply for present and future periods.

Example: Shoosh Ski Company has manufactured a well-known line of quality fiberglass skis for the last ten years. The company was one of the first to experiment with fiberglass skis and as a result of early technical gains has become very successful. Of late, however, the company faces a threat to its long-run success. Many competitors have entered the market, and the competition has reduced Shoosh's prospects for continued increases in its sales of skis.

The president of the company has been very unhappy with the prospect of a declining share of the market. In searching for alternatives, she has concluded that whereas many competitors make finished skis, few suppliers can produce high-quality metal edges used in making skis. Shoosh

Company, however, has the know-how to do the job. But to make the edges for sale to other ski manufacturers, Shoosh Company will need an immediate factory and equipment expansion that will have a ten-year life, costing $120,000, with no salvage value in the end. The company has enough money to pay for the expansion. But is it worth diverting the $120,000 from other possible uses in order to begin production of the new product?

The president understands the concept of present value and intends to use it in her decision. She has already determined that the company can invest the $120,000 in projects of risk equal to that of the plant expansion and receive an annual rate of interest of 10 percent. She therefore reasons that unless the present value (at 10 percent) of the net cash inflows from the production and sale of edges equals or exceeds $120,000, that is, unless the *net* present value (at 10 percent) of the factory expansion is equal to or greater than zero, the project is not worth implementing. With that she turns the project over to the company accountant, who must now provide the necessary information to value the choice.

The first step in determining the net present value of the factory expansion is estimation of the future cash inflows and outflows associated with the project. Unfortunately, in practice no one is going to tell the accountant directly what these amounts are going to be, except for the initial outlay of $120,000. Instead he has to work with the sales manager, production engineer, plant manager, and others who will plan and control the new manufacturing operation in order to determine what new cash inflows and outflows to expect from the operation.

First he approaches the sales manager and requests estimates of how many pairs of edges will be sold and at what price in each of the next ten years. The sales manager estimates that $30 would be a competitive price for the edges (per pair). At that price he estimates that on the average 5,000 pairs of edges can be sold each year for the next ten years.

Meanwhile the production engineer has determined the quantities of material, labour, and miscellaneous other resources required for production in addition to the new factory facilities. He estimates the following resource requirements:

Materials: Each pair of edges requires a 10' × 1/8" × 3/16" bar of cold rolled steel alloy.

Manufacturing labour: Two hours of skilled labour will be required in total to complete each pair of edges.

Other costs-annual:Supervisor's salary Cleanup, repairs, and maintenance Insurance, taxes, etc.

With the information based on physical production plans, the accountant turns to the personnel manager and the purchasing agent to determine the cash costs of the production requirements for the edges. He estimates the *annual* net cash inflow from production and sales of the edges.

The accountant then presents the company president with decisionready information relevant to the factory expansion. Assuming that the president has confidence in the accountant's ability to gather the necessary information and make the necessarily uncertain projections of cash flows as well or better than anyone else in the organization, she will undertake the plant expansion, since it has a positive net present value of $15,080.

Example: brings into focus two important aspects of all managerial activity. First, it illustrates an important feature of the accountant's role in the business enterprise, alluded to earlier. Notice that the accountant has actually prepared a ready-made decision value for the decision maker, that is, the net present value of the decision alternative. Recall that we noted earlier that there usually is (or should be) a close working relationship between the accountant and an internal decision maker.

As a result, the decision maker can communicate to the accountant features of his specific decision model, including such things as the time preference rate that he feels is appropriate for discounting the expected cash flows from a particular project, to which the accountant does not have access in the case of external parties. Hence, at the discretion of the decision maker, the managerial accountant may perform not only the information-gathering step in the decision process but parts of the problem definition and evaluation steps as well. It is important to note, however, that as more of the decision process is assumed by the accountant, the risk increases that the accountant will intentionally or unintentionally introduce his own biases into the decision. The accountant should of course maintain a detached attitude insofar as possible. But the decision maker should nevertheless be aware of this risk in determining the degree to which decision responsibility is delegated to the accountant.

The second important aspect of managerial accounting (also alluded to earlier) is the managerial accountant's responsibility as a translator. Since the management of the enterprise is almost always interested in the effects of the decisions on cash flows, an important part of the managerial accounting function is the translation of the resource flows connected with a product, project, or programme into financial or money flow implications. One of the most general sets of skills or tools employed by managerial accountants to execute their role as translators is *cost behaviour analysis*, a set of techniques described in the following section.

ANALYSIS AND USE OF COST (AND REVENUE) BEHAVIOUR PATTERNS

The discovery and application of cost and revenue behaviour patterns are relevant in producing information for all types of management decisions. Hence it is appropriate that we turn next to some discussion of this important topic. The introduction to long-run management decisions and the related accounting contribution provides the context in which to examine the application of cost behaviour patterns.

Cost Behaviour Analysis: A Flexible Tool

As noted earlier, an important task in managerial accounting is the association of financial (money) flows with the resource flows that are expected from various decision alternatives. One very general concept employed in performing this task is the *concept of cost* (the "cost principle" in conventional financial accounting is a special application of the concept of cost): Cost: A cost is a resource sacrifice, usually measured in money terms, *associated* with a particular decision alternative, for example, conduct of an activity, production of a product, acquisition of a resource, or operation of an organization.

Costs measured in money terms are associated with various kinds of management decision alternatives in order to evaluate the alternatives in the context of the long-run goal of the enterprise, that is, profit maximization. The basis of association of costs with particular decision alternatives is usually cost behaviour patterns derived through cost behaviour analysis.

Cost behaviour pattern: A cost behaviour pattern is a functional relationship between various activities or events that represent a decision alternative and the cost that is expected to be incurred in connection with that alternative.

Cost behaviour analysis: Cost behaviour analysis is the process of discerning and describing forms of cost behaviour patterns.

Basic Types of Cost Behaviour Patterns: Experience in discerning cost behaviour patterns in practice has led accountants to expect certain recurring patterns. The simplest, most frequently encountered, and most easily recognized patterns of cost behaviour are the patterns we refer to as *fixed* and *variable* costs.

Fixed costs: Fixed costs are costs whose amounts do not change regardless of the level of enterprise activity (within certain limits called the relevant range).

Relevant range: The relevant range is that *range of activity* within which the level of actual activity is expected to occur in the normal course of events.

Spectrum Sales Company is planning a new sales territory. It is considering opening a new branch sales office. Activities will start with one salesman; additional sales staff will be added when monthly sales exceed $20,000 per salesman. But the territory will not grow beyond a staff of five salesmen, since it is company policy to split off a new territory at that point. If the new territory is opened, office space sufficient to accommodate a secretary and from one to five salesmen will be rented. The monthly rent for the office will be $500 regardless of how many people use it. Thus, within the relevant range of activity for the new sales territory, the monthly cost of rent is a fixed cost.

The pattern inherent in fixed costs. On the horizontal axis is measured the level of activity in terms of monthly sales dollars (in thousands) for the territory. (The maximum of $100,000 is determined by a maximum of five salesmen at $20,000 each before a new territory is split off.) On the vertical axis is the level of monthly rent cost. The horizontal line at a level of $500 above the horizontal axis shows that within the relevant range of $0 to $100,000 sales, rent cost is invariant (fixed) with respect to activity.

Fixed-Cost Behaviour Pattern

Variable costs can exhibit a variety of patterns but they all have a common definitional characteristic:

Variable costs: Variable costs are costs whose amounts increase as activity increases and decrease as activity decreases—though not necessarily proportionately. If Spectrum Sales Company opens its new territory, it intends to compensate its sales staff with salaries plus commissions of 5 percent of sales dollars.

Monthly commission costs therefore vary proportionately with the level of sales dollars. If sales are $20,000 per month, sales commissions will be $1,000 (.05 X $20,000). If sales double to $40,000, sales commissions also double to $2,000 (.05 X $40,000).

Although many kinds of variable costs actually vary proportionately, not all variable costs behave in this way. For example, if an activity doubles but the related variable cost increases less than double, we say it varies with the activity at a decreasing rate. If a cost more than doubles as activity doubles, we say it varies with activity at an increasing rate. The three patterns. Many variations in cost behaviour lie between the simple extremes of strictly variable and strictly fixed costs. Although it is not our intention to be exhaustive, it might interest the reader to see some additional patterns that have been suggested to describe other frequently encountered types of cost behaviour.

Discerning Cost Behaviour Patterns. One of the great challenges of managerial accounting is to discover the behaviour of various costs with respect to activities that are of concern in managerial decisions. Although many cost behaviour patterns are rather obvious, others are not clear or intuitively obvious at all.

Example: In manufacturing its product, Stunning Beauty Company uses one pound of material at $2 per pound for every unit of product produced. Thus material costs vary proportionately with total activity measured in units of product produced. Maintenance costs, on the other hand, do not seem to obey any such strict rule.

Some kinds of maintenance requirements are necessary from time to time regardless of the level of activity, but they do not seem to occur at regular intervals. Other kinds of maintenance requirements occur regularly and increase with activity but not proportionately. All in all, specification of the expected behaviour of maintenance costs with respect to activity is considerably more difficult than specifying the expected behaviour.

In discerning patterns of cost behaviour, particularly nonobvious patterns, accountants typically use one (or all) of the following techniques:

- Construction of cost behaviour schedules from engineering or production specifications of a product or process
- Analysis of past cost data to discern evident patterns
- Experience with cost behaviour of similar products or processes in the past, plus judgment and intuition

Within the limits of time and other resources available for cost analysis, accountants generally prefer more objective and scientific approaches (number 1 and some techniques embraced by number 2) rather than resorting strictly to experience, judgment, or intuition.

Applying Cost Behaviour Patterns to Decision Problems

How are cost behaviour patterns used in managerial decision making? First the cost behaviour implications of various activities and events are used to construct an overall cost function for a decision alternative or decision variable. Then the cost function (usually together with a revenue function) is manipulated to generate decision-relevant information about the alternative or variable.

Since managerial decision making often focuses on the production and sales of products and services, accountants are frequently concerned with using cost behaviour patterns to supply information for production-sales decisions. This type of application has the special label of *cost-volume-profit analysis* (sometimes called *break-even analysis*). Cost-volume-profit analysis is so frequently used in practice that it is a most appropriate context for acquainting the reader with the application of cost behaviour patterns.

Constructing Cost and Revenue Functions: The accountant's role in a long-run capital-budgeting decision (new product line) with Example Shoosh Ski Company). That capital-budgeting decision involved determination of the net present value of the set of future cash flows associated with production and sale of the proposed product over a ten-year period. Most of the accountant's task involved estimation of the annual costs and benefits (cash outflows and inflows) from production and sales of the product.

Then, since the president of the company had already specified the appropriate time preference rate for the risk involved, the stream of annual net cash inflows was discounted and compared with the initial outlay.

Though highly simplified, the example served to illustrate how the accountant constructed from various physical production, sales, and price data the annual net cash inflow to be expected from the product. But many potential benefits of that construction were ignored at the time. By returning to the basic situation described in Example, we can elaborate the further potential that recognition and use of cost behaviour patterns offer.

Example: Suppose that after the accountant prepared the net present value of the new product line (edges) for Shoosh Ski Company, the president changed her mind about the appropriateness of the 10 percent discount rate. The president had some misgivings about her original assessment of risk associated with the new product line and asked a number of questions about the annual net cash to be expected for the coming ten years. Some of her questions were as follows:

- Suppose a presently unknown competitor enters the market at the same time we do, and we end up splitting annual sales right down the middle, that is, 2,500 pairs of edges per year each?
- How low can our annual sales be without cash outflows exceeding cash inflows from sales in any given year?
- By how much can we lower selling price to sustain sales at 5,000 pairs of edges in any given year and still not experience losses (net cash outflows) in that year?

The accountant for Shoosh is chagrined by all these questions. He thought he had done a good job of satisfying the president's original request, but now he feels he has to retrace all of his steps to answer this barrage of questions. How could the accountant have avoided his chagrin? These types of questions are very common. Therefore, it is usually worthwhile to be prepared for them by making certain assumptions and constructing (or specifying) revenue, cost, and profit (net cash flow) functions in advance and stating them in terms (variables) of interest to management. To do this in the case of production-sales-type situations, accountants make certain simplifying assumptions on which they often base uncomplicated but useful revenue, cost, and profit functions. Typical simplifying assumptions include the following:

- Within the relevant range virtually all costs can be classified into the two simple behaviour categories of *fixed* and *variable.*
- Variable costs vary (approximately) proportionately with activity.
- A short-run analysis (typically no more than one

year) is sufficient to encompass all significant consequences of decisions to be made.

- All sales are for cash (or there is no net buildup of accounts receivable during the period), meaning that revenue and cash inflow from sales are approximately equal.
- All products produced are sold (or no net buildup of inventory takes place), so that production activity (in units of product) approximately equals sales activity.
- All units sold, within the relevant range, in any given period will be sold at the same price.

The Simplified Cost-Volume-Profit Model: On the basis of assumptions such as the foregoing, the accountant can formulate simplified revenue, cost, and profit functions. For instance, based on assumption number 6 above, the total revenue (*TR*) for a period will equal the number of units sold (q) times the price per unit (p).

Similarly, based on assumptions 1 and 2, total cost (*TC*) will equal the sum of a fixed component (f) and a proportionate variable component equal to the number of units produced and sold (q) times the per-unit variable cost (v). Profit or net cash flow represented by p will equal total revenue minus total cost. These simple relationships can be represented symbolically.

Basic Cost-Volume-Profit Relationships

$$TR = pq$$

$$TC = vq + f$$

$$\pi = TR - TC$$

substituting Equation for *TR* and Equation for *TC* in Equation, we get

$$\pi = pq - (vq + f)$$

$$\pi = pq - vq - f$$

Cost-Volume-Profit Analysis. The advantage of the cost-volume-profit model, provided the six assumptions are approximately applicable to the individual situation, the accountant can answer a wide variety of management questions.The value of any one of the model variables in a given situation can be found by solving Equation after determining the values of the other variables for that situation.

Example: Suppose, for instance, that the Shoosh Company accountant had been alert to cost behaviour patterns when he estimated the annual net cash inflow from production and sales of the new product line. He found that the material and labour costs per pair of edges were $4 and $16, respectively. Suppose that he had then checked with the production engineer and found that those per-unit costs would apply for production levels from 2,000 to 6,000 pairs of edges per year. The other production costs, including the $10,000 supervisory salary, $15,000 cleanup and maintenance, and $3,000 insurance, taxes, and so forth, would remain the same as long as actual production activity fell within that range.

Similarly, suppose the sales manager, upon inquiry, had confirmed that all sales in any given year would be made at the same price, that is, no preferential prices would be quoted to any customer. He had estimated earlier that $30 would be a competitive price for a pair of edges. If the accountant had thus been alert to the general expected patterns of behaviour of costs and revenues associated with the new product line, he could have readily answered the president's three questions as follows:

- If a competitor enters the market for edges at the same time Shoosh enters and halves Shoosh sales to 2,500 pairs per year, Shoosh will experience an annual net cash outflow of $3,000, calculated as follows:
  p = \$30; v = \$20; q = 2,500; f = \$28,000
  Solve for
  π
  $\pi = pq - vq - f$
  π = (\$30 – 2,500) – (\$20 2,500) – \$28,000 π = \$75,000 – \$50,000 – \$28,000
  π = \$75,000 – \$78,000
  π = – \$3,000
- Sales have to reach a level of at least 2,800 pairs in order for cash inflows to equal cash outflows in any given year, that is, for profit to equal zero (this is

often referred to as the break-even point in sales volume):
$p = \$30$; $v = \$20$; $f = \$28{,}000$; $p = 0$
Solve for q
$0 = (\$30 \bullet q) - (\$20 \bullet q) - \$28{,}000$
$0 = (\$30 - \$20) \bullet q - \$28{,}000$
$0 = \$10 \bullet q - \$28{,}000$
$\$10 \bullet q = \$28{,}000$
$q = 2{,}800$ pairs of edges

- Selling price could be lowered by \$4.40 to \$25.60, and the company would still break even if it sustained sales of 5,000 pairs of edges per year:
  $p = 0$; $v = \$20$; $q = 5{,}000$; $f = \$28{,}000$
  Solve for p
  $0 = (p \bullet 5{,}000) - (\$20 \bullet 5{,}000) - \$28{,}000$ $(p - \$20) \bullet 5{,}000 = \$28{,}000$
  $p = \$28{,}000$ ——— $+ \$20$ $5{,}000$
  $p = \$25.60$

Clearly, the plausible variations on the kinds of questions asked by the company president in the example are virtually unlimited. The great advantage of cost-volume-profit analysis is that by summarizing cost behaviour patterns into simple functional forms, many of the answers can be supplied with the same set of basic cost data through relatively simple algebraic manipulation. It should be recognized, however, that cost-volume-profit analysis and the several other applications of cost behaviour patterns are subject to two important limitations. First, the simplifying assumptions limit the applicability of information generated by manipulations of *simplified* cost functions to the extent that the assumptions are not descriptive of reality in a given situation.

Second, although manipulation of cost data within the simplified cost-volume-profit framework is relatively easy once the data are available, it is often difficult to discern actual cost behaviour patterns and to secure the necessary data. Nevertheless, these two limitations are overcome in practice sufficiently often to make cost-volume-profit analysis a most important management accounting tool.

Since the advent and proliferation of computing machinery, the problems associated with manipulating more complex cost functions have lessened consider-ably.

Managements can therefore be provided with more accurate information from more realistic revenue, cost, and profit models, provided they acquire or rent the expensive computers to perform the manipulations. Even though the functions used in such cases will be more complex, the process of constructing and utilizing them to provide information for management is the same as for the simple model. Thus our illustration of the simplified model is sufficient to highlight the analysis and use of cost behaviour patterns and functions for management decisions.

DIFFERENTIAL COST ANALYSIS

How often have you heard the expression, "A dollar is a dollar"? Quick reflection on the inflation phenomenon convinces us that a dollar is *not* a dollar when purchasing power changes. We can make a similar observation about costs (and revenues). Even though a cost presumably always represents a resource sacrifice, one can usefully distinguish between *differential* and *nondifferential* costs (revenues) for any given decision situation.

Differential cost (revenue): A cost (revenue) whose level differs between decision alternatives, that is, different courses of action. Nondifferential cost (revenue): A cost (revenue) that does not differ between decision alternatives.

This distinction is significant because decisions are based on the expected consequences of choosing one alternative versus another. Nondifferential costs (revenues) are consequences that do not differ between alternatives and therefore should not affect the decision maker's preference for one alternative over another. Differential costs (revenues), on the other hand, are expected consequences that differ between the alternatives and therefore ought to influence the decision maker's choice. In general, then, differential costs (revenues) are relevant to the given decision, and non-differential costs (revenues) are irrelevant. The important thing, therefore, is to be able to distinguish between differential and non-differential costs and revenues in providing information for all kinds of management decisions. What makes this most challenging is that a given cost item may be differential for one decision purpose and non-differential for others.

Example: Assuming that the Shoosh Ski Company actually invested in the new ski edge production facility, recall the estimates of variable costs of $20 per pair of edges and fixed costs of $28,000—for volumes up to an annual production level of 6,000 pairs of edges. Further assume that the company sells 5,000 pairs of edges as planned during each of the first three years of ski edge production.

Early in year four the president of Shoosh Company receives an urgent telephone call from a well-known Swiss ski manufacturer. His company's edge-making facility has just been destroyed by fire and he is offering to buy 1,000 pairs of quality Shoosh edges for $24 a pair on a "one-time-only" basis. Should the president accept this offer?

For purposes of this decision, the Shoosh Company fixed costs of $28,000 are non-differential—that is, they do *not* vary whether the Swiss offer is accepted or not. The only differential costs are the variable costs of $20 per pair of edges. If the sale to Switzerland takes place, Shoosh Company will have a net additional cash inflow of $4,000 in the year of the sale. Thus the Swiss offer should be accepted.

But suppose now that before the Swiss manufacturer's offer, Shoosh was already producing and selling 6,000 pairs of edges per year and was thus operating at the top of the range of production at which the $28,000 fixed costs could be assumed to be constant.

Further suppose that in the range of production from 6,000 to 10,000 pairs of edges, fixed costs can be expected to be $33,000. Under these assumptions, the Swiss offer of $24,000 for 1,000 pairs of edges should not be accepted because it is insufficient to cover both the differential variable costs of $20,000 and the differential fixed costs of $5,000 that will be incurred in accepting the offer. The foregoing example demonstrates some important points, including the following:

- That variable costs are differential and fixed costs non differential *when the decision alternatives being considered are alternate levels of activity within a "relevant range,"* and
- That in other cases *fixed costs can be differential* costs (e.g., when decision alternatives are alternate levels of activity in different "relevant ranges" or when alternate production methods are being considered). Thus differential cost analysis is applied on a case-by-case basis, with the nature of the decision (alternatives) determining what is a differential and a non differential cost. Perhaps the only generalization that cuts across all decision situations is that past expenditures (often referred to as "sunk costs") are always non differential, since nothing that a decision maker may do in the present or future can alter the level of past costs incurred.

Example: In 19X6 the Port Authority of Silver City purchased twelve hand-luggage screening devices for its airport security operations. The cost of these devices was $48,000. Early in 19X7 the CAB (Civil Aeronautics Board) ruled these devices illegal as a hazard to public health. Recourse to the manufacturer of the devices was not available, since the manufacturer had acted in good faith in 19X6.

The Port Authority of Silver City had to decide immediately between screening by security guards and screening devices of an approved mechanical type. The $48,000 cost of the old devices is a non differential (sunk) cost to the new decision, even though this expenditure represented a bona fide cost in 19X6. Analysis of differential cost can be refined for application in complex industrial equipment "make-versus-buy" decisions, leasing decisions, general plant replacement policies, and the like. It therefore ranks with cost behaviour analysis as an important tool of the management accountant.

Chapter 2

Accounting for Public Sector

Each decade more and more economic resources in the United States are directly devoted to the public interest. In fact, the significant growth of economic activities outside the private sector in our essentially market-oriented economy is without doubt one of the most striking developments of the twentieth century.

Prevailing political and social attitudes point to further expansion of this segment of economic activities. Society-at-large demands that certain public and nonproprietary services be provided for the benefit of all of its citizens regardless of their ability to pay. Profit-motivated enterprises are not able to make such services available to everyone within socially acceptable norms.

Moreover, upon investigation it appears that the free-enterprise system (like any other known economic system) is incapable of alleviating all perceived inequities within our society. The result has been that society, usually via governmental and charitable institutions, has made economic commitments to not-for-profit activities as a means of correcting perceived inequities. For these and a number of more technical reasons there exists a sector of economic activity for which the profit motive is absent by design.

NATURE AND SIZE OF NOT-FOR-PROFIT ECONOMIC ACTIVITY

Economists generally divide the production activities of our economy into a private and a public sector. The simplest way to define the public sector is to include within it all organizations not privately owned and operated, that is, nonproprietary organizations, as well as all not-for-profit organizations. This public sector can be subdivided by placing all governmental units (local, state, and federal) into one category and all nongovernmental not-for-profit organizations into another. However, the foregoing delineations are not clear-cut.

Despite the hybrid nature of some nonproprietary and some not-for-profit organizations, the public sector is treated. Accounting and reporting problems are quite similar between units of governments and privately organized associations having no deliberate or avowed profit motive. Hence, the general frame of reference for not-for-profit organization or agency, generally without specific regard for the public versus private ownership question.Not-for-profit organizations have the following main characteristics:

- Contributors of resources receive no direct financial interest in these resources nor proportionate benefits from the organization's operations.
- There are no individual shares of ownership. Ownership is public and cannot be sold or traded.
- Performance of services occurs on the basis of perceived social need rather than in response to strict market-related demand.
- A framework of public authorization and control is utilized. In governmental units this authorization typically covers specific financial budgets. Government constitutions grant taxing authority and usually restrict modes of expenditures. Voluntary boards of trustees often control private nonprofit organizations.
- Accountability to the public is essential, since the public supports these organizations through direct contributions and grants many special privileges, such as a tax-exempt status. Sometimes this accountability is weak (in practice at least) for privately organized not-for-profit organizations.

Growth of Public Sector Activities

Not-for-profit activities have experienced substantial growth in our society over the last forty years when measured in terms of the resources committed to them. One interesting comparison is that all government expenditures prior to 1940 do not equal the amount presently spent in one year by the federal government alone. Of our total Gross National Product, which currently exceeds $1 trillion a year, approximately one-fifth comes from federal government sources.

Federal Outlays for Social Programs During Selected Years 1960-1973 (in billions of dollars)

Category	*Actual*			*Estimates*		
	1960	*1965*	*1970*	*1971*	*1972*	*1973*
Community Development and Housing	1.0	0.3	3.0	3.4	4.0	4.8
Education and Manpower	1.1	2.3	7.3	8.7	10.1	11.3
Health	0.8	1.7	13.0	14.5	17.0	18.1
Income Security	18.2	25.7	43.8	55.7	65.2	69.7
Total Social Programs	21.1	30.0	67.1	82.3	96.3	103.9
Total Federal Outlays for All Programs	92.2	118.4	196.6	211.4	236.6	246.3
Percent Social Programs to Total Programs	23%	25%	34%	39%	41%	42%

State and local government expenditures over the past ten years have also increased. Their growth rate has been nearly double the rate of growth of the Gross National Product. Thus governmental units of all types spend about one-fourth of the economic resources of the total economy as represented by the Gross National Product.

Beyond government-related activities, there has been a significant growth in resources committed to the remainder of the not-for-profit sector of our economy. These non-government, not-for-profit activities include hospitals, private colleges and universities, religious institutions, private social agencies, the Red Cross, the March of Dimes, the Scout movements, and thousands of other similar organizations. In total, the size of not-for-profit economic endeavors is huge.

We should note here that comparable public interest resource commitments are relatively as large, and in some instances even larger, in countries outside the United States. While many other Western nations-like Canada and the Scandinavian countries-devote proportionately greater resources to federal level expenditures, the United States leads in efforts devoted to nongovernmental not-for-profit activities.

Profit-Motivated and Not-for-Profit Organizations Compared

A central theme of economics is that resources are scarce and that human wants are without limit. This condition produces many continual allocation problems. We must also recognize that we live in a social environment which imposes limitations on the use of available resources.

Efficient use of limited resources once fell into the category of conventional political and individual judgment. Today it is clearly a social obligation and possibly even a moral obligation. It seems reasonable, then, that every effort should be made to maximize the benefits coming from the use of available resources.

Profit-motivated and not-for-profit organizations are alike in that both must strive in principle to marshall resources as best they can. Both must ultimately justify to society the commitment of resources to their respective operations. Both have the responsibility to operate as efficiently as possible in their resource conversion processes or in their outright consumption of resources. In this important aspect of social responsibility, no differences exist between the two types of organizations.

In another important respect, profit-motivated and nonprofit organizations are fundamentally different. In a market-oriented economy, a private enterprise that continuously consumes resources unwisely does not survive. If it is unable to produce market-acceptable goods or services efficiently and thereby provide adequate returns to its employees, creditors, and investors, it will go out of existence after a period of time. An unalterable process of elimination, perhaps a Darwinian "survival of the fittest," thus operates in the private sector of our enterprise system.

The potential elimination process operates quite differently in the public sector. Perceived social needs dictate the establishment and possible later termination of not-for-profit organizations without direct or singular reliance on a market system of economic checks and balances (though economic stress may be an overriding factor in the closing of a small private not-for-profit school or college).

Some public sector organizations may even be forced to operate in an economically inefficient manner for a time because public interest considerations demand it. In a financial control sense, profit-oriented organizations focus heavily on producing appropriate returns for creditors and investors. Hence they have accounting systems that emphasize the periodic measure-ment of results of operations.

Public sector organizations are often concerned primarily with the size of their available cash resources, since the continued existence of public sector organizations or their programs generally depends quite heavily on cash availabilities. Therefore measurements of financial position, including cash reserves and outstanding obligations, dominate public sector accounting.

Accounting Objectives

The objectives of accounting for not-for-profit organizations can be stated as follows:

- To provide the information necessary for efficient, effective, and economical management of a nonproprietary entity and of the resources entrusted to it. This is a management control objective analogous to its counterpart for private enterprises.
- To provide information that enables managers to

report to third parties and to the general public on the discharge of their responsibilities in administering the programs of the entity and the use of the resources under their direction.

- To permit public officials to report generally on the results of organizational operations and the use of public funds.
- To confirm and report legal compliance with statutory or administrative rules and regulations that relate to the acquisition and expenditure of resources.

Accounting entities in the public sector can be categorized into five different levels of operation. Each of these levels involves one or more of the following:

- A government-city, state, or national.
- An organizational unit within a government-a department, an agency, a bureau.
- A separately organized not-for-profit organization comparable to a governmental subunit-a college, a church, or a community health centre.
- A programme-usually a specified set of goal-oriented activities which, at times, cuts across organizational lines in large not-for-profit organizations.
- A fund-usually a pool of resources subject to special restrictions or requirements.

Since the notion of a "fund" has a specific connotation in public sector accounting, we call attention to the definition provided by the National Committee on Governmental Accounting in its 1968 edition of *Governmental Accounting, Auditing and Financial Reporting:*

A fund is an independent fiscal and accounting entity with a self balancing set of accounts recording cash and/or other resources together with all related liabilities, obligations, reserves, and equities which are segregated for the purpose of carrying on specific activities or attaining certain objectives in accordance with special regulations, restrictions, or limitations.

The nature of these entities dictates an accounting orientation that seeks to substitute *effectiveness* in meeting specified objectives for the *periodic net income* measure of private enterprise performance. A second difference relates to *compliance* with laws, special limitations and restrictions, or organizational statutes. While legality is an ever-present ancillary goal of the private enterprise accounting process, it takes on the importance of ensuring specific statutory compliance in public sector accounting.

Compliance-efficiency-effectiveness are interlocking goals when it comes to public sector accountability. *Compliance* is a measurement of congruence with statutory or quasi-legal requirements.

Example: The Bel Ami Fellowship Fund requires that grants from its resources be made only to undergraduate students at accredited colleges and universities who can establish descendancy from French ancestors. Accountability for Bel Ami funds does not concern grade point averages, financial need, or subject area of study. Compliance is established so long as awards are made only to students with French forebears.

The notions of efficiency and effectiveness. *Efficiency* is related to economic performance. It is a measure of relationships for the entity between resource inputs and outputs. Different types of efficiency measures may be specified, for example, output efficiency or input efficiency.

Example: Output efficiency relates to specified levels of resource inputs. If the seating configuration of a commercial airliner is changed from five to six persons abreast in its coach passenger section, greater output efficiency (i.e., more passenger miles per flight) is achieved.

Example: Input efficiency is measured against a desired level of output. The city of Bellevue requires 250 transit buses to run an average of fifteen hours per workday. Higher input efficiency is achieved if the average cost per mile of operating a bus can be reduced from thirty-one to twenty-nine cents. *Effectiveness* measures achievement against specified technological, social, or other performance goals. It is normally difficult to quantify effectiveness measures precisely.

*Example:*The buses of the city of Bellevue operate over a

route network which covers the entire city. Outlying areas have less frequent bus service due to a relatively lower demand for it. But there are persons everywhere within the city limits who depend completely on public bus transportation! A fully effective system would provide the same bus service to all citizens of Bellevue. Differential service frequency reduces public bus transportation effectiveness. Note also that greater effectiveness often means a sacrifice in efficiency.

Compliance, efficiency, and effectiveness all require control procedures that may be built into underlying accounting systems and processes.

THE TRADITIONAL ACCOUNTABILITY SYSTEM

The traditional mainstay of accountability in the public sector has rested with expenditure control. Expenditure control is largely a compliance-oriented activity.

Expenditure Control

Managers of not-for-profit organizations cannot spend funds comparatively as easily as managers of private enterprises. This is not surprising, since controlling expenditures is the important constraining factor in not-for-profit organizations.

Expenditure control is typically effected in four separate, sequential steps:

- Preliminary approval by a legislative body or a board of trustees to appropriate funds to a given programme.
- Actual appropriation of funds to an approved programme.
- Obligations or encumbrances incurred against the funds appropriated.
- Disbursement of funds.

This four-step expenditure control process is especially important for governmental units. Preliminary *approval* to appropriate funds to a given programme starts the programme by providing a blueprint on how programme expenditures are to be made eventually. But approval represents *no more* than eventual permission to request funds. Many tentatively approved programs falter every year in national, state, and local governments due to the failure of the respective legislative branches to appropriate funds for projects or programs fully endorsed at an earlier stage.

An *appropriation* grants authority from a legislative body or a city council or a board of trustees to an agency of government or to a not-for-profit organization (for example, the local boys' club receiving an appropriation from the Central United Crusade) to either disburse funds as approved or obligate the respective government or not-for-profit organization for the future payment of money. The act of appropriation is significant for accounting because it is at this point that the accounting process in not-for-profit organizations begins.

Step 3 entails recognition of planned use of appropriated funds. If contracts are actually made but not yet fully completed, an *obligation* is recognized. Definite commitments to spend funds for specified purposes in the future result in so-called *encumbrances* (defined below) against appropriated funds. The formal recognition of an encumbrance illustrates an act of accounting in advance of a completed transaction. Recognition of obligations to expend funds provides a necessary control against incurrence of total obligations and expenditures exceeding available appropriations.Finally, *disbursements* are cash payments either liquidating public sector obligations or making direct payments for products and services as authorized.

The distinction between cash payments and obligations or encumbrances made on behalf of the not-for-profit unit is most important. New encumbrances must cease as soon as the appropriations level is reached—irrespective of actual cash payments to date. Moreover, since direct operating cash payments are usually needed to the very end of an individual programme, advance encumbrances must typically stop short of the appropriated funding level.In the public sector, then, accountants must provide continuing information to programme administrators on the following:

- Total appropriations available
- Total obligations and encumbrances to date
- Estimated funds needed to complete the programme
- Cash payments made to date
- Balances (for example, unused appropriations less obligations and encumbrances needed to complete programme, and obligations and encumbrances to date less cash payments made)

The Accounting Process Illustrated

A highly simplified example of a small federal government agency is used to illustrate the accounting process just described. In accounting for profit-motivated enterprises, the financial position equation is usually stated as:

Assets = Liabilities + Owner's Equity, however, represents the following relationship:

Cash Fund = Obligations Payable + Agency Account

Agency (fund) account:

The agency account, or fund account, is the accounting quantity measuring the unencumbered or otherwise uncommitted amount of appropriated funds. As a book-keeping convenience, a nominal or subaccount for encumbrances is provided as an elaboration of the agency account.

Encumbrance

An encumbrance is an internal authorization to expend agency funds in the future for a specific purpose. An encumbrance is neither an actual expenditure nor an obligation already incurred.

The actual accounting process begins by formal recognition of appropriations becoming available to allow future expenditures. The typical process also recognizes commitments (encumbrances) as soon as they are made against available appropriations. The process does not await evidence of a completed transaction, as is usually the case for business enterprise accounting.

Financial Position and Analysis of Changes

The agency starts the current period with a cash fund balance with the U.S. Treasury of $50,000. It has obligations (accounts) payable of $20,000 and a balance in the agency account of $30,000. The latter amount represents earlier appropriations not expended. In this case, periodic appropriations do not lapse at the end of the period for which an appropriation is made.

Line 1: A current appropriation of $300,000 is made to the agency through the federal department with which it is affiliated.

Line 2: The agency director authorizes the current item-by-item budget for the next period of operation.*Line 3*. Subcontracts are let for a number of agency subprograms. If a position statement were prepared at this point, it would appear as follows:

Cash balance with U.S. Treasury		$350,000
Obligations and contracts payable	$230,000	
Encumbrances for estimated future expenditures	80,000	
Agency account (Fund balance)	40,000	$350,000

Line 4: Orders are placed for miscellaneous office furniture, fixtures, and supplies in the amount of $10,000. This is technically an encumbrance.

Line 5: Salaries, wages, and other office expenses amounting to $75,000 became payable. In technical jargon, this is called an "expenditure."*Line 6*. Progress payments of $180,000 are made to subcontractors. This is a disbursement.

Line 7: Payment is made of various liabilities now due, including some that were outstanding at the beginning of the period and others recorded on line 5.

Line 8: Direct expenses amounting to $14,000 are paid for items like unbudgeted travel and office expenses. A summary of the final financial position is best expressed in statement form.

Cash balance with U.S. Treasury	$62,000

Obligations and contracts payable	$31,000	
Encumbrances carried forward	15,000	
Agency account (Fund balance)	16,000	$62,000
	————	======

From the earlier definition of an encumbrance, we note that the agency has $31,000 ($15,000 + $16,000) in cash resources not yet legally payable.

The $15,000 represents authorized future expenditures, and therefore the remaining $16,000 is the uncommited, unencumbered amount of funds with which the agency will start its forthcoming budget year. Since balances carry forward, the agency:

- Had a total of $330,000 to spend during the current year instead of the appropriated $300,000.
- Incurred cash disbursements of only $288,000, even though its operating expenses were higher (financed by an increase in the amount of obligations payable).
- Made commitments to expend funds during the next operating year and thereby anticipated its continued existence (this can only be done on the basis of appropriate legal or administrative stipulation).

Refinements.

The foregoing illustration was constructed to show that not-for-profit organizations usually expend funds for two purposes:

- To acquire directly various goods and services needed for their programs, and
- To make payments on obligations incurred for services performed by others (i.e., local contractors).

  The first category represents the largest amount of non-private funds spent each year in the United States. Accounting processes surrounding it can become very complex.

  They may involve special recognition of inventories and long-lived depreciable assets. On the other hand, the second category may call for renegotiations with subcontractors or elaborate payment schemes tied to production performance. Furthermore, complicated expenditure allocation devices may have to be used, as is the case when Medicare or other programs cover health maintenance furnished by physicians and private hospitals. Yet the basic accounting process is the same in all of these instances.

Control of Resources

Expenditure control, is the traditional mainstay of *compliance* accountability in the public sector. How does this traditional system of accounting achieve resource input control in not-for-profit activities? Three major resource control techniques are used:

- Precise specifications for appropriations of funds
- Creation of special-purpose funds
- Use of various cost concepts

Expenditure

Specification. One of the more effective cost control devices in not-for-profit organizations is the exact specification of the uses of funds at the time appropriations are authorized. Almost invariably the total amount of money is specified for a given appropriation. This places an upper limit on the cost that an agency or a programme can incur within the authorized appropriation. When cost overruns occur, the additional sums of money requested are separately identifiable and hence susceptible to management and public scrutiny and review.

Public sector appropriations are typically also quite specific as to the time period for which a given appropriation is available. This control technique ensures that unauthorized expenditures will not be made from carry-forward or carry-backward appropriations (our earlier illustration notwithstanding). When used in conjunction with other control efforts, the limitation on the length of time to complete an expenditure serves a good purpose.

However, when used by itself, it may well induce expenditures not actually needed because "the appropriation will be lost if not expended by *x* date," and, moreover, "next year's budget will probably be cut because we didn't need all that was appropriated this year." Agency case histories are filled with instances when public monies were consumed almost solely to avoid *under*spending an established budget (appropriation).

Another possible appropriations specification concerns specific identification of the purposes for which designated funds are to be used (i.e., so-called line item budgets). This technique circumscribes the ability of administrator-managers to use funds at their own discretion outside the specified purposes. Specification of purpose is an effective control too. It is particularly helpful in audit and review functions.

The auditors can match, after the fact, the purposes contemplated in the approval and appropriation processes with the purposes served by actual expenditures. If variations are identified, corrective actions can be recommended or required.

Fund Designation

Probably the oldest control technique utilized for not-for-profit organizations is the segregation of appropriations into separately established funds. For example, a small city government may have a fire department fund, a water department fund, a traffic court fund, a street and engineering fund, a planning commission fund, a public school fund, and so on. A local YMCA organization may have a capital project fund, a special programme fund, a scholarship fund, and an office and operations fund. Since specification of nonproprietary resources into large batteries of individual funds is still used almost universally, accounting for not-for-profit organizations is often identified by accountants as "fund accounting." Under this concept, an individual fund becomes an *accounting entity* unto itself, and financial records and controls are established with a specific fund focus. Sometimes separate funds and separate accounts for them are required by law, especially in municipalities.

In fund accounting, it is common to distinguish between a general fund and special purpose funds. The general fund normally provides the resources needed to operate the unit or agency on a day-by-day basis. Salaries of employees, building maintenance, and general office expenses are items chargeable to a general fund. In contrast, special funds are established to yield accountability for separately identifiable activities which make individual control procedures necessary or desirable.

The pervasiveness of fund accounting is illustrated by the fact that the semiannual Uniform Certified Public Accountants Examination usually contains at least one lengthy problem on this subject. Undergraduate accounting curricula of colleges and universities often devote at least one quarter or semester course to fund accounting.

Various Cost Concepts

Following the lead of private enterprise, accountants and administrators in the public sector have recently begun to utilize different concepts of cost behaviour for specified control purposes. The essence of cost behaviour distinctions is that different cost measurements are most useful for different managerial control decisions if specific and directly related cost measurements are established for individual circumstances. For example, the cost of acquiring an asset can be distinguished usefully from the cost of using that asset in a not-for-profit programme. Similarly, the cost of replacing an old asset with an equivalent new asset may be more important in certain decisions than original acquisition cost of the old assets.

MATCHING EFFORTS AND ACCOMPLISHMENTS

Compliance with expenditure authorizations is a key objective of the public sector accounting function. Measures of compliance are easier to establish than measures of efficiency or measures of effectiveness, since the output of not-for-profit organizations is by and large intangible and not market oriented.

Our market-oriented economic system serves, among others, the crucially important roles of allocating resources and continually threatening the survival of weak or inefficient enterprises. Thus the profit motive ensures that the entire private sector runs relatively efficiently.

For private enterprises, periodic costs (efforts) and revenues (accomplishments) are accounted for systematically, and the difference between them is reported as period net income. For larger companies, this reporting must conform absolutely to the requirements of the federal SEC. Moreover, it must be reviewed and audited at least once a year by independent outside professionals.

Determination of periodic net income is presumably the most critical performance measurement for a private enterprise. Even though in the future we are likely to see greater emphasis upon measuring and reporting a company's social, legal, and environmental performance, the latter will not replace the basic measures of economic performance. So long as private capital finances enterprise investments, economic performance will retain its prominence in the overall system.

With the absence of the profit motive in the public sector and the compounding difficulty of producing intangible and quite often elusive products, periodic matching of efforts and accomplishments in terms of concise quantitative reports has proved difficult. Thus, for many years, the public sector did little more than measure and report its dollar performance.

Dollar Performance

Traditional financial accounting systems and reports of not-for-profit organizations are oriented to identifying and summarizing how money is expended and to what extent such expenditures are consistent with authorizations or budgets. This system provides dollar accountability, but it furnishes few clues about the results that may have been achieved. The degree of efficiency in operations cannot be determined from dollar performance reports.

As we have seen, dollar performance is predominantly oriented to compliance. Dollar inflows are a measure of accomplishment for private enterprises if such inflows represent revenues. However, no implication of accomplishment can be attached to the donated or appropriated dollars flowing to a not-for-profit organization.

Moreover, matching of costs and revenues in the private sector produces a measure of performance (however conventionally or arbitrarily defined) which, if consistently applied, is a useful economic indicator.

Neither money inflows alone nor calculations of *net* money inflows and outflows allow evaluation of the efficiency and effectiveness of a not-for-profit organization's activity. A system of accounts and reports primarily aimed at compliance is both necessary and desirable for the public sector. However, such a system does not adequately serve today's social needs and concerns.

PPBS System

During World War II, several federal government agencies and various units of the armed services began to distinguish between monetary expenditures and operational efficiency. Moreover, the stated objectives of an organization began to be distinguished from measured accomplishments of these objectives.

These developments were the forerunners of an accounting process known as planning, programming, and budgeting system (PPBS), which is increasingly being used in not-for-profit organizations. PPBS came fully into its own when, in 1965, the late President Lyndon B. Johnson requested that all government agencies adopt this system.

PPBS is designed to create a framework within which each not-for-profit organization can consider its anticipated outputs (accomplishments) in relation to probably required inputs of resources (efforts) before it makes a commitment to the programme. Under PPBS, the supporters of an organization or programme begin their justification for financial support by identifying the goals (accomplishments) that the organization or the programme expects to achieve.

Measurement is facilitated if goals can be stated in quantitative terms, though not necessarily dollar terms. After programme goals are established, alternative courses of action are evaluated in terms of their probable achievement of the goals (i.e., probable effectiveness) and their probable costs (i.e., probable efficiency). Decision makers then choose the plan that allows optimal goal achievements in terms of required resource inputs (i.e., optimal effectiveness-efficiency). With PPBS, some proposed programs are never initiated because analysis shows excessive resource input requirements or low probabilities of achieving desired results. Also, PPBS allows periodic reporting just like most other formal accounting systems.

Goals in Relation to Accomplishments

The statement is made in the preceding section that identification of goals is the first significant step in a PPBS system. This statement needs elaboration. Goal-setting procedures in not-for-profit organizations technically involve

- Specification of objectives and
- Specification of measures of accomplishment. Operationally, these two steps constitute the goal structuring needed in not-for-profit organizations.

Example: The stated objective of Unified School District 205 is to provide kindergarten, primary, and secondary education for all residents in its district through grade level 12. From this broad objective a hierarchy of sub objectives is established, like minimizing the number of high school dropouts per year, operating a special education programme for physically or mentally handicapped students, running summer school programs for exceptionally able students, and providing various health care and counseling services for all students in the district.

The entire hierarchy of objectives is subsequently used to measure accomplishments. College admission percentages of high school seniors wishing to enter college may be one measure of accomplishment. Lower in the hierarchy, performance on verbal and quantitative aptitude tests may measure math and language achievements of district sixth graders against national test scores.

Not only do statements of objectives influence the selection of measures of accomplishment, but the selection of measures of accomplishment may influence statements of objectives. Therefore the establishment of objectives and of criteria for the measurement of these objectives are interacting processes in the goal formation stage in PPBS.

PPBS Data Bases

As knowledge stands at present, most PPBS applications are plagued by inadequate data bases. Notwithstanding developmental efforts by the General Accounting Office (GAO), the American Accounting Association, and other concerned professional groups, relatively little is known about non-financial measures of efficiency and effectiveness, particularly where several different data bases have to be used. What information to seek and how to measure it are the two most significant barriers to making PPBS fully operational.

INDICATORS OF ACCOMPLISHMENT

Accounting for efforts expended in public sector programs or organizations is similar to its counterpart in the private sector. Although there are certain operational differences, these are not extraordinary in nature. Accounting for costs of not-for-profit organizations can simply and directly be carried forward to any PPBS matching of efforts and accomplishments for not-for-profit activities.

The same cannot be said for the revenue or resource inflow side of the coin. Revenue measurements are not appropriate measures of accomplishment in the public sector. Even if changes in revenue flows were one of the objectives of a programme or an organization, achievement of that particular objective would still not give any indication of overall efficiency or effectiveness. Consequently, we need something other than measures of revenue or cash flows before any effort and accomplishment relationships can be established. The missing link needed for activity evaluation in the public sector has been identified as "indicators of accomplishment." These indicators are most conveniently classified as

- Operations indicators and
- Programme impact indicators.

Operations Indicators

These measures relate to output activities and are often non-financial expressions of products or services produced by an agency or organization.

Examples are miles of highways built in a given period, number of automobile licenses issued, number of tests administered, and number of families visited by a social worker. In many instances, these indicators are merely statistics that measure neither efficiency nor effectiveness. Operations indicators can be classified in many ways, including, for example, measures of volume, quality, and comparison.

Example: Street lighting in Ritzville is measured in three different ways. The number of street lights maintained is a volume indicator. An illumination index in terms of kilowatts made available is an indicator of the quality of service. Kilowatt hours of electricity used per street mile during December 197X is an example of a comparative indicator. None of these measures effectiveness of street lighting as a deterrent to crime or for the prevention of automobile accidents.

Of course, operations indicators may also be expressed in financial terms. For instance, federal assistance to minority business programs during fiscal year 1971 produced these indicators, among others:

- Government grants, loans, and guarantees by programme agencies rose from approximately $200 million in 1969 to $434 million in fiscal 1971.
- SBA direct and guaranteed loans to minority enterprises increased from $105.4 million in 1969 to an estimated $254 million in 1971.
- The dollar value of government 8(a) procurement contracts for minority owned business enterprises rose from $8.8 million in 1969 to $66 million in 1971.
- Minority firms received $77.8 million in direct Federal procurement in fiscal 1971, almost 10 times the $8.2 million of the previous year.

Operations indicators generally provide little qualitative information. They are not very useful in measuring how well public needs are being met. Often these measures are selected on the basis of simplicity and ease of calculation and understanding rather than on the basis of relevant performance measurement.

Programme Impact Indicators

Indicators of this type are often directly expressed in, or at least implied by, programme objectives. They relate directly to public or social needs or policies. Here outputs of programs are evaluated comprehensively vis-à-vis

- Other programs,
- Actual planned accomplishments, or
- Public or social needs or policies.

Example: (Efficiency vis-à-vis another programme.) The primary objective of the Space Shuttle is to reduce substantially the cost of space operations and provide a capability designed to support a wide range of scientific, defence, and commercial uses.

The National Acronautics and Space Administration contracted with Mathematical, Inc., for an analysis of how economical the Shuttle would be compared with the present launch systems which are used only once. NASA and Mathematical officials stated that this study demonstrated the Shuttle to be economically justified.

Senator Walter F. Mondale asked the General Accounting Office (GAO) to review the cost-benefit analysis used by NASA. With the senator's agreement, GAO's report was released to the Congress in view of widespread interest in the Space Shuttle. GAO identified critical areas of uncertainty in the Mathematical study. GAO also identified the percent of cost increase before an investment in the Space Shuttle programme would become uneconomical compared to the present launch systems.

Example: (Efficiency in meeting a social need.) The Detroit Management Information Systems Group of the international CPA firm

Touche Ross & Co. participated in a programme concerned with measurement of one aspect of the so-called war on poverty. Welfare recipients were analyzed for certain personal characteristics, such as health, work experience, and educational background. On these indicators, deficiencies were scaled and multiplied by weights to develop an index of needs. Total needs were then aggregated to develop guides to the most effective areas for investment.

Problems with measuring programme impact indicators abound. Without technical elaboration, we can observe that some scale must be devised to measure each characteristic to be included in the analysis. This often proves most difficult, especially if some type of index has to be constructed and a number of indices aggregated to develop a single composite measure of programme accomplishment. Despite these difficulties some public sector organizations, the Sierra Club Foundation for example, have begun public reporting of some of their programme performance in their annual reports. Other organizations, including private enterprises, seem certain to follow this lead.

SELECTED SPECIAL TOPICS

The scope of accounting for public sector organizations is as wide as the accounting scope in the private sector. Many special accounting problems arise along the line of this spectrum. Accounting for public revenues is singled out as a fairly comprehensive illustration of a special topic. As a second point of general interest, some recent standard-setting efforts are described.

Accounting for Public Revenues

Not-for-profit organizations, like all other units in our economic system, must generate resource inflows before continued resource outflows are possible. Quite naturally, the inflows and the outflows seldom match completely.

Example: If total revenue collections for the same period amounted to, let us say, $220 billion, a deficit of $26.3 billion would arise. This deficit is the difference, during 1973, between new monetary resources flowing to the federal government and its total monetary expenditures for the same period. To finance this deficit the federal government must borrow, and the national debt will increase by the difference.

Example: The Open Door Clinic is a university district medical and social aid facility. It was established with an initial grant from the federal government which was not renewed. United Crusade and state, county, and city governments were also unable to provide funds. The clinic's future revenue possibilities were not bright, and hence it could borrow very little money on its own account. Private contributions kept the clinic open, but on a much reduced scale of operations. As implied in these examples, nonproprietary organizations have two major sources of funds:

- Current revenues and
- Borrowing from the public or the private sector. Public borrowing occurs largely through the sale of bonds—U.S. savings and treasury bonds at the national level and state, county, city, or school district bonds at the local level. Most governmental units have statutory power to tax citizens under their jurisdictions and consequently can offer their bonds as virtually risk-free investments. The low-risk feature accounts for the comparatively low interest rate on major government bond issues. Income tax exemption for interest from state and municipal bonds is also a factor, which is explored at greater length.

Public Revenue Origins.

For not-for-profit accounting purposes, revenues are increases in expendable funds which have no corresponding liability increases and do not represent bookkeeping adjustments within the public sector.

Governmental revenues derive predominantly from tax collections. The right to levy taxes is among the most basic powers of our form of government. Other not-for-profit organizations rely heavily on voluntary contributions and transfer, payments. Both governments and other not-for-profit organizations collect revenues from both involuntary and voluntary sources. The largest single involuntary source of public revenues, namely, federal tax collections. Readers should note that, in turn, the largest single source of federal government revenue is the personal income tax. Voluntary contributions are the major source of revenue for private nonprofit organizations. Again private individuals make the largest amounts of such contributions.

There is an impressive array of different types of sources (e.g., taxes, gifts, investment earnings, collections, contributions, etc.) from which public sector organizations derive their revenues. This is in sharp contrast to the relatively small number of types of sources (i.e., primarily consumer groups) from which revenues can be earned by private enterprises. Also it should be noted that revenue collection control is often a problem. For example, private not-for-profit organizations depend heavily on volunteers for fund raising and for some administrative activities. The use of "nonaccountable" employees often leads to loose control over the collection processes. This is an ethical rather than an accounting question but one of which we should be aware.

Public Revenue Accounting Process

Accounting for public sector revenues is similar to accounting for business revenues. In both instances, care must be taken to separate revenues from funds inflows not representing revenues. Proceeds from borrowing no more represent revenue in the public sector than in the private sector.

In several ways, however, revenue accounting for not-for-profit organizations presents problems not found elsewhere. One issue relates to accrual (recognition) of public revenues. Conventional accounting in the private sector recognizes revenue as soon as a relatively certain claim to cash is established. To satisfy the realization principle, this occurs typically after goods have been manufactured and sold or after services have been performed. In the not-for-profit setting, revenue recognition is closely related to actual cash collection. There is no criterion of "earning" public sector revenue. Hence the notion of revenue accrual is also absent in most existing practices.

Example: Wiley Township is on a July 1 to June 30 fiscal year. Real estate tax bills for 1973-74 are prepared in March 1973 and are mailed late in April 1973, with one-half of the annual tax assessment due and payable October 31 and the other half April 30, 1974.

Technically, these real estate taxes accrue proportionately month by month during the entire 1973-74 fiscal year. However, for traditional municipal accounting purposes, one-half is recognized October 31 and the other half April 30 of each year.

Example: The YWCA is planning a branch in South City. It needs a new building, furniture, and fixtures, plus a director and staff for the facility. A special fund-raising effort is undertaken which yields pledges promising payment of $XX each September 15 for the next five years. Does the total pledge constitute revenue in year one? Since it is easier to pledge than to contribute money, would it be best to wait until cash is actually received before any revenue is recognized in this case?

Acceptable accounting practice would be to recognize each yearly pledge on the date it becomes due and payable. Past experience may be used to establish estimated uncollectible amounts in connection with each revenue accrual. However, the accrual method of revenue recognition could be useful in the public sector. For instance, month-by-month revenue recognition could yield better financial information.

A second issue in the not-for-profit revenue accounting area centers on reporting. Conventional reports of not-for-profit organizations relate revenues to cash collections and costs to cash disbursements. But are revenues really independent variables in the operations of not-for-profit units?

Or should revenues be related to the expenditures they make possible? Or should revenues be compared to the benefits that result from the expenditures? These questions remain largely unresolved.

Generally, the authors favour independent revenue and cash collection reports together with separate cost-benefit reports. This solution does, however, treat revenues and costs as separate variables.

Abbreviated Accounting Process Illustration

Utilizing the worksheet format developed, it is not difficult to illustrate the accounting process relating to public revenue recognition and collection. A hypothetical case of a municipality so that taxation effects can be shown. To avoid repetition, the worksheet reflects *only* revenue transactions. Our hypothetical city started the current accounting period with a cash balance of $45,000, obligations payable of $20,000, and a General Fund balance of $25,000. The "General Fund" designation used here has the same meaning as the "Agency Account" designation used. Revenue transactions for the year are described below.

Line 1: Memorandum records are made when the city council adopts a budget for the current year by authorizing expenditures of $6,400,000 and a General Fund increase of $100,000. Consequently the annual revenue needs are established at $6,500,000. These revenue needs are then compared with the estimated available revenues from all sources. After this comparison the property tax rate for the current year is set. Depending upon local statutes, a public vote may have to ratify the tax rate so established. The budget is not recorded in the worksheet.

Line 2: Property tax statements, representing taxes due of $4,800,000, are mailed to all property owners in the city.

Line 3: Throughout the year, city sales taxes are collected on all retail sales transacted within the city, and various fees and fines are assessed. The total amounts to $1,200,000.

Line 4: Some years ago, a wealthy resident established a large endowment for use by the city. The endowment was placed in a special investment fund which yields interest income. Also, certain temporary investments were placed in the investment fund. Together these resources yield $500,000 in interest and dividends during the year.

Line 5: Property tax collections amount to $4,750,000.

Line 6: At the end of the year, the assessor's office determined that $50,000 in property tax assessments could not be collected. This amount was charged off, even though additional collection efforts or public auctions of properties involved were planned. A revenue statement for our hypothetical city for the current year would show:

Net property tax revenues collected	$4,750,000
Revenue from city sales tax, fines, and fees	1,200,000
Interest and dividends revenue from special investment fund	500,000
Total addition to available cash	$6,450,000

Setting of Accounting Standards in the Public Sector

Efforts to set broad accounting standards for public sector accounting are widespread and intense. These efforts are relatively less unified than the comparable private sector efforts supporting the activities of the Financial Accounting Standards Board.The United States General Accounting Office (GAO) has statutory responsibility for all accounting systems and standards used by federal government units and agencies.

Hence the GAO, with assistance from advisory councils and national commissions, is a key accounting standard setter in the public sector.State auditors usually have authority to set accounting standards at the state government level. Since state and local governments interact frequently on many public service activities, state auditors also have considerable indirect influence on accounting for local and municipal government operations.

A national association of municipal treasurers and financial officers has produced an authoritative set of recommended accounting standards for municipal governmental accounting. This group regularly updates its standards. The nongovernmental portion of public sector accounting is literally inundated with accounting standards suggestions. Each branch of private nonprofit organizations appears to have a national association eager to propose accounting standards for its members. A list of such organizations includes, among many others:

- American Hospital Association
- American National Red Cross
- Club Managers Association of America

- Evangelical and Reformed Churches
- National Association of College and University Business Offices
- National Health Council
- United Cerebral Palsy Associations
- United Community Funds and Councils of America

Fairly detailed accounting standards have been set and come into use for health and welfare organizations. The bases of these standards are

- The 1964 publication by the National Health Council jointly with the National Social Welfare Assembly of a book entitled Standards of Accounting and Financial Reporting for Voluntary Health and Welfare Organizations, and
- The 1967 AICPA audit guide entitled *Audits of Voluntary Health and Welfare Organizations*. Other comprehensive standards are available for colleges and universities, independent elementary and secondary schools, and hospitals. It appears imperative that a major harmonization effort be initiated to streamline the many accounting standards and procedures presently found in the public sector so that the financial statements of public sector organizations become more comparable and more easily understandable.

PRIVATE AND PUBLIC SECTOR ACCOUNTING COMPARED

Many accounting writers attribute a certain mystique to public sector accounting in that they portray it as substantially different, more complicated, and differently oriented than private sector accounting. We disagree. Private and public sector accounting have more in common than is generally recognized. The existing differences are in form and procedure rather than substance. The principal differences between private and public sector accounting into five points:

- *Cash versus accrual accounting*: Private enterprises generally keep financial records on an accrual basis. Cash basis or modified cash basis accounting still prevails in much of the public sector.

- *Use of fund accounting:* Most businessmen are unfamiliar with fund accounting. This type of accounting, however, facilitates expenditure control and stewardship reporting in the public sector. The concept of separate record keeping for separate funds is not particularly difficult. Care must be taken that fund accounting based financial reports are presented in a straightforward manner, since separate reporting on a large number of separate "funds" quickly becomes confusing.
- *Treatment of long-lived assets.* In the public sector, current appropriations of funds must cover current operating expenditures as well as acquisitions of long-lived assets. The need for full current funding of even very long-term assets has generally led to non recognition of such assets as long-term items. Hence depreciable assets (and often inventories) may or may not be carried forward to future periods (i.e., recorded as assets). This mixed practice is often confusing to readers of public sector financial reports.
- *Transfer payments, appropriations, and encumbrances.* These terms are found in public sector accounting without private sector counterparts. Transfer payments are simply reallocations of existing funds from one agency or programme to another. Appropriations and encumbrances are *not* items of revenue and expense as the latter are understood in commercial usage.
- *Contributions, pledges, and non cash contributions.* Pledges to not-for-profit organizations may or may not be legally enforceable. Non cash contributions include donations of securities, works of art, equipment and supplies, and personal services. Recording of this type of "income" causes timing and measurement problems. Conventional financial accounting also has problems of this type, but their frequency and dimension differ. Thus a private enterprise may sue to collect a business receivable, whereas a church might not seek legal remedy to enforce an overdue pledge.

Chapter 3

Accounting Management Theory

Management accounting is generally understood as a process or as referring to the use of techniques. For example, the 1958 Committee on Management Accounting defines it as "the application of appropriate techniques and concepts in processing the historical and projected economic data of an entity to assist management in establishing a plan for reasonable economic objectives, and in the making of rational decisions with a view towards achieving these objectives."

Similarly the emergent conceptual framework of management accounting started by the National Association of Accountants defines it as the process of identification, measurement, accumulation, analysis, preparation, interpretation and communication of financial information used by management to plan, evaluate, and control within an organization and to assure appropriate use of and accountability for its resources. Management accounting also comprises the preparation of financial reports for non-management groups such as shareholders, creditors, regulatory agencies, and tax authorities.

Those techniques are further explicated as follows:

Identification: The recognition and evaluation of business transactions and other economic events for appropriate accounting action.

Measurement: The quantification, including estimates, of business transactions or other economic events that have occurred or may occur.

Accumulation: The disciplined and consistent approach to

recording and classifying appropriate business transactions and other economic events.

Analysis: The determination of the reasons for, and the relationships of, the reported activity with other economic events and circumstances.

Preparation and Interpretation: The meaningful coordination of accounting and/or planning data to satisfy a need for information, presented in a logical format, and, if appropriate, including the conclusions drawn from those data.

Communication: The reporting of pertinent information to management and others for internal and external uses.

Plan: to gain an understanding of expected business transactions and other economic events and their impact on the organization.

Evaluate: To judge the implications of various past and/or future events.

Control: To ensure the integrity of financial information concerning an organization's activities or its resources.

Assure accountability: To implement the system of reporting that is closely aligned to organizational responsibilities and that contributes to the effective measurement of management performance.

A generally accepted definition of a theory, as it could apply to management accounting, is that a theory represents the coherent set of hypothetical, conceptual, and pragmatic principles for a field of inquiry. Accordingly, management accounting theory may be defined as a frame of reference in the form of a set of postulates and/or principles from different disciplines by which management accounting techniques are evaluated. The task of justifying the existence of a management accounting theory lies in the definition of appropriate postulates and principles. Given the differences in the objectives between management accounting and financial accounting, the postulates of financial accounting, with some exceptions, do not hold true for management accounting.

In fact, the 1961 AAA Management Accounting Committee, charged with determining the relevance of financial accounting concepts to management accounting, concluded that the concepts underlying internal reporting differ in several important respects from those of external public reporting;

These differences are due to differences in the objectives of both areas; and it is justified to develop a separate body of concepts applicable to internal reporting. There is a need, then, for the accounting profession to develop a conceptual framework in management accounting to guide the development and use of techniques. Similar to financial accounting, such a framework would include the following elements:

The *objectives* of management accounting as the first and important step for the development of the elements of the conceptual framework for management accounting.

Qualitative characteristics to be met as essential attributes of management accounting information.

Management accounting concepts as the foundation for the body of knowledge contained within the conceptual framework.

Management accounting techniques and procedures that constitute the internal accounting systems.

Although these elements and the total integrated framework have not yet been formalized through a deductive reasoning process, they do exist in the literature as separate attempts to resolve these issues. Each of the proposed elements of management accounting will be examined next.

Objectives of Management Accounting

The objectives of management accounting are the first and essential step to the formulation of a management accounting theory. Then, the management accounting concepts will be true because they will be based on accepted objectives. In spite of the importance of management accounting objectives, there has never been a formal attempt by the profession to accomplish such a task. One noticeable exception, which may serve as *de facto* objectives of management accounting, was provided by the 1972 AAA Committee on Courses in Managerial Accounting. Four objectives were presented:

Management accounting should be related to the planning functions of the managers. This involves:

Goal identification. Planning for optimal resource flows and their measurement. Management accounting should be related to organizational problem areas. This includes:

Relating the structure of the firm to its goals. Installing and maintaining an effective communication and reporting system. Measuring existing resource uses, discovering exceptional performance, and identifying causal factors of such exceptions. Management accounting should be related to the management control function. This includes:

Determining economic characteristics of appropriate performance areas that are significant in terms of overall goals. Aiding to motivate desirable individual performances through a realistic communication of performance information in relation to goals. Highlighting performance measures indicating goal incongruity within identifiable performance and responsibility areas. Management accounting should be related to operating systems management, by function, product, project, or other segmentation of operations. This involves: Measurement of relevant cost input and/or revenue or statistical measures of outputs.

Communication of appropriate data, of essentially economic character, to critical personnel on a timely basis. The NA's emerging conceptual framework defines the objectives of management accounting as well as management accountants in terms of providing information and participating in the management process. More specifically the true objectives are defined as follows:

Providing Information: Management accountants select and provide, to all levels of management, information needed for:

Planning, evaluating, and controlling operations; safeguarding the organization's assets; and communicating with interested parties outside the organization, such as shareholders and regulatory bodies.

Participating in the Management Process: Management accountants at appropriate levels are involved actively in the process of managing the entity. This process includes making strategic, tactical, and operating decisions and helping to coordinate the efforts of the entire organization. The management accountant participates, as part of management, in assuring that the organization operates as a unified whole in its long-run, intermediate, and short-run best interests.

While these objectives reflect some of the priorities facing management accounting, they do not necessarily represent all the facets of the environment of management accounting. A formal study for the objectives of accounting is a definite must for the profession.

Qualitative Characteristics of Management Accounting Information

Management accounting information should have certain desirable properties so that benefits are achievable. The 1969 AAA Committee on Managerial Decision Models explored the application to internal reporting of the standards of relevance, verifiability, freedom from bias, and quantifiability. These standards for accounting information were suggested in the AAA Statement of Basic Accounting Theory. This effort was pursued by the 1974 AAA Committee on Concepts and Standards—Internal Planning and Control. The Committee offered the following closely related properties as representatives of the benefits information or information systems:

Relevance/mutuality of objectives
Accuracy/precision/reliability
Consistency/comparability/uniformity
Verifiability/objectivity/neutrality/traceability
Aggregation
Flexibility/adaptability
Timeliness
Understandability/acceptability/motivation/fairness.
The findings of the Committee are discussed next.

Relevance/Mutuality of Objectives

Relevant information is that which bears upon or is useful to "the action it is designed to facilitate or the result it is desired to produce." For example, given different alternatives, the relevant costs and revenues are those expected costs and revenues that will be different for at least one of the alternatives. Historical costs may be only the basis for estimating expected future costs.

Relevance depends on the structure of the objective function. In other words, relevant information is the information on any variables in the user's objective function and must be very close to the definition implicit in the objective function. Relevance is a qualitative rather than a quantitative characteristic in the sense that information is either relevant or not. Finally, relevance depends on the particular user receiving the information and on his or her particular decision. Some variables may be relevant to one user and not to others, and to one type of decision and not to others.

Mutuality of objectives refers to the consistency and congruency of the goals of the information users with those established by top management for the whole organization. The information provided by the internal reporting system may contribute to internal goal congruency if the signals of success or failure have the same meaning for both the total organization and its different segments. The mutuality of objectives applies also to the management accountants or the "internal information processors." Their goals should be consistent with the organizational goals.

Accuracy/Precision/Reliability

These properties are statistically interrelated in the sense that the notion of accuracy is statistically expressed by the concepts of precision and reliability. The specification of precision requires the specification of reliability, and vice versa. These concepts as follows: "reliability is commonly used to describe the chances that a confidence interval will contain the true value being estimated precision is often used in describing the interval about a sample estimate." While it is generally impossible to reach 100 percent accuracy, it is advisable to specify upper and lower bounds within which accuracy may be an effective property of management accounting information.

Consistency/Comparability/Uniformity

Consistency refers to the continued use of the same rules and procedures by the same firm over time, leading to comparability of its own statements with each other for one year to another. Uniformity refers to the use of similar rules by different firms. Consistency, uniformity, and the ensuing comparability are considered desirable criteria for financial accounting. Their relevance to management accounting differs between long-term and short-term decisions.

A long-range planning decision relies on diverse, unstructered information and non-repetitive situations, and it may be unduly hampered by an internal accounting system stressing consistency/comparability/uniformity. However, the areas of short-run planning and performance control rely more on carefully structured information and repetitive situations, and lend themselves to an internal accounting system stressing consistency/comparability/uniformity.

Verifiability/Objectivity/Neutrality/Traceability

Verifiability and objectivity refer to measurements that can be duplicated by independent measurers using the same measurement methods. It is usually operationally measured by the dispersion of the data in terms of the variance of the data. If the measurement rules are well-specified, the verifiability of the measurement may be accomplished through a reconstruction of the initial measurement process and on the basis of evidential documents referred to as the audit trail. Traceability refers to the availability of such an audit trail. Finally, neutrality refers to the impartiality of the data in terms of its impact on different groups.

A personal interest of the measurer in the data will not likely lead to neutral measurements. The degree of verifiability/objectivity/traceability of the data generated for management accounting is not as pronounced as when applied to financial accounting. However, neutrality of the information is a desirable objective, especially when the data are used for information evaluation or as a basis for distributing resources or settling claims.

Aggregation

This refers to the process of reducing the volume of data. A loss of identifiability or information is generally attributed to the process of aggregation, which may be compensated by cost savings in accounting for the information. An optimal level of aggregation is difficult to specify for either financial or management accounting. For financial accounting, the preparation of standard financial statements according to well-defined rules has led to a tendency to aggregate the information at an early stage of information processing. For management accounting, the lack of homogeneity in the reports, the flexibility in the choice of rules for preparing these reports, and the objective to meet a variety of information needs argue in favour of a management accounting system with less aggregated data, but that takes into account the user's limitations in handling voluminous data.

Flexibility/Adaptability

Flexibility refers to the degree to which data may be the basis for several types of information and reports. It depends on both the classification used for the data base into definite categories and the level of aggregation used in each of the categories. For example, purchase data may be classified under the following categories:

- By individual product or service,
- By individual purchaser,
- By supplier, and so on. These data may be aggregated under the following categories:
  - By transaction,
  - By day,
  - By month, and so on.

Adaptability refers to the extent to which information derived from the data base may be tailored to, or harmonized with, the decision processes of the firm. The adaptability of an accounting system requires not only the presence of flexibility, but also an explicit process of harmonizing it with the decision process. The Committee suggested the following procedures for harmonizing:

Such harmonizing is often accomplished iteratively through an understanding of the planning and control process, representing the latter in terms of information parameters and specifying the aggregation rules to be used in going from data base to information and analyzing the impact of such information on the planning processes.

Again, given the lack of homogeneity in the management accounting reports, the large number of these reports and the desire to meet various decision needs, management accounting requires higher levels of flexibility and adaptability than financial accounting.

Timeliness

Timeliness refers to the age of the information. It has two components: interval and delay. Interval is the period of time elapsing between the preparation of two successive reports. Delay is the period of time necessary to process the data, prepare the reports, and distribute them. Timeliness is also related to the concept of real time. Wayne Boutell provides the following definition:

"It [real time] refers to the time in which information is received by the particular decision maker. If the information is received in sufficient time for a decision to be made without a penalty for delay, the information is said to be received in real time." Although timeliness is a uniquely desirable property of management accounting information, it is affected by cost considerations and may conflict with other criteria, such as accuracy.

- Understandability/acceptability/motivation/fairness. This refers to the extent to which the user is able to use the information. Understandability refers to the ability of the user to ascertain the message transmitted. Acceptability is the recognition by the user that the problem specification and measurement criteria have been met. Fairness refers to the neutrality of the information as defined earlier. Finally, motivation refers to the attempt to secure goal congruences between the user and the organization.

In brief, management accounting information should be understandable, acceptable, fair to the user, and a motivation to the user to perform in the desired manner.

Management Accounting Concepts

Management accounting concepts based on both the objectives and qualitative characteristics of management accounting would constitute the basic foundation for a management accounting conceptual framework.

Although the development and formalization of a management accounting conceptual framework remains to be accomplished, the literature contains references to certain identifiable management accounting concepts.

For example, the 1972 AAA Committee on Courses in Managerial Accounting identified measurement, communication, information, system, planning, feedback, control, and cost behaviour as some of the management accounting concepts "which represent a necessary, if not minimum, foundation for the body of knowledge contained within the structure." Accordingly, each of these concepts will be explained next.

- Applied to accounting, *measurement* has been defined as "an assignment of numerals to an entity's past, present, or future economic phenomena, on the basis of past or present observation and according to rules." This concept is very essential to management accounting.
- As defined by Claude Shannon and Warren Weaver, *communication* encompasses "the procedures by means of which one mechanism affects another mechanism."
- Information represents significant data upon which action is based. It refers to those data that reduce the uncertainty on the part of the user. Thus, data produced by management accounting should be evaluated in terms of their informational content. Although not exhaustive, management accounting information includes the following categories:
  - Financial information resulting from the flow of financial resources within the organization,

- Production information resulting from the physical flow of resources within the organization,
- Personnel information resulting from the flow of people within the organization,
- Marketing information resulting from the interaction with the market for the organization's products.

- System refers to an entity consisting of two or more interacting components or subsystems intended to achieve a goal. Management accounting is generally a subsystem of the accounting information system, which is itself a subsystem of the total management information system within the organization. The interaction of the management accounting system with all the other systems within the organization, and especially the integration of all these systems, is essential for an efficient functioning of the organization.

  A management accounting system may be defined as the set of human and capital resources within an organization that is responsible for the production and dissemination of information deemed relevant for internal decision making.
- Planning refers to the management function of setting objectives, establishing policies, and choosing means of accomplishment. Planning may be practiced at different levels in the organization, from strategic to operational, and may have behavioral implications.
- Feedback refers to the output of a process that returns to become an input to the process in order to initiate control. It is basically a revision of the planning process to accommodate new environmental events.
- Control refers to monitoring and evaluating of performance to determine the degree of conformance of actions to plans. Ideally, planning precedes control, which is followed by a feedback corrective action or a feedforward preventive action.

- Cost Behaviour: cost results from the use of an asset for the generation of revenues. The identification, classification, and estimation of costs is essential to any evaluation of courses of action.

Although not exhaustive, this list represents concepts that are representative of those foundation components essential to a grasp of the management accounting process. This is very much in line with the NA's definition of the responsibilities of a management accountant:

- Planning. Quantifying and interpreting the effects on the organization of planned transactions and other economic events. The planning responsibility, which includes strategic, tactical, and operating aspects, requires that the accountant provide quantitative historical and prospective information to facilitate planning. It includes participation in developing the planning system, setting obtainable goals, and choosing appropriate means of monitoring the progress toward the goals.
- Evaluating. Judging implications of historical and expected events and helping to choose the optimum course of action. Evaluating includes translating data into trends and relationships. Management accountants must communicate effectively and promptly the conclusions derived from the analyses.
- Controlling. Assuring the integrity of financial information concerning an organization's activities and resources; monitoring and measuring performance and inducing any corrective actions required to return the activity to its intended course. Management accountants provide information to executives operating in functional areas who can make use of it to achieve desirable performance.
- Assuring accountability of resources. Implementing a system of reporting that is aligned with organizational responsibilities. This reporting system will contribute to the effective use of resources and measurement of management performance.

The transmission of management's goals and objectives throughout the organization in the form of assigned responsibilities is a basis for identifying accounta-bility. Management accountants must provide an accounting and reporting system that will accumu-late and report appropriate revenues, expenses, assets, liabilities, and related quantitative information to managers. Managers then will have better control over these elements.

- External reporting. Preparing financial reports based on generally accepted accounting principles, or other appropriate bases, for non-management groups such as shareholders, creditors, regulatory agencies, and tax authorities. Management accountants should participate in the process of developing the accounting principles that underlie external reporting.

MANAGEMENT ACCOUNTING TECHNIQUES

Management accounting techniques should be derived and supported by the management accounting conceptual framework.

Given the absence of such a framework, there is no consensus on a list of management accounting techniques. Most management accounting textbooks include standard cost accounting techniques and only a few attempts at introducing behavioral and/or quantitative considerations.

What is needed is a structure that will allow an integration of accounting, organizational, behavioral, quantitative, and other techniques of relevance to internal decision making. The AAA Report of the Committee on Courses in Managerial Accounting proposes such a structure:

Introductory Material
Systems theory and accounting
Communications, measurement, and
information concepts
Criteria development
Feedback and control mechanisms
Information systems

Accounting for management planning and control
Cost concepts and techniques
Cost Determination for Assets
Job order and process costing
Standard costing system
Direct versus absorption costing
By-product and joint product costing
Cost allocation practices
Accounting for human resources
Planning
Strategic planning
Continuous planning
Investment decisions
Comprehensive budgets
Cost-volume-profit analysis
Problems of alternative choice
Management Control
Responsibility accounting
Cost centers
Financial performance centers
Investment centers
Centralized versus decentralized structures
Concern for goal congruence
Transfer pricing
Evaluation methods
Performance reporting
Operational Control
Internal control
Project control
Inventory control

Although not exhaustive, this list represents most of the techniques included in management accounting textbooks, but still fails to incorporate behavioral, organization, and decisional models essential to an adequate performance of a management accounting system of knowledge known as management accounting.

This is particularly due to the absence of a conceptual framework for management accounting.

In addition, there is no consensus on what are the appropriate techniques for each of the management accounting topics included. The following overhead variance analysis problem to illustrate the varieties of treatment existing in management accounting:

Problem: The Following Information is Available:

Budgeted production	9,000 units
Actual production	9,450 units
Standard DIRECT LABOUR HOURS (DLHs) per unit	3
Actual DLHs (total)	28,000
Standard DLHs (total) (9450 3)	28,350
Actual FIXED OVERHEAD (FOH)	$56,700
Actual VARIABLE OVERHEAD (VOH)	$54,000
FOH Rate (per DLH)	$2
VOH Rate (per DLH)	$1

- Management and cost accounting topics are differentiated following R. N. Anthony's distinctions between the themes of the two subdisciplines: the primary theme of cost accounting is to measure full cost while the pricing theme of management accounting is different purposes.
- The accounting information system (AIS) pulsator is characterized by continuous flow dimensions, including nonfinancial and external data.
- The data for internal use are filtered out before any GAAP influences are introduced.

THE ACCOUNTING FOUNDATIONS

Management accounting is one of the areas in the field and profession of accountancy. As suggested by the 1958 American Accounting Association (AAA) Committee on Management Accounting, it "involves consideration of the ways in which accounting information may be accumulated, synthesized, analyzed, and presented in relation to specific problems, decisions, and day-to-day tasks of business management." An appreciation of management accounting requires a good understanding of the different facets of accounting in organizations. A clarification of each accounting area will help identify the scope of management accounting, the possibility of a management accounting theory, and a taxonomy of management accounting techniques.

The role of management accounting in the field of accounting per se, and to argue for a management accounting theory as a frame of reference for the justification of present and new management ac- counting techniques.

NATURE OF ACCOUNTING

The financial community has always regarded the accounting discipline as one of its principal tools in the decision-making process. The primacy of decision has been stressed by both William Paton and the AAA *"Statement of Basic Accounting Theory"*:

The purpose of accounting may be said to be that of interpreting the financial data... to provide a sound guide action by management, investor and other interested parties. The committee defines accounting as the process of identifying, measuring, and com-municating economic information to permit informed judgments and decisions by users of the information.

Thus, accounting is perceived as utilitarian in purpose and descriptive in nature. Stated in means-end terms, the end sought is good information and the means employed are descriptions. Accounting provides information for two distinct but closely related purposes:

- Reporting to managers within the organization and
- Reporting to persons outside the organization who have a legitimate interest in its affairs.

More precisely the accounting system provides information for three broad objectives: Internal routine reporting to managers to provide information and influence behaviour regarding cost management and the planning and controlling of operations.

Internal non routine, or special, reporting to managers for strategic and tactical decisions on matters such as pricing products or services, choosing which products to emphasize or de-emphasize, investing in equipment, and formulating overall policies and long range planning. External reporting through financial statements to investors, government authorities, and other outside parties. The first two areas are those of internal or management accounting, the third is of external or financial accounting. What is the extent of the differences in scope of both financial and management accounting?

FINANCIAL VERSUS MANAGEMENT ACCOUNTING

Financial accounting deals with reporting information that pertains to the financial position, performance, and conduct of a firm for a given period to a set of users and the market in general. Management accounting is more oriented toward internal decision making and purposively channels relevant and timely information to internal managers. Both are production processes of different accounting data for different problem-solving situations.

Financial accounting is the result of applying generally accepted accounting principles (GAAP) to the recording of transactions between different entities. As such, financial accounting statements conform to a set of rules established by the profession. Management accounting, however, reflects the use of techniques from different disciplines, including accounting, for internal problem solving. Therefore, management accounting techniques may differ from GAAP techniques and from one firm to another. They do not conform to any set of prescribed rules, and much may be left to the decision-maker's philosophies.

In short, the frame of reference used in management accounting is much broader than that used in financial accounting. Vergil Boyd and Date Taylor considered the specific difference to be the following: The managerial approach places the student in the role of a *user* of financial data in decision making. The conventional approach assigns the student the role of *preparer* of financial statements for use by others.

The student of managerial accounting is called upon to

use his or her entire knowledge of the business world in making business decisions based upon accounting data. Conventional accounting limits itself to accounting techniques, principles, and prac-tices, and rarely deals with decisions other than those required in the preparation of financial statements.

An attempt is made to consider the external and internal business environment in managerial accounting. Conventional accounting usually ignores these conditions. The arrangement and emphasis of topical material differs under the two methods because of the differences in objectives. The purpose of managerial accounting is to make a decision related to a business problem.

Conventional accounting has as its end the ability to prepare adequate financial statements. To this list of differences, it may be also added that financial accounting data are required to be objective and verifiable, while management accounting emphasizes relevance and flexibility.

MANAGEMENT VERSUS COST ACCOUNTING

Although the relationship between cost accounting and management accounting has not been explicitly clarified, it is usually believed that it is one point of emphasis. Cost accounting deals mainly with cost accumulation, inventory val-uation, and product costing. It emphasizes the cost side. The objective function is implicitly perceived to be cost minimization. Similarly, management account-ing deals with the efficient allocation of resources.

The objective function may be perceived to be profit maximization. It is also believed that the cost accountant and the management accountant are performing different activities; cost control is in the domain of the cost accountant, while cost reduction is in the domain of the management accountant. A cursory examination of accounting textbooks shows that, in general, those labeled *cost accounting* emphasize cost control while those labeled *management accounting* or *managerial accounting* emphasize planning, which may have reinforced the belief in a difference between both areas.

It is advisable, however, not to stress those differences,

but rather to conceive of management accounting as an attempt to bring techniques from other disciplines into the area of cost accounting. In fact, in recent years, the scope of cost accounting has been enlarged in various ways:

It emphasizes not only the explanatory but also the predictive ability of accounting data. It develops normative models to be applied in the accounting context with an emphasis on mathematical, statistical, and operations research techniques. It stresses the behavioral impact of accounting information on the users. It uses non accounting information—economic, environmental, and qualitative to improve the relevance of management accounting data.

It merges economic and social goals and consequently draws the accountant into programme budgets and "performance" auditing in not-for-profit organizations. It relies on more frequent and heavier use of computers, leading to a centralization of information and the expected candidature of the management accountant for the job of the "information manager" having overall responsibility of this resource. This enlargement of the scope of cost accounting into management accounting leads to the problem of the modern education of management accountants, which can be resolved by an exposure of students to either a proliferation of courses in the computer, quantitative, and behavioral sciences, or to an integrated multidisciplinary approach as advocated. Following the same line of reasoning, the 1972 AAA Committee on Courses in Managerial Accounting made the following appropriate assumptions:

The role of managerial accounting encompasses the entire formalized information function of an organization. The accountant is the best candidate for a manager of this information system.

Managerial accounting should be developed around a framework for the information wide perspective in the analysis and design of the information function. Managerial accounting should integrate material from the computer, the quantitative, and the behavioral sciences areas.

Management accounting should continue the traditional

emphasis on problems while using more sophisticated approaches to problem solving.

In brief, management accounting should go beyond cost accounting and integrate various material from organization theory, behavioral sciences, information the-ory, and so on, in a multidisciplinary approach aimed at facilitating the production of information for internal decision making. In spite of these diversifications in the background of management accountants, they remain professionals, as evi-denced by the growing popularity of the Certificate in Management Accounting programme of the National Association of Accountants (NAA; also NA). The following excerpt from a brochure issued by the NAA highlights the new scope of the management accountant's activities:

More and more people—inside the business world and out—realise the significant changes which have been taking place for years in accounting and the role of the accountant in business. No longer is he simply a recorder of business history. He now plays a dynamic role in making business decisions, in future planning and in almost every aspect of business operations.

This new accountant is called a Management Accountant and he sits with top management because his responsibility is developing, producing and analyzing information to help management make sound decisions. Many management accountants make their way to top management positions. In response to the needs of business and at the request of many in the academic community, the National Association of Accountants has established a programme to recognize professional competence in this field—a programme leading to the Certificate in Management Accounting.

The CMA programme requires candidates to pass a series of uniform examinations and meet specific educational and professional standards to qualify for and maintain the Certificate in Management Accounting. NA has established the Institute of Management Accounting to administer the programme, conduct the examinations and grant certificates to those who qualify.

The objectives of the programme are threefold: to establish management accounting as a recognized profession by identifying the role of the management accountant and the underlying body of knowledge, and by outlining a course of study by which such knowledge, can be acquired; to foster higher educational standards in the field of management; to assist employers, educators and students by establishing objective measurement of an individual's knowledge and competence in field of management accounting.

Those management accountants are to occupy important positions in organizations and therefore have to abide by high ethical standards. Accordingly the NAA has promulgated the following ethical standards for management accountants:

Competence

Management accountants have a responsibility to: Maintain an appropriate level of professional competence by ongoing development of their knowledge and skills. Perform their professional duties in accordance with relevant laws, regulations, and technical standards. Prepare complete and clear reports and recommendations after appropriate analyses of relevant and reliable information.

Confidentiality

Management accountants have a responsibility to: Refrain from disclosing confidential information acquired in the course of their work except when authorized, unless legally obligated to do so. Inform subordinates as appropriate regarding the confidentiality of information acquired in the course of their work and monitor their activities to assure the maintenance of the confidentiality. Refrain from using or appearing to use confidential information acquired in the course of their work for unethical or illegal advantage either personally or through third parties.

Integrity

Management accountants have a responsibility to: Avoid actual or apparent conflicts of interest and advise all appropriate parties of any potential conflict. Refrain from engaging in any activity that would prejudice their ability to carry out their duties ethically. Refuse any gift, favour, or hospitality that would influence or would appear to influence their actions. Refrain from either actively or passively subverting the attainment of the organization's legitimate and ethical objectives. Recognize and communicate professional limitations or other constraints that would preclude responsible judgment or successful performance of an activity.

Communicate unfavorable as well as favorable information and professional judgments or opinions. Refrain from engaging in or supporting any activity that would discredit the profession.

Objectivity

Management accountants have a responsibility to: Communicate information fairly and objectively. Disclose fully all relevant information that could reasonably be expected to influence an intended user's understanding of the reports, comments, and recommendations presented.

Chapter 4

Inflation in Accounting

GENERAL VERSUS SPECIFIC INFLATION

The wholesale price index is a general indicator of inflation of the aggregate weighted price of manufacturers' purchases. Specific items within the index have their unique inflation rates. As an example, the wholesale price index in the United States rose by 5.8 percent between 1987 and 1988. This does not mean that every component within this index rose by 5.8 percent. On the contrary, prices for machinery and equipment climbed by 16.3 percent and metals by 1.7 percent, whereas prices for pulp and paper fell by 16.4 percent and energy by 3.2 percent. However, the weighted average of these, and the other components to the index, caused the wholesale price index to increase by 5.8 percent.

Labour costs are usually tied to the general consumer price index because wage earners want to maintain their purchasing power for consumer goods and services. But a company's other costs are affected by specific price indices associated with material costs (e.g., steel, copper, and plastic) and transportation costs (vehicle acquisition, maintenance, and fuel costs). If a company produces a variety of consumer products, its revenue may track the general consumer price index, but this may not be true if it makes a single consumer item or industrial goods.

Consequently, price hikes in the product line may under- or overcompensate for cost escalations caused by inflation. The general consumer price index, although of interest in the conduct of business in a highly inflationary environment, is only one of many possible indices of inflation and may not be relevant for a particular company.

MANAGEMENRS REACTION TO INFLATION

Inflation is linked to government fiscal and monetary policies and to the productivity of a nation's industries and its people. Most blame inflation on government deficit spending, which is papered over by printing more currency or expanding of bank credit, rather than by raising taxes. This lack of fiscal responsibility to balance the budget usually ends up with a monetary policy that creates excess amounts of currency and bank credit by which the government pays or borrows to cover its deficits.

Managers view inflation as something beyond their control. On an individual basis, this is true. Yet the growth in the productive capacity of a nation's industrial base is a consequence of decisions made by business interests, which are, in turn, influenced by government policies toward business. Presumably, productivity gains by businesses and corporations equal to the speed of the government monetary printing presses can keep inflation under control. If incremental output of goods and services were equal to incremental growth of the money supply, prices might not go up—the definition of inflation. It is far easier for a government to add currency and credit than it is for industry to add productive capacity.

OBJECTIVITY IN HISTORIC COST ACCOUNTING

Businessmen and accountants obviously prefer a stable currency for all sorts of good sound reasons, one of which is historic cost accounting. Historic cost accounting depends on a stable currency because transactions are recorded at actual cost with no further adjustments as the value of money changes. This, allows for objectivity in accounting, in that no "guesstimtes" are made with regard to what an item might have cost. The original $1 million cost of a factory remains on the books at $1 million.

There have been instances when historic cost accounting

did not fulfill the dictum to present the true and fair view of a company's financial state. Several U.S. airlines have showed profits right up to the moment of financial oblivion. These airlines originally acquired their fleets at cheap prices. Their financial reports, based on historic cost accounting, showed a profit on the original investment.

They provided no hint that the airlines were in danger of ceasing to be ongoing concerns. Yet this occurred because the accumulated profits fell far short of enabling the companies to preserve themselves as ongoing concerns when the time arrived to replace the aircraft. In one instance, the cost of the door on the new airplane was equal to the acquisition cost of the original aircraft.

The revenue generation of these airlines provided a margin of profitability on the historic cost of their aircraft, but fell far short in servicing the financing charges of the replacement aircraft.

In extreme cases, financial reports can show profits up to the moment of a company's demise and do not present a true and fair view of its financial state.

This problem becomes particularly acute in an inflationary environment. Historic cost accounting in an inflationary environment leads to an overstatement of earnings because depreciation is based on the historic cost of the productive assets, whereas their replacement is based on much higher current costs.

Insufficient depreciation also may result in the overpayment of taxes, which takes away from the capacity to accumulate sufficient funds to replace productive assets. In addition, a manager operating a company in a highly inflationary environment must deal with continual demands for increases in wages and dividends.

Workers need more money to feed their families. Investors need more money to provide a real return on their original investment.

Governments in highly inflationary nations are apt to take actions to deal with the rapid loss of purchasing power of their currencies that are inimical to the interests of business. An obvious solution is to balance the budget. But this requires that government officials cut spending, which may be politically painful. Less painful moves are price controls and excess profits taxes, both of which hinder the accumulation of funds for replacement of productive assets.

SUBJECTIVITY IN INFLATION ACCOUNTING

There are several ways to measure inflation and to adjust the financial accounts for inflation. The choice of a measure of inflation and the choice of a methodology to recast financial statements to reflect inflation introduce an element of subjectivity that is not present in historic cost accounting. Some argue against this introduction of subjectivity in the preparation of financial reports because of the consequential loss of objectivity.

However, in a highly inflationary environment, there is a greater degree of fairness in financial reports that attempt to take into consideration the impact of inflation, which admittedly introduces subjectivity, than in financial reports that rely on the objectivity inherent in historic cost accounting.

GENERAL APPROACHES

Financial reports consist of both monetary and non-monetary items. Receivables and payables are monetary items, expressed in fixed amounts of money. Inventories and fixed assets are non-monetary items, expressed in monetary terms. A general guideline for inflation accounting is that all items in financial reports should disclose the net effect of inflation on a company's accounts. The two principal approaches are general price level accounting and current cost accounting.

General price level accounting changes the values of all assets and liabilities to reflect the loss of the underlying purchasing power of the currency. Historic costs are adjusted to a new number of currency units representing the present equivalent amount of purchasing power. The conversions are based on a general price index of inflation, such as the consumer price index. Current cost accounting differs in that historic costs are recast in terms of replacement costs.

Replacement costs usually escalate at a different rate than a general price level indicator. Current cost accounting, which applies to both assets and expenses, is tied to specific indices of inflation, not to a general index of inflation.

Examination of how various nations deal with currency inflation shows that there is a variety of approaches to this accounting challenge and that these approaches generally depend on whether a nation is experiencing a low, medium, or high inflation rate. Moreover, accounting practices within a single nation change in response to changes in that nation's underlying inflation rate. As the inflation rate climbs, there is a call for adjusting financial statements to reflect inflation despite the introduction of subjectivity. As the inflation rate falls, there is a call to return to the objectivity inherent in historic cost accounting.

UNITED STATES

U.S. generally accepted accounting principles (GAAP) and U.S. tax law require the exclusive use of historic cost accounting both for financial reports and calculation of tax liabilities. In the 1930s, the problem of accounting in an inflationary economy was first debated, but was really of no great concern in the midst of the nation's worst depression, where price and wage deflation, not inflation, was the worry of the day. The subject became relevant in the 1970s. In 1974, the Financial Accounting Standards Board (FASB) issued an exposure draft on the subject of "Financial Reporting in Units of General Purchasing Power.

This was followed in 1976 with the Securities and Exchange Commission issuance of Accounting Series Release No. 190 (ASR 190) "Notice of Adoption... Requiring Disclosure of Certain Replacement Cost Data." This required footnote disclosure of replacement costs on the basis of "the lowest amount that would have to be paid in the normal course of business to obtain an asset of equivalent operating or productive capacity."

About one thousand of the nation's largest companes had to comply with footnote disclosure of replacement costs. ASR

190 was rescinded with the issuance in 1979 of FASB 33, "Financial Reporting and Changing Prices." The footnote disclosure requirements of FASB 33 in the 1985 annual report of GTE, a large, partially regulated communications company and manufacturer of communications equipment and electrical products.

GTE suffered a loss in operations of $198 million (MM) in 1985. This was an audited loss based on historic cost accounting. In accordance with FASB 33, GTE made an unaudited assessment that regulated communication rates were not recovering $377 MM in depreciation charges based on accounting in terms of replacement rather than historic costs. In addition, $124 NM was not being recovered in its unregulated business lines, and $3 MM in the company's cost of sales. There was another $349 MM in nonrecovery of investment in shifting from an index based on general prices to one that was industry-specific.

Interestingly, GTE felt that investors in GTE debt and preferred stock offerings were suffering $505 MM in capital losses—the loss of purchasing power between making the investment and receiving interest and dividends plus repayment of the principal of debt and the preferred stock. Their loss was the company's gain.

This is a footnote disclosure of management's assessment of the foolishness of investors buying the company's fixed income securities in an inflationary environment. This also shows one way for companies to pass the ravages of inflation on to others. If the interest rate is less than the inflation rate, then a company can borrow funds, invest in tangible assets, and reduce its monetary exposure to the ravages of inflation at the investors' expense.

GTE lost $198 MM in operations and $348 MM in erosion of the equity of the company from inadequate depreciation associated with historic cost accounting practices, resulting in a total loss of $546 MM after inflation was taken into consideration. The 1980s became a period of more subdued inflation. At the end of 1984, FASB 82, "Financial Reporting and Changing Prices: Elimination of Certain Disclosures," made footnote disclosures on inflationary losses voluntary. As inflation waned, so did investors' interest in reading, and companies' desire to calculate, disclosures on inflationary losses. Inflation accounting in the United States ended, at least for the time being, with FASB 82.

JAPAN

Japan is a low inflation country. Accounting rules, set forth by the Ministry of Finance, call for historic cost accounting, a footnote from the 1990 annual report of Sumitomo Chemical. As an aside, note that the entire annual report is drawn is an English translation of the Japanese annual report, which is prepared in accordance with Japanese GAAP. Certain modifications have been made in presenting the financial reports to "facilitate understanding by non-Japanese readers," without changing the accounting practices.

The report also translates yen entries to U.S. dollars and is fully consolidated, reflecting another recent change in Japanese financial reporting practices. A company wishing to attract the attention of the global investment community is under pressure to issue fully consolidated financial reports, expressed in both the language and the currency convenient for potential investors.

A more rapid declining balance method of depreciation is being substituted for straight line depreciation. This increases depreciation expense and reduces reported income. It is an admission by management that straight line depreciation is "too slow" in writing off productive assets. Changes in the characteristics of products, and in manufacturing processes, are occurring at a faster pace in today's world.

Depreciation, which is usually based on the physical life of productive assets, may not adequately reflect their economic life. A manufacturing process may be technologically obsolete long before it has to be physically replaced. The decision to "speed up" the depreciation probably reflects management's assessment of the anticipated economic, rather than the physical, life of the assets.

NETHERLANDS

Accounting practices and business economics are closely allied in the Netherlands. The Dutch philosophy on accounting for profit is based on the concept of a company remaining in business as a going concern far into the future. Profit is measured on the basis that an ongoing concern should be as well off at the end of a period of time as it was in the beginning. A profitable concern is one that can accumulate sufficient funds to replace its existing productive assets at current replacement costs.

From the Dutch viewpoint, replacement value accounting makes more sense than historic cost accounting. Dutch accounting practices require that profit determination and valuation methods be acceptable to business interests. Current cost accounting is preferred because the inflation rate is keyed to a specific index that best reflects the cost of replacing productive assets.

The 1983 annual report of the Royal Dutch Petroleum Company. The corporate view of current cost accounting practices and difficulties therewith, the nature of subjectivity inherent in inflation accounting. Although it is common to adjust profits for the effects of inflation on land, buildings, equipment, machinery, and inventories, some companies have attempted to incorporate technological changes in their estimates of replacement value. Advocates of this approach argue that, as an example, a manufacturing plant is hardly ever replaced with a replica. In time, technological advances change the characteristics and design features of a new plant.

Generally speaking, technolo-gical progress tends to increase the capital cost of a replacement plant for the benefit of producing goods at less unit cost. The obvious hindrance in taking this approach is that management may not be able to foresee the direction of technological progress in determining replacement cost, or for that matter, changes in the market for its product line that call for an entirely different investment in productive assets. Mention of this is made, where management expresses doubt whether productive assets, primarily in the form of oil and gas reserves, would be "replaced in their present form." The Netherlands experienced less inflation in the 1980s than in the 1970s, which reduced the incentive to account for inflation and to surmount the difficulties associated with current cost accounting. Royal Dutch Petroleum had virtually abandoned supplementary current cost accounting by 1990, because of difficulties in estimating the replacement costs of its productive assets, namely, oil reserves.

Earnings were adjusted to reflect the current cost of supplies rather than using the first in, first out method of inventory accounting. This adjustment is easily made because inventory supplies are primarily oil, for which the current market price is a reliable measure of replacement cost.

AG-AMEV/VSB is a Dutch financial services company whose business is concentrated in the Netherlands, Belgium, and the United States. Its auditors' report, signed by a Dutch accounting firm and the Belgian office of a U.S. accounting firm, states that the generally accepted accounting principles with regard to valuation and profit determination are in accordance with "international usage and developments," without reference to any particular GAAP. The annual report states the principles by which the financial statements are prepared, illustrating the practical business orientation of Dutch accounting practices. Assets (real estate and stock holdings) are written up or down as their values change.

Unrealized gains or losses for assets above historic cost are added to shareholders' equity. If below historic cost, they are applied to unrealized capital gains/losses. The financial statements for this company are presented in three currencies: Dutch guilders, Belgian francs, and ECUs.

EXCERPT FROM ROYAL DUTCH PETROLEUM COMPANY 1983 ANNUAL REPORT

Supplementary Information-current Cost Accounting

The assessment of trends in profit and net assets measured under the historical cost accounting convention is complicated by changing prices, since current revenues are matched with out of date costs and net assets are stated on the basis of an unspecified mixture of historical costs. Current cost accounting (CCA) attempts to portray the profit which would have been achieved had both inventories and property, plant and equipment consumed been charged to income at their current prices and to present net assets on a current cost basis.

Departure from the basis on which historical cost accounts are compiled inevitably introduces a considerable degree of subjectivity and imprecision due to the approximations and assumptions involved.

Current cost data	**1981**	**1982**	**1983 £ million**
Summarized income data			
Historical cost net income	1,989	1,993	2,754
deduct Current cost adjustm-ents: Depreciation, depletion and amortization	1,105	1,319	1,296
Cost of sales1,033	211	(51)	
Earnings of associated companics 164	79	54	
Income applicable to minority interests	(162)	(222)	(208)
Income.(loss) from continuing operations	(151)	606	1,663
Gearing adjustment	555	307	215
Current cost net income	404	913	1,878
Summarized statement of assets and liabilities			
Property, plan and equipment - net	28,326	33,449	37,405
Investments in associated companies2,564	3,382	3,958	
Inventories7,994	8,263	7,747	
Other assets, less liabilities (other than long-term debt)	(4,757)	(5,923)	(5,645)
Capital employed	34,127	39,171	43,465
deduct: Long-term debt and capitalized lease obligations	5,518	6,858	6,825
Minority interests	3,815	4,361	4,942
Current cost net assets	24,794	27,952	31,698

The difficulties are compounded when account has to be taken of whether, in fact, the revalued assets would be replaced in their present form. There is a particular problem in presenting in current cost statements the capitalized cost of oil and gas exploration and development activities.

The cost of replacing oil and gas reserves is dependent on the location in which new reserves are found and the conditions under which they are developed. As these are not known, the capitalized costs are represented in current cost accounts only by the equivalent value of past expenditures at today's prices. For this reason and because of the approximations and assumptions referred to above, caution should be exercised in drawing conclusions from the current cost data. It is considered that at the present stage of development of current cost accounting there is no adequate alternative to the historical cost accounting convention for the oil industry and that this convention should therefore continue as the basis for the primary financial statements. The present experimental nature of CCA is manifested in differing accounting practice in the Netherlands, the United Kingdom and the United States over the items which should be reflected in current cost accounts. The accounting standard setting bodies of each of these countries are considering or reviewing alternative methods of calculating and presenting price change data, but the inherent difficulty of the subject makes it unlikely that effective and fully compatible solutions will be developed in the near future. Existing differences between the three countries relate to the treatment of monetary items and taxation. The information shown in the table on this page has been presented to reflect the current cost adjustments common to the three countries.

In addition, a gearing adjustment has been included to recognize the offsetting effect of borrowing on cost increases arising from changing prices. The basis of restatement for this purpose is set out below. Further details are provided under the heading. 'Additional information' to facilitate the appreciation of the Group current cost data in the light of Netherlands, United Kingdom and United States practice.

	1981	1982	1983 £ million
Netherlands			
If the provision for deferred taxation were to include the potential tax effects of current cost revaluations, current cost net assets would become	19,600	22,600	**25,800**
If the historical tax charge were reduced to recognize tax effects related to the CCA additional depreciation and cost of sales adjustments and in addition the gearing adjustment (for which there is no standard practice in the Netherlands) were excluded, current cost net income would become	900	1,300	**2,200**
United Kingdom			
If the Group current cost data were to include only provisions for those taxes that are likely to be paid within the foreseeable future in conformity with the UK accounting practice, current cost net income would become	700	1,400	**2,500**
United States			
Were the Group to adopt the LIFO basis of inventory accounting, which is common in the USA and which, after excluding any inventory drawdown profits, charges cost of sales on a current cost basis, the tax charge would be reduced in 1981 and 1982 and increased in 1983. In the USA adjustments for monetary items in the form of gearing are not recognized, but companies disclose the gain on net monetary items arising from changes in purchasing power. If the gain on net monetary items is included instead of the gearing adjustment and the above tax effects of valuing inventory on a LIFO basis are recognized, current cost net income would become	1,100	1,200	**2,300**

Basis of Restatement

The accounting policies used are the same as those applied in the Group financial statements except as modified below.

Property, plant and equipment of Group companies has been restated to year-end current cost by applying appropriate indices to historical local currency acquisition costs or by estimating the current cost of acquiring assets of approximately equivalent productive potential where technological change renders the use of an index inappropriate. Property, plant and equipment of associated companies has been restated on a basis as far as possible consistent with that of Group companies.

Inventories have been restated to their approximate year-end current cost. Historical cost operating expenses have been adjusted to reflect the current cost of sales as at the date of sale. Depreciation, depletion and amortization charges have been calculated as an appropriate proportion of the restated property, plant and equipment at current cost, on the basis of the same asset lives as those used for historical cost accounting. Income tax and provisions for deferred tax included in the income statement are the same as those included in the historical cost financial statements.A gearing adjustment has been made to quantify the proportion of the depreciation and cost of sales adjustments which relates to assets financed by borrowing.

The proportion is calculated by reference to the ratio of average net borrowing to the average net operating assets over the year, taken at their current cost values. For this purpose net monetary working capital, which is not otherwise recognized in the current cost income statement, is included in the calculation of average net borrowing. All figures are expressed in pounds of the years to which they relate.

Additional Information

Were the Group to adopt the LIFO basis of inventory accounting, which is common in the USA and which, after excluding any inventory drawdown profits, charges cost of sales on a current cost basis, the tax charge would be reduced in 1981 and 1982 and increased in 1983. In the USA adjustments for monetary items in the form of gearing are not recognized, but companies disclose the gain on net monetary items arising from changes in purchasing power. If the gain on net monetary items is included instead of the gearing adjustment and the above tax effects of valuing inventory on a LIFO basis are recognized, current cost net income would become 1,100 1,200 2,300

EXCERPT FROM ROYAL DUTCH PETROLEUM COMPANY 1990 ANNUAL REPORT

Accounting Policies

The annual accounts on pages 26 to 30 have been prepared under the historical cost convention. The determination of Royal Dutch's share in the net income of the Royal Dutch/Shell Group of Companies is explained in Note 3. The valuation of Investments in companies of the Royal Dutch/Shell Group is explained in Note 4. The assets and liabilities are stated at the amounts at which they were acquired or incurred, unless indicated otherwise. Administrative expenses, Interest income and Taxation are stated at the amounts attributable to the financial years. Amounts in foreign currency relating to the.

Balance sheet have been expressed in guilders at appropriate rates ruling at the balance sheet date, and those relating to the Profit and loss account at average rates. Supplementary current cost information is not disclosed by the Royal Dutch/Shell Group of Companies because of the impossibility of satisfactorily determining current costs that reflect the cost of replacing existing oil and gas reserves. In explaining the results from operations of the Royal Dutch/Shell Group of Companies, however, use is also made of information on the estimated current cost of supplies, as this information does not involve the uncertainties associated with the replacement of oil and gas reserves.

UNITED KINGDOM

The United Kingdom experienced a higher degree of inflation than the United States, Japan, Germany, and the Netherlands. The Institute of Chartered Accountants in England and Wales issued the Provisional Statement of Standard Accounting Practice (SSAP) No. 7 in 1974, entitled

"Accounting for Changes in the Purchasing Power of Money." Several interim reports and recommendations were made leading up to SSAP 16, *"Current Cost Accounting."* In 1983, SSAP 16 was declared to be effective for a three-year experiment in dealing with inflation. In 1985, SSAP 16 became voluntary and continues to be so.

The 1987 annual report of Bass, shows the impact of writing up of assets. "Freehold" means owned property, whereas "leaseholds" are leased properties, some for over a century of remaining time. These properties are primarily public houses (pubs), which totaled 1,638.1 million pounds in 1987. Although there is virtually no depreciation (0.8 million pounds) associated with these properties, there is significant depreciation associated with plant and machinery and fixtures and fittings. Depreciation of these items infers the need for replacement, quite unlike the situation pertaining to pubs.

Management states that depreciating pubs on the basis of historic costs is not appropriate because they are gaining in value, mainly from inflation. Management also notes elsewhere in the report that the pubs are maintained in a condition such that there is no foreseeable end to their useful lives. The valuation of properties is based on an in-house appraisal of market values. The 1986 valuation of all properties was 1,868.4 million pounds, as compared to a 1987 valuation of 3,060.8 million pounds. The 1987 value of all properties under historic cost accounting would have been 1,227.1 million pounds. Therefore, the aggregate net write-up in the value of the pubs has been of the order of 1,833.7 million pounds. The low depreciation associated with properties is justified on the basis that it makes little sense to depreciate a tangible asset that is being written up in value.

Write-ups of properties do not flow through the income statement. Shareholders' equity is adjusted to reflect changes in valuation of assets under the line item "Revaluation Reserve," which increases the book value of the company. Depreciation, on the other hand, does flow through the income statement and the reduced depreciation associated with properties does affect reported profitability.

FRANCE

France experienced rampant inflation after World War II. This necessitated a departure from historic cost accounting, which was restored in 1959 with the issuance of a new currency. Changes in the Finance Acts in the 1970s mandated the use of current cost accounting. The financial statements of publicly traded companies were to report all assets on a current replacement cost basis. The prescribed methodology involved writing up the book value of the asset by an official coefficient. The applicable official coefficients, in turn, were based on price level changes of wholesale price indices of those commodities, including labour, which largely determine the cost of manufacturing fixed assets. This is a price-oriented adjustment system that does not take into account technological change.

Peugeot S.A. is a large French automobile manufacturer. The individual companies making up the Peugeot group prepare their financial statements in accordance with the GAAP of their respective nations. For those Peugeot companies located in France, financial reports are prepared in accordance with French GAAP, including any required write-up of assets. The beginning of the notes to its 1990 consolidated financial statements.

Since 1979, the company has presented the consolidated financial statements of its activities in fortyfour nations in accordance with U.S. and IASC (International Accounting Standards Committee) GAAP, "which the group considers best adapted to the international context of its activities."

The principles of consolidation follow U.S. GAAP with specific references made to FASB 94 and 21 in paragraph (a) Paragraph (b) states that the legal revaluations required by French law, which are contained in the financial reports filed by the Peugeot companies in France, have been recast to historic costs in the consolidation process. Noted elsewhere in the report, a French company has the option to pay taxes based on the consolidated taxable income of its French activities, or on the results of each separate company within France. Peugeot elected to switch methods in 1990.

Accounting Policies

The financial statements of group companies, prepared in ac- cordance with the accounting principles applicable in their respective countries, have been restated, for comparison pur- poses, in accordance with accounting principles generally ac- cepted in the United States of America, which the group con- siders best adapted to the international context of its activities. These principles, which are essentially those described in note 1 (a) to (k) below, are in conformity with international.ac- counting principles promulgated by the I.A.S.C. and the legal requirements for consolidation in France.

Consolidation The financial statements of significant subsidiaries in which Peugeot S.A. holds directly or indirectly a majority interest are consolidated, with the exception of finance subsidiaries, which are included in the consolidated financial statements on an equity basis. Companies in which Peugeot S.A. holds directly or indirectly an interest of 20 to 50 % and exercises significant influence over operating and financial policies, as well as finance sub- sidiaries, are included in the consolidated financial statements on an equity basis (note 4). According to the "U.S.

Financial Accounting Standard Board" (FASB) bulletin n° 94 banks and finance companies in which Peugeot S.A. holds directly or indirectly a majority in- terest should have been consolidated in the financial state- ments. Peugeot S.A. Provides the presentation required by the FASB in note 21 and continues as in prior years to carry banks and finance subsidiaries on the equity basis in its main financial statements.

There is no difference between the finan- cial statements presented in note 21 and the main financial statements in respect of consolidated net income and stock- holders' equity. Investments representing an interest of less than 20% in the companies concerned are valued at cost except in the case of permanent decline in the value of the investment. All significant inter company transactions are eliminated. b) Property Land, plant and equipment are carried at cost, including capitalised interest expense since January 1, 1979.

The French legal revaluations (laws of December 29, 1976

and December 30, 1977) and foreign revaluations are not reflected in the con- solidated financial statements. Maintenance and repair costs are expensed as incurred, except for those which enhance the productivity or prolong the useful life of an asset. Depreciation is calculated on a straight-line basis over the èsti- mated useful lives of the respective assets as follows:

	Useful lives, in number of years
Buildings	16 to 20
Material and equipment	6,66 to 16
Data processing equipment	3 to 4
Transport and handling equipment	4 to 7
Furniture and fixtures	10
Land improvements	25

High inflation nations in Table 8.3 qualify as hyperinflationary under FASB 52. Generally speaking, the conditions contained in FASB 52 result in the local currency (LC) being declared the functional currency and the selection of the current method of translation. Under the current method of translation, fixed assets are translated at the current conversion rate of a currency. Suppose that a factory is built for 10 MM LC and the local currency rate is 10 LC per U.S. dollar (/$). The initial translation of the fixed asset to U.S. dollars is $1 million. Neglecting depreciation, suppose that the LC devalues to 100 LC/$ over the subsequent year.

The plant is translated at the current rate, or 100 LC/$, and the original 10 MM LC plant, costing $1 MM, is now shown on the balance sheet for $100,000. If the conversion rate falls to 1,000 LC/$ in the following year, the original $1 million plant has a translated value of $10,000 on the balance sheet. The plant, which physically exists and is in production, is literally disappearing from the financial statements. To counter this disappearing plant phenomenon, FASB 52 requires that an affiliate operating in a hyperinflationary environment must declare the U.S. dollar as the functional currency and translate its financial statements in accordance with FASB 8. FASB 8 calls for the temporal method of translation, which uses the current rate of translation for cash, receivables, payables, and long-term debt and the historic rate for inventories, fixed assets, intangible assets, and contributed capital.

The plant is now translated at the historic rate of exchange. The translation of the original value of the plant is at the conversion rate that was in effect when the plant was built, or 10 LC/$. Neglecting depreciation, the 10 MM LC investment in the plant is always translated at the historic rate of 10 LC/$, and the plant remains on the balance sheet at $1 million. Under the temporal method, translation gains or losses are reported in the income statement, not in the equity section of the balance sheet.

In contrast to U.S. practice, the International Accounting Standards Committee permits a company with a subsidiary in a hyperinflationary nation to adjust the financial statements for inflation before translation to the currency of the parent company, or to use a variation of the temporal method.

BRAZIL

For Brazilian companies operating in Brazil, there is no FASB 52, no U.S. dollar as a functional currency, and all accounting is done in accordance with Brazilian GAAP. Brazil recognized that high inflation rates destroy the validity of historic cost accounting and was the first nation to officially introduce indexing in the preparation of financial statements. It was also the first nation to have indexing apply to the calculation of taxes.

This reduced government revenue from corporate taxes, but permitted corporations to more easily accumulate the funds necessary for replacement of their productive assets to continue as going concerns. This, by the way, is atypical behaviour on the part of tax authorities. Most governments consider inflation their ally in revenue collection, neglecting, naturally, the impact of inflation on government spending.

The Corporation Law of 1976 requires that all companies adjust owners' equity and "permanent assets" to a government compiled price index. Permanent assets are property, plant, equipment, long-term investments, plus deferred charges and associated amortization.

The difference between the adjusted owners' equity and the permanent assets is called the net monetary correction. This may be applied to a capital account entitled "Reserve for Unrealized Profit" or may be charged to income depending on the circumstances.

Indexing permeates the financial life of Brazil. It applies to the face value of bonds and mortgages, to salaries and wages, to savings, and to calculation of taxes. Indexing is a series of calculations that follow a prescribed set of procedures. An illustration of the complexity associated with indexing is shown for Mexico.

MEXICO

The Mexican peso was a stable currency until the explosion in oil prices made Mexico, an oil exporter, rich. For reasons that perhaps defy the imagination of economists, the floodtide of oil money pouring into Mexico transformed a once stable peso to a currency of dubious value.

Mexican accounting practices are closely allied to U.S. GAAP and the standards set forth by the International Accounting Standards Committee, with one glaring exception. Whereas U.S. GAAP is based on historic cost accounting, Mexico practices inflation accounting. All monetary assets and liabilities (cash, receivables, and payables) are restated in pesos of constant purchasing power as calculated from the National Consumer Price Index (NCPI).

The NCPI is a general index of inflation published quarterly by the Bank of Mexico. Any gain or loss on the net monetary position is recorded in the income statement as the line item "Monetary Gain (Loss)."

For nonmonetary items such as inventory and fixed assets, Mexican companies are given a choice of revaluation methods. Inventory can be adjusted on the basis of replacement cost, last production purchase price, the NCPI, or a specific price index. Fixed assets can also be revalued on the basis of appraisals, in addition to the aforementioned methods. The net effect of revaluing inventory and fixed assets is an adjustment to the line item "Accumulated Gain (Loss) on

Nonmonetary Assets" in the stockholders' equity section of the balance sheet.

The National Consumer Price Index at the end of 1988 was 16,147.3 and 19,327.9 at the end of 1989. On the last day of 1990, the NCPI had a published value of 25,112.7, and at the end of 1991, 29,832.5. Suppose that a company was formed at the end of 1990, and had the following balance sheet at that time.

BALANCE SHEET 31 December 1990 (Figures in 1990 pesos)

Cash	240	Payables	96
Receivables	0		
Inventory	96		
Fixed assets	240	Equity	480
Total	576	Total	576

At year-end 1991, the first step is to restate the opening (prior year's) balance sheet, and the prior year's cash flow and income statements using the end-ofcurrent-year (1991) purchasing power of the peso. The year-end 1991 NCPI was 29,832.5, whereas the year-end 1990 NCPI was 25,112.7. The factor to be applied to the 1990 balance sheet to adjust it for year-end 1991 peso purchasing power is 1.188 (29,832.5 divided by 25,112.7).

BALANCE SHEET 31 December 1990 (Figures in 1991 pesos)

Cash	285	Payables	114
Receivables	0		
Inventory	114		
Fixed assets	285	Equity	570
Total	684	Total	684

The balance sheet in pesos at year-end 1991 is shown in the next table.

BALANCE SHEET 31 December 1991 (Unadjusted)

Cash	180	Payables	62
Receivables	74		
Inventory	120	Equity	480
Fixed assets	230	Retained Earnings	62
Total	604	Total	604

The unadjusted 1991 balance sheet must take into consideration the changing value of the peso during the course of the year in order to state the balance sheet strictly in terms of the value of the peso on 31 December 1991. Inventory is recalculated using either first in, first out or replacement cost on the last day of the year or by applying a specific price index or the NCPI to historic costs. These adjustments are done quarterly using the appropriately adjusted conversion factors and/or replacement costs.

Suppose that the adjusted inventory is 125 pesos. Having readjusted inventory, cost of goods sold must now be recalculated using last in, first out, using the last purchase price paid, or by applying specific indices. Obviously, the choice of methodology determines the outcome, and ultimately, the profitability of the company. An accountant, in selecting the methodology, is also selecting the final version of the reported profits. This is an example of the subjectivity introduced into accounting in attempting to recast the financial statements to reflect the impact of inflation on the operations of a company.

This adjustment is done quarterly to express cost of goods sold throughout 1991 in terms of the value of the peso on the last day of the year. Suppose that the adjusted cost of sales is 240. The fixed assets are next to be revalued to current cost either by independent appraisal or by applying a specific price index or the NCPI. There are limits in writing up assets—they cannot exceed "net realizable value," which is a measure of future aggregate earnings. Depreciation expense is recalculated on the adjusted value of individual fixed assets and their respective remaining useful lives. Suppose that the result of this calculation is a value of 300 pesos for fixed assets and a depreciation charge of 12 pesos.

After cost of goods sold and depreciation have been adjusted, the remaining item to be adjusted on the income statement is revenue. Again, using quarterly NCPI figures, adjustments are made to transform sales in pesos throughout the year into the purchasing value of year-end pesos. Suppose that the adjusted sales are 293 pesos.

The line item *"Monetary Gain (Loss)"* is in the section of the income statement containing interest expense and foreign exchange gains or losses. The restated 1990 balance sheet has cash of 285 and payables of 114, less payables (none), for a net monetary asset position of 71 pesos. The 1991 balance sheet has cash of 180 plus receivables of 74 less payables of 62 for a net positive monetary position of 192 pesos. Inflation adversely impacts the purchasing power of net monetary assets resulting in a monetary loss. Had the company a net monetary liability, inflation would have created a monetary gain.

Starting with the net monetary asset at year-end 1990, adding in quarterly sales less quarterly purchases of inventory, adjusted to reflect the end 1991 value of the peso, and netting the year-end net monetary asset position of 192 pesos, results in the calculation of the net monetary loss.

Suppose that this is 31 pesos, thereby reducing reported profit to 10 pesos. After adjusting the original capital contribution by 1.188 to reflect the change in value of the peso during 1991, the balance sheet and income statements can be cast in their final form. The item "Holding Gain on Nonmonetary Assets," or "HGNA" herein, is simply a derived figure that balances the balance sheet. The amounts shown in these examples are illustrative in nature. The actual calculations for a real company are quite cumbersome and more complex than indicated in the discussion. Perhaps one lesson to be learned is that accounting is much more straightforward in a nation with a stable currency.

OPERATING IN A HYPERINFLATIONARY ENVIRONMENT

Many businessmen naturally shun operating in an environment where annual inflation may be 100 percent, 1,000 percent, or more. One factor to realise is that inflation is relative to the beholder. Brazil, with its high inflation rate, may be considered a citadel of financial stability to someone from Argentina. The Canadian inflation rate may be considered low by an Italian businessman and high by a businessman from Germany or Japan.

Another factor to keep in mind is that the usual assumption that inflation, once entrenched in an economy, will only get worse, is not necessarily true. Although government officials are usually not eager to give the economy the necessary medicine to treat the disease of inflation, there are exceptions. In the late 1980s, Bolivia was able to commit itself to a fiscal austerity programme that reined in inflation from 20,000 percent per year to 10 percent per year. During the 1980s, the industrialized nations in Europe and North America have intentionally pursued policies, such as high interest rates, that slowed their economic growth and subdued the high inflation rates of the 1970s.

Another difficulty in running a business in a hyper inflationary environment is the matter of measuring success. How does one know if he or she is ahead in making an investment in a hyperinflationary environment? The fact that there is a positive return of, say, 10 percent on the original investment doesn't mean success if the currency has lost half its purchasing power in the interim. Therefore, the accounting data of a company must be adjusted, because, left unadjusted, the information is useless, misleading, or wrong.

Ultimately, only net cash flows can be used to reinvest in a firm and provide a return to equity holders through the payment of dividends. In hyperinflationary nations, cash flows must be managed on a daily basis to protect against the rapid decline in purchasing power. During the German inflation after World War I, workers were paid twice a day to allow them to spend the money immediately. A company operating in this type of inflationary environment manages its cash flow on a hourly basis.

A manager in a highly inflationary nation needs an effective cash management control system. Cash is not an asset in a hyperinflationary nation—in some ways it can be considered a liability that generates losses just by holding it. Greater demands are placed on the financial acumen of managers in dealing with a company's pricing policy and its inventory and cost containment strategies.

Deviations from projected cash flows must be more carefully attended to because the repercussions can be devastating. For instance, the slow collection of receivables in a nation with a stable currency may result a higher financing charge on borrowings to supply the company with necessary cash until the receivables are collected. In a hyperinflationary nation, the same slow collection of receivables may bankrupt the company.

Money received two months later than anticipated for payment of a given quantity of product may no longer be sufficient to purchase the material and components necessary to manufacture the same quantity of product. The loss in purchasing power caused by a delayed payment of a receivable does not allow the company to replace the sales represented by the receivable, thereby jeopardizing the company as a going concern.

In a hyper inflationary environment, the accounting system must be modified to reflect the ravages of inflation on the income statement and balance sheet. Only then can financial reports perform their intended function of measuring the performance of a company. If some means of accounting for inflation is not incorporated in adjusting the financial reports, then the owners of the company have no way of knowing whether they have made a successful investment. This is one reason why Brazil, and later Mexico, introduced a formal system of indexation.

Highly inflationary environments make classic return-on-investment (ROI) analysis very difficult. Assumptions regarding future inflation rates, as applied to sales prices and cost of goods sold, can dramatically impact the calculated ROI of the investment. In fact, the analyst is in a position to select those rates that make a project either economically attractive or not, according to some preconceived notion in the analyst's mind. As noted in the tables on inflation rates, there is no constancy in inflation rates from one year to the next. This makes selection of the appropriate inflation rate to be incorporated in an ROI analysis of a multiyear project more difficult, because there is no single inflation rate that is suitable for a multiyear project. ROI models, which have been devised in stable currency nations, have little validity in nations with high inflation rates.

However, something has to be used to determine the

desirability of a project. Often, an ROI model assumes that present prices and costs are also the projected prices and costs without taking inflation into account. The analysis is done in units of "constant" local currency or equivalent dollars. The discounted cash flow is measured against the amount of the investment to judge its rate of return. The basic assumption in this approach is that escalation of costs from inflation can be passed on to the consumer in terms of price hikes. But this is inadequate.

Price increases have to be greater than increases in costs to provide a real return in terms of net cash flow to the company, or dividends to the investors. Even this may not be adequate. Price hikes have to be sufficient to accumulate sufficient funds for replacing productive assets at some point in the future. This is the Dutch approach for measuring success. This is no easy task to accomplish in a hyperinflationary environment, but realization of its necessity is the first step to understanding business practices in these nations.

The financial earnings from a business venture in a hyperinflationary environment cannot be kept as a monetary asset, because it is unlikely that bank interest rates will compensate for the loss of purchasing power of the currency. This presents another challenge to operating a firm in a highly inflationary nation. Managers of companies, along with private citizens, avoid holding currency for any length of time. Individuals and businesses become adept at preserving purchasing power by spending cash immediately for needed items to run a home or a business and converting any remaining cash to a more desirable currency, if possible. For soft currency nations, the latter alternative is usually hampered by local currency exchange restrictions. Aside from a black market to accommodate those fleeing from a currency, the alternative is to purchase tangible assets with excess currency holdings. When currency is needed, a portion of these assets are sold. Tangible assets tend to preserve the purchasing value of a currency, a characteristic lacking in the currency itself.

Businesses operating in highly inflationary countries tend to have large inventories and small amounts of cash on hand.

Businesses operating in low inflationary countries tend to minimize inventory holdings because they represent a cost in terms of storage, insurance, spoilage, obsolescence, and pilferage, besides generating financial charges. Because inventory is widely recognized as a cost of doing business in nations with stable currencies, excess inventory holdings must be viewed as another cost of doing business in hyperinflationary nations.

This is a means of preserving purchasing power, not a means of providing for the smooth operation of a company. Cash management is a critical function in high inflation nations. Often inventory is the likely investment for excess holdings of cash, but one has to select whether raw material or finished goods inventory should be the chosen investment medium. Another consideration in managing cash is borrowing money in order to reduce the net monetary asset exposure of a company.

The borrowings are usually invested in inventory, which can transform a company from an exposure to net monetary assets to net monetary liabilities.A company with net monetary liabilities is thought to be better positioned to deal with inflation than one with net monetary assets. In theory, the company stands to win in an inflationary climate.

This strategy depends, of course, on interest rates charged by banks. There have been times when bank interest rates on corporate borrowings were so high that there was serious doubt as to the efficacy of borrowing to enhance inventory holdings as a successful strategy for dealing with inflation. In other words, the real financing costs associated with having a net monetary liability exposure may not have been matched by unrealized inventory profits. There is a risk in holding excessive inventory. If a company makes shoes and borrows money to put more shoes into inventory as a means of protecting itself from inflation, what happens to the value of the inventory when shoe fashions change? Or if raw material inventory holdings are performing this function, what happens to the value of inventory when degradation of the leather occurs from sitting too long in a warehouse?

The purchasing power of currency invested in inventories of out-of-style shoes and rotting leather will not be preserved. And, of course, even if the adjusted soft currency income is adequate to provide a return on a hard currency investment, the question of how to convert the soft currency back into a hard currency still exists. Selling a portion of the goods for hard currency, transfer pricing, and management fees for services and for transfer of tangible and intangible assets are means by which a company can obtain a hard currency return on a hard currency investment. But local currency restrictions may bar the way. Inflation sometimes indicates underlying political and social problems in addition to government fiscal and monetary problems.

Companies operating under the threat of nationalization, changing government regulations, and the arbitrary administration of regulations and rules by those in power without means of appeal, or social and political instability react to the situation by changing the criteria associated with making investments.

The greater the political, economic, or social risks, the shorter the desired time horizon in recouping an investment, and consequently, the higher the required ROI. Businessmen become reluctant to invest if the higher ROI cannot be achieved. This impedes the ability of a nation to raise the standard of living of its people, which is often the underlying reason for the political and social unrest.

MANAGERIAL GUIDELINES

Some of the guidelines for managing a company in a highly inflationary environment, which are not present, or are present in a subdued way in nations with stable currencies, follow. Management of prices and costs has to be conducted in a manner to ensure a cash flow sufficient to provide a real return on investment. This involves daily attention to cash flow and quick reaction to deviations in the projected cash flow.

- Management of monetary assets and liabilities is necessary to avoid losses from currency devaluations. This sometimes leads a company to assume a net monetary liability position by borrowing from banks and investing the proceeds in tangible assets such as inventories.

But, this may lead to a liquidity crisis if the tangible assets cannot be sold. This course of action can also be nonproductive if interest rates on bank loans become extremely high and are not compensated by gains in inventory values.

- Accounting for inflation should be done in a fashion that permits the appraisal of the success of a company in terms of a real return on investment and the accumulation of sufficient funds to remain a going concern. This means that there has to be a correct choice of accounting methods and indices of inflation to take into consideration losses in the purchasing power of the currency and the concomitant increases in the replacement cost of productive assets.
- Classic ROI models for evaluating new projects must, at the least, be viewed with suspicion. Such models cannot be dismissed out of hand because some methodology is needed to assess whether an investment, or which of a choice of investments, should be made. Performing the analysis in constant units of the local currency, or equivalent units of a hard currency, is common, but this does not address the ramifications of different rates of inflation affecting prices and various elements of cost.
- In making new investments that require hard currency either in the form of the investment itself, or in importing parts and components to sustain an investment, some means of transferring goods or monetary assets, or of paying fees, should be arranged before these investments are made. This is necessary to amortize the hard currency investment, along with providing a return on the investment and/or paying for hard currency imports.
- A realistic assessment of political risk and arbitrary action taken against a company by what may be a

hostile government has to be made. The latter is sometimes influenced by those managing a company. One of the potential strengths of local management is their knowledge of both the regulatory and administrative requirements and those who are in charge of such matters. Local management can often deal more effectively with problems than managers from the parent company organization, who often lack the cultural appreciation of the way things are done in a different nation.

- There has to be careful selection of personnel to ensure that an operation is well managed under the trying circumstances of buying and selling in a hyperinflationary currency. Here, again, local management, who have been raised in a hyperinflationary environment and have learned to cope with the system since childhood, may have an advantage over a manager brought up in a hard currency nation.

The management evaluation system should be designed to ensure that managerial motivations and corporate objectives are more or less in harmony. Such a measuring system goes beyond conventional measuring of performance by financial results commonly found in nations with relatively stable currencies. The measuring system should also include an evaluation of the effectiveness of management to protect the company against the continual erosion of the purchasing power of its monetary assets.

All currencies are heading down the road to worthlessness, some more rapidly than others. Many businessmen, however, have been commercially successful in highly inflationary environments. As long as increases in corporate revenue compensate for the ravages of inflation, one can prosper where others may not survive. Businessmen can more easily manage cash flow and monetary assets when inflation rates are low and interest rates substantially compensate for the loss of purchasing power. Cash can be held as cash. Games do not have to be played with inventories, receivables, payables, bank loans, and currency conversions to protect a company from erosion of the purchasing power of its monetary assets.

The simple reaction to avoid doing business in highly inflationary environments is understandable. A special financial acumen is necessary to stay ahead of inflation surging at several hundred percent per year. A company that decides to avoid the pitfalls of operating in highly inflationary economies restricts its activities to those areas where business is conducted in relatively stable currencies. There is a much larger market, in terms of population, called the third world. It is obvious by the size of third world economies that many businessmen and companies have learned to cope, and apparently to thrive, in less than desirable monetary environments.

INFLATION VARIES WITH TIME AND PLACE

A cursory examination of consumer price indices listed in the *International Financial Statistics*, published by the International Monetary Fund, shows that the rate of inflation is unique to a nation and varies with the times. Inflation was more subdued among the industrialized nations in the 1980s than it was in the 1970s. It is possible to group nations in terms of low, medium, and high rates of inflation, although nations can shift their position among these broad classifications over time. Generally speaking, low inflation nations are the leading industrialized nations. They also exhibit social and political stability, which suggests that inflation of a nation's currency is not just a consequence of a government's fiscal and monetary policies.

The medium inflation nations have inflation rates more closely akin to low inflation nations than high inflation nations. Although France is listed as a nation with a medium rate of inflation, which was true for the 1970s, it should be listed among the low inflation nations in the 1980s. Both Italy and the United Kingdom have cut their inflation rates substantially during the 1980s. Two conditions, among others, for the European Currency Unit (ECU) becoming a common European currency are that interest and inflation rates be at comparable levels among the European Community nations, to permit the simultaneous conversion of all European currencies into a single currency.

Table: Annual Inflation Rates of Low Inflation Nations

	Japan	Germany	Netherlands	United States
1975	11.9%	5.9%	10.5%	9.2%
1976	9.3	4.5	8.8	5.8
1977	8.1	3.9	6.4	6.5
1978	3.8	2.8	4.1	7.5
1979	3.6	4.1	4.2	11.3
1980	8.0	5.5	6.5	13.5
1981	4.9	6.3	6.8	10.4
1982	2.6	5.3	5.9	6.2
1983	1.9	3.3	2.8	3.2
1984	2.3	2.4	3.3	4.3
1985	2.0	2.2	2.2	3.6
1986	0.6	-0.1	0.1	1.9
1987	0.0	0.2	-0.7	3.7
1988	0.7	1.3	0.7	4.0
1989	2.3	2.8	1.1	4.8
1990	3.1	2.7	2.5	5.4
1991	3.3	3.5	3.9	s4.2

The considerable reduction in inflation rates during the 1980s suggests that inflation can be controlled if nations have the will to do so. It is apparent in examining the disparity in inflation rates between the medium inflation nations and the high inflation nations that there appears to be a point where citizens and businessmen abandon a currency as a storehouse of value.

This occurs when the inflation rate exceeds the interest rate on financial instruments by a sufficient margin to convince all that holding the currency, even in the form of an interest-bearing bank deposit, is a losing proposition. Once money has lost its attribute as a storehouse of value through a succession of rapid losses in purchasing power, the currency is essentially repudiated. Money is spent on receipt. Excess cash is exchanged for tangible assets to preserve purchasing power. This increases the velocity of money, or the number of transactions per period of time, which adds to the inflation rate and brings a nation to a point of hyperinflation.

An inflation rate of 100 percent means that prices are doubling every year, 1,200 percent means, neglecting compounding, doubling every month, such as occurred in Brazil in 1989. Inflation of 2,400 percent means doubling of prices every two weeks, such as in Argentina and Brazil in 1990. In 1989, prices were doubling in Argentina in less than two weeks' time, posing quite a challenge for financial managers and accountants.

CUMULATIVE LOSSES IN PURCHASING POWER

Not apparent from these numbers is the cumulative loss of purchasing power over a period of time. In 1915, Henry Ford doubled the salary of his work force to $5 per day, which meant that workers at that time could survive (feed, house, and clothe their families) on $2.50 per day, or about $750 per year. When Ford doubled their pay to $5 per day, or $1,500 per year, the workers not only could increase their standard of living but they had enough money to buy a Model T automobile. Today, the poverty level for a family in the United States is around $15,000 per year, which is not adequate to purchase a new automobile. Viewed in this light, the cumulative loss in purchasing power of the U.S. dollar over the course of this century is on the order of 95 percent.

Cumulative loss of purchasing power is more severe in other nations. For highly inflationary nations such as Brazil, which, by the way, does not have the worst inflationary record, money is called in from time to time and exchanged for new money with a new name, the cruzerio or the cruzado. The exchange of 1,000 cruzerios for 1 cruzado to be followed some time later by the exchange of 1,000 cruzados for 1 cruzerio avoids confusion among Brazilians as to which currency is in vogue. The lopping off of three zeroes reduces the expense of having to print a wheelbarrowful of money to buy a quart of milk and of having to expand numerical data fields in the banks' computer systems.

The record for the highest cumulative loss in the shortest time by an industrialized nation is probably held by Germany. During the Weimar Republic, a mark, which was worth about \$0.25 at the end of World War I, was reduced in value to I trillion marks per postage stamp over the course of about four years. When new money was issued, the conversion rate was several trillion old marks per new mark—the lopping off of twelve zeroes in one blow.

Chapter 5

International Accounting

The International Accounting Standards Board (IASB) founded on April 1, 2001 is th e successor of the International Accounting Standards Committee (IASC) founded in June 1973 in London. It is responsible for developing the International Financial Reporting Standards (new name for the International Accounting Standards issued after 2001), and promoting the use and application of these standards. The International Accounting Standards Board is an independent, privately-funded accounting standard-setter based in London, UK.

FOUNDATION OF THE IASB

In March 2001, the International Accounting Standards Committee Foundation (IASCF) was formed as a not-for-profit corporation incorporated in the State of Delaware, US. The IASC Foundation is the parent entity of the International Accounting Standards Board, an independent accounting standard-setter based in London, UK. On 1 April 2001, the International Accounting Standards Board (IASB) assumed accounting standard-setting responsibilities from its predecessor body, the International Accounting Standards Committee. This was the culmination of a restructuring based on the recommendations of the report Recommendations on Shaping IASC for the Future.

The IASB structure has the following main features: the IASC Foundation is an independent organization having two main bodies, the Trustees and the IASB, as well as a Standards Advisory Council and the International Financial Reporting Interpretations Committee. The IASC Foundation Trustees appoint the IASB members, exercise oversight and raise the funds needed, but the IASB has sole responsibility for setting International Financial Reporting Standards (international accounting standards).

IASB Members

The IASB has 14 Board members, each with one vote. The members are selected chiefly upon their professional competence and practical experience. A unanimous vote is not necessary in order for the publication of a Standard, exposure draft, or final IFRIC Interpretation. The approval by nine of the IASB's fourteen members is however required. At 28/01/2008 the IASB Chairman was Professor Sir David Tweedie. The Vice-Chairman was Thomas E Jones.

INTERNATIONAL FINANCIAL REPORTING STANDARDS

International Financial Reporting Standards (IFRS) are standards and interpretations adopted by the International Accounting Standards Board (IASB). Many of the standards forming part of IFRS are known by the older name of International Accounting Standards (IAS). IAS was issued between 1973 and 2001 by the board of the International Accounting Standards Committee (IASC).

Adoption of Ifrs

IFRS are used in many parts of the world, including the European Union, Hong Kong, Australia,India, GCC countries, Russia, South Africa and Singapore Nearly 100 countries currently require or permit the use of, or have a policy of convergence with, Firs. For a current overview see IAS PLUS's list of all countries that have adopted IFRS.

Australia

The Australian Accounting standards, previous to 1 January 2005, were based around accounting standards developed by the Australian Accounting Standards Board (AASB). As a result of pressure towards international harmonisation, the AASB had been working towards a convergence between the Australian Standards and the Australian equivalent of IFRS has been fully implemented as AASB 101 - 141. It is a requirement that all reporting entities adopt the standards as they have replaced the previous Australian generally accepted accounting principles.

Due to the accounting standards operating halfway through the year, the requirements can be summarised as follows:

- Year ended 30 June 2004-Prepare under pre IFRS standards and state in notes the expected effect of the adoption of IFRS
- Year ended 30 June 2005-Prepare under pre IFRS standards and prepare a reconciliation to IFRS standards
- Year ended 30 June 2006-Prepare under Australian Equivalents to IFRS standards

Canada

The use of IFRS will be required in 2011 for Canadian publicly accountable profit-oriented enterprises. This includes public companies and other *"profit-orientated enterprises that are responsible to large or diverse groups of shareholders."*

European Union

All listed EU companies (including banks and insurance companies) have been required to use IFRS since 2005. Prior to 2005, there were around 350 publicly listed companies that used IFRS. In order to be approved for use in the EU, standards must be endorsed by the Accounting Regulatory Committee (ARC), which includes representatives of member state governments and is advised by a group of accounting experts known as the European Financial Reporting Advisory Group. As a result IFRS as applied in the EU may differ from that used elsewhere. Parts of the standard IAS 39: *Financial Instruments*: Recognition and Measurement were not originally approved by the ARC. IAS 39 was subsequently amended, removing the option to record financial liabilities at fair value, and the ARC approved the amended version. The IASB is working with the EU to find a way to an acceptable way to remove a remaining anomaly in respect of hedge accounting.

As the standards are part of European law the approved standards and approved subsequent changes must be published in the Official Journal of the European Union. On October 13, 2003 the first publication of the standards was included in PBL 261. Changes to the earlier published IAS and IFRS can be monitored using the Web site of the Directorate Internal Market of the European Union on the implementation of the IAS in the European Union. From 2007 companies traded on the Alternative Investment Market in the UK will be required to prepare their accounts using IFRS.

Russia

The government of Russia has been implementing a programmed to harmonize its national accounting standards with IFRS since 1998. Since then twenty new accounting standards were issued by the Ministry of Finance of Russian Federation aiming to align accounting practices with IFRS. Despite of these efforts essential differences between national accounting standards and IFRS remain. From 2004 all commercial banks are obliged to prepare financial statements in accordance with both national accounting standards and IFRS.

Turkey

Turkish Accounting Standards Board translated IFRS into Turkish in 2006. As of 31 December 2006 Turkish companies listed in Istanbul Stock Exchange are required to prepare IFRS reports.

Singapore

Until 2007, the Council of Corporate Disclosure and Governance (CCDG) was in charge of standard setting in Singapore. The CCDG had multiple responsibilities and thus, it was decided that in order for greater transparency and independence, these responsibilities would be divided up. Currently, the Accounting Standards Committee (ASC) is in charge of standard setting.

Singapore closely models its Financial Reporting Standards (FRS) according to the IFRS, with appropriate changes made to suit the Singapore context. Before a standard is enacted, consultations with the IASB are made to ensure consistency of core principles.

This also allows both parties to engage in constant feedback in an effort to improve the IFRS general frameworks. Companies listed on the Singapore stock exchange are required to follow the latest sets of FRS, to be audited by one of the Big 4 Accounting firms.

Small Medium Enterprises (SMEs) have their own set of accounting standards and private firms are encouraged to adopt FRS for greater accountability.

UNITED STATES AND CONVERGENCE WITH US GAAP

In 2002 at a meeting at Norwalk, Connecticut, the IASB and the US Financial Accounting Standards Board agreed to harmonise their agenda and work towards reducing differences between IFRS and U.S. generally accepted accounting principles (GAAP or the Norwalk Agreement). In February 2006 FASB and IASB issued a Memorandum of Understanding including a programmed of topics on which the two bodies will seek to achieve convergence by 2008. US companies registered with the United States Securities and Exchange Commission must file financial statements prepared in accordance with US GAAP.

Until 2007, foreign private issuers were required to file financial statements prepared either

- Under US GAAP or
- In accordance with local accounting principles or IFRS with a footnote reconciling from local principles or IFRS to US GAAP.

This reconciliation imposed extra expense on companies which are listed on exchanges both in the US and another country. From 2008, foreign private issuers are additionally permitted to file financial statements in accordance with IFRS as issued by the IASB without reconciliation to US GAAP.

IASB CURRENT PROJECTS

Convergence Projects with FASB

- Government grants
- Joint ventures
- Impairment
- Income tax
- Investment properties
- Research and development
- Subsequent events

Projects under Research

- Derecognizing (Asset and/or liabilities)
- Financial instruments (replacement of existing standards → Merge all 3 standards)
- Intangible assets
- Liabilities and Equity

STRUCTURE OF IFRS

Firs are considered a "principles-based" *set of standards in that they establish broad rules as well as dictating specific treatments.*

International Financial Reporting Standards comprise:

- *International Financial Reporting Standards (IFRS):* standards issued after 2001.
- *International Accounting Standards (IAS):* standards issued before 2001.
- *Interpretations originated from the International Financial Reporting Interpretations Committee (IFRIC)-* issued after 2001.
- *Standing Interpretations Committee (SIC)* - issued before 2001.

There is also a Framework for the Preparation and Presentation of Financial Statements which describes some of the principles underlying IFRS.

FEATURES OF IFRS

References

References to IFRS standards given in the standard convention, for example refers to paragraph 14 of IAS1, Presentation of Financial Statements.

Content of Financial Statements

IFRS financial statements consist of

- A balance sheet
- Income statement
- Either a statement of changes in equity or a statement of recognised income or expense ("*SORIE*")
- A cash flow statement
- Notes, including a summary of the significant accounting policies

Comparative information is provided for the previous reporting period. An entity preparing IFRS accounts for the first time must apply IFRS in full for the current and comparative period although there are transitional exemptions. On 6 September 2007, the IASB issued a revised IAS 1 Presentation of Financial Statements.

The main changes from the previous version are to require that an entity must: Present all non-owner changes in equity (that is, 'comprehensive income') either in one statement of comprehensive income or in two statements (a separate income statement and a statement of comprehensive income). Components of comprehensive income may not be presented in the statement of changes in equity.

Present a statement of financial position (balance sheet) as at the beginning of the earliest comparative period in a complete set of financial statements when the entity applies an accounting policy retrospectively or makes a retrospective restatement. Disclose income tax relating to each component of other comprehensive income. Disclose reclassification adjustments relating to components of other comprehensive income.

IAS 1 changes the titles of financial statements as they will be used in Firs: 'balance sheet' will become 'statement of financial position' 'income statement' will become 'statement of comprehensive income' 'cash flow statement' will become 'statement of cash flows').

Entities are not required to use the new titles in their financial statements. All existing Standards and Interpretations are being amended to reflect the new terminology. The revised IAS 1 resulted in consequential amendments to 5 Firs, 23 IASs, and 10 Interpretations. The revised IAS 1 is effective for annual periods beginning on or after 1 January 2009. Early adoption is permitted.

Consolidated Financial Statements

The ultimate parent company of a group must produce consolidated financial statements including all of its subsidiaries. A subsidiary is an entity which is controlled by another entity; control is the power to govern the financial and operating policies. In preparing consolidated financial statements, balances, transactions, income and expenses with other group members are eliminated.

Acquisition Accounting and Goodwill

All business combinations are accounted for by applying the purchase method, requiring that one entity is identified as acquirer. The acquiring entity assesses the fair value of the separate assets, liabilities and contingent liabilities in the business it has acquired; this can include identification of intangible assets, for example customer relationships, which are not commonly recognised except on acquisitions. The difference between the cost of the business combination and the fair value of the assets and liabilities acquired represents goodwill.

Goodwill is not subject to amortisation, but is assessed for impairment at least annually. Impairment is charged to the income statement. Impairment provisions on goodwill are not subsequently reversed.

Property, Plant and Equipment

Property, plant and equipment is measured initially at cost. Cost can include borrowing costs directly attributable to the acquisition, construction or production if the entity opts to adopt such a policy consistently. Property, plant and equipment may be revalued to fair value if the entire class of assets to which it belongs is so treated (for example, the revaluation of all freehold properties). Surpluses on revaluation are recognised directly to equity, not in the income statement; deficits on revaluation are recognised as expenses in the income statement.

Depreciation is charged to write off the cost or valuation of the asset over its estimated useful life down to the recoverable amount. The cost of depreciation is recognised as an expense in the income statement. The depreciation method and recoverable amount is reviewed at least annually. In most cases the method is "straight line", with the same depreciation charge from the date when an asset is brought into use until it is expected to be sold or no further economic benefits obtained from it, but other patterns of depreciation are used if assets are used proportionately more in some periods than others.

Joint Ventures, Associates and other Investments

Joint ventures are investments other than subsidiaries where the investor has a contractual arrangement with one or more other parties to undertake an economic activity that is subject to joint control. Joint ventures may be accounted for using either:

- Proportionate consolidation, accounting for the investor's share of the assets, liabilities, income and expenses of the joint venture.
- Equity method. The investment is stated initially at cost and adjusted thereafter for the investor's share of post-acquisition changes in net assets. The income statement includes the investor's share of profit or loss of the investment.

Associates are investments, other than joint ventures and subsidiaries, in which the investor has a significant influence (the power to participate in financial and operating policy decisions). It is presumed that this will be the case if the investment is greater than 20% of the investee unless it can be clearly demonstrated not to be the case. Associates are accounted for using the equity method.

Investments other than subsidiaries, joint ventures and associates are accounted for at their fair values unless:

- They have fixed or determinable maturity periods and are expected to be held to maturity, in which case they are stated at amortised cost (providing a constant rate of return until maturity.
- There is no reliable market value, in which case they are measured at cost.

Inventory (Stock)

Inventory is stated at the lower of cost and net realisable value. Cost comprises all costs of purchase, costs of conversion and other costs incurred in bringing items to their present location and condition.

Where individual items are not identifiable, the *"first in first out"* (FIFO) method is used, such that cost represents the most recent items acquired.

"Last in first out" (LIFO) is not acceptable. Net realisable value is the estimated selling price less the costs to complete and costs to sell.

Receivables (Debtors) and Payables (Creditors)

Receivables and payables are recorded initially at fair value. Subsequent measurement is stated at amortised cost. In most cases, trade receivables and trade payables can be stated at the amount expected to be received or paid; however, it is necessary to discount a receivable or payable with a substantial credit period. If a receivable has been impaired its carrying amount is written down its recoverable amount (the higher of value in use and its fair value less costs to sell). Value in use is the present value of cash flows expected to be derived from the receivable.

Borrowing

Borrowing is stated at amortised cost using the effective interest method. This requires that the costs of arranging the borrowing are deducted from the principal value of debt and are amortised over the period of the debt.

Provisions

Provisions are liabilities of uncertain timing or amount. Provisions are recognised when an entity has, at the balance sheet date, a present obligation as a result of a past event, when it is probable that there will be an outflow of resources (for example a future cash payment) and when a reliable estimate can be made of the obligation. Restructuring provisions are recognised when an entity has a detailed plan for the restructuring and has raised an expectation amongst those affected that it will carry out the restructuring.

Revenue

Revenue is measured at the fair value of consideration received or receivable. Revenue for the sale of goods cannot be recognised until the entity has transferred to the buyer the significant risks and rewards of ownership of the goods. Revenue for rendering of services is accounted for to the extent that the stage of completion of the transaction can be measured reliably.

Employee Costs

Employee costs are recognised when an employee has rendered service during an accounting period. This requires accruals for short-term compensated absences such as vacation (holiday) pay. Profit sharing and bonus plans require accrual when an entity has an obligation to make such payments at the reporting date.

Share-based Payments

Where an entity receives goods or services in return for the issue of its own shares or equity instruments it accounts for the fair value of those goods or services as an expense or as an asset. Where it offers options and other share based incentives to its employees it is required to assess the market value of the instruments when they are first granted and then to charge the cost over the period in which the benefit vests.

Income Taxes

Taxes payable in respect of current and prior periods are recognised as a liability to the extent they are unpaid at the balance sheet date.

Deferred tax liabilities are recognised for taxable temporary differences at the balance sheet date which will result in tax payable in future periods (for example, where tax deductions have been claimed for capital expenditure before the cost of depreciation has been charged in the income statement).

Deferred tax assets are recognised for deductible temporary differences at the balance sheet date (for example, tax losses which can be used in future periods) to the extent that it is probable that these will reverse in future and that there will be taxable profits against which they can be offset.

Cash Flow Statements

IFRS cash flow statements show movements in cash and cash equivalents. This includes cash on hand and demand deposits, short term liquid investments readily convertible to cash and overdrawn bank balances where these readily fluctuate from positive to negative. IFRS cash flow statements do not need to show movements in borrowings or net debt.

Cash flow statements may be presented using either a direct method, in which major classes of cash receipts and cash payments are disclosed, or using the indirect method, whereby the profit or loss is adjusted for the effect of non-cash adjustments. Items on the cash flow statement are classified as operating activities, investing activities and financing activities.

Leasing (accounting by lessees)

Leases are classified:-

- Finance leases, being a lease which transfers substantially all the risks and rewards incidental to ownerships to the lessee. Finance leases are recognised on the balance sheet as an asset (the asset being leased) and as a liability (liability to the lessor).
- Operating leases, being a lease other than a finance lease. The cost of an operating lease is recognised in the income statement as the asset is used.

Fair Value

Fair value is the amount for which an asset could be exchanged, or a liability settled, between knowledgeable, willing parties in an arm's length transaction.

Amortised Cost

Amortised cost uses the effective interest method to provide a constant rate of return on an asset or liability until maturity. This term is used in IAS 39, for examples, Financial Liabilities at amortized cost, Loans and receivables at amortized cost and Held to maturity investments at amortized cost.

DIFFERENCES IN INTERNATIONAL ACCOUNTING

The Birth of an Accounting Harmonization Process? Financial reporting now concerns all listed companies in the EU. By the year 2005 all of them will be reporting according to the International Accounting Standards that are uniform throughout the EU. This is quite a radical change from the past. For continental Europe IAS is very much an Anglo-Saxon inspired reporting model. Applying and understanding IAS in other European countries requires considerable effort in getting to know the new concepts and the approach of the standard setters.

On the other hand, there is virtually no UK listed company yet that already applies IAS. Although the requirement to apply IAS does not extend to small and medium sized companies (at least not as an EU requirement), many member states of the EU will, as a result of the modernization of their Accounting Directives, amend their national accounting legislation in a manner which brings it closer to IAS.

MODERN FINANCIAL REPORTING

Broadly speaking, accounting is about the provision of figures to people about their resources. It can be seen mainly as technical manipulation of figures characterizing various points of interest. In accounting much of the emphasis is likely to be on 'doing things with figures'.

But the question arises as to which figure or figures should actually be built into the system. Or more fundamentally, how is one going to decide which figures to put in? In general terms, we can answer this question by going back to the original definition of accounting. The figures the accountants should provide to people are the figures that they need to know for their own practical purposes.

This raises questions about the users of accounting information, and the purposes for which each particular type of user requires the independently, and often very differently in different countries. Practice, regulation and especially the mode of regulation differed often very greatly.

Financial reporting in general can be viewed as a part of the communication process. The nature and functions of reporting with respect to organizations differ depending on the nature of the sender and the receiver as well as the nature of the information transferred.

The sender and the receiver form an integral part of the environment. Initially financial reporting was mainly internal reporting. It provided company owners with a vehicle to manage the company.

Later on, in the early 1800s private capital alone was insufficient to finance business activities. Capital was gathered from sources outside the company. The owners delegated the managing function to directors and provided them with the necessary authority.

Nowadays the external financial report provides a means of reporting the results and accounts to owners. Financial reporting evolved from internal to external reporting, but for a long time external reporting meant providing information within the borders of a specific country.

Thus, because national authorities perceive that there are alternatives for recognition and measurement and presentation they have chosen those recognition, measurement, consolidation and presentation policies which best fitted their national environments.

The annual report, for example, provides information on the financial position of a company and its results. Although the general purpose is similar in most countries, many differences occur resulting from different environmental and cultural influences in the individual countries.

Differences in Accounting

Among the most important causes of differences referred to in the literature are:

- Sources of finance,
- The existing legal system,
- The link between accounting and taxation, and
- Cultural differences between societies.

Sources of Finance (Provision of Finance)

'This difference in providers of finance (creditors/insiders) versus (equity/owners) is the key cause for international differences in financial reporting'. Companies in different countries responded differently to the increased need for finance.

In Germany, France, Italy, Belgium, banks became the major supplier of additional funds. Thus companies relied more on debt financing. On the contrary, in the UK and in the US shareholders provided extra funds, which has given rise to active stock exchanges.

Existing Legal System

In the past two types of legal system have developed in

the West: 1) the common law system (zvykové právo), and 2) the code law system (kodifikovaný systém).

The common law system originated in England and developed from case law. Common law is characterized as a legal system which develops case by case and which does not prescribe general rules, which could be applied to all cases. In common law countries accounting regulation is in the hands of professional organizations in the private sector. Company law is kept to a minimum and detailed regulation is produced by the private standard setter.

The code law system originated in Roman law and has developed in continental Europe. It is characterized by a wide set of rules which attempt to give guidance in all situations. In the code law countries the company law is very detailed and accounting standards are often embodied in the company law. Accounting regulation in code law countries is in the hands of the government and financial reporting is in those circumstances often reduced to complying with a set of very detailed legal rules.

Link between accounting and taxation

In some countries fiscal authorities use information provided in the financial statements to determine taxable income. In some countries the costs are only tax deductible if they are also recognized in the P&L account. This may lead to the danger, that financial reporting becomes tax influenced or even tax biased. This link is often found in those countries that do not have an explicit investor approach, e.g. Germany, Belgium, and the Czech Republic.

In the UK, the US and in the Netherlands the link between taxes and accounting is much weaker. Separate accounts are filed for tax purposes. The measurement and recognition rules are different from the valuation rules used in financial reporting. This relation between accounting income and tax income varies over time.

Cultural Differences

Cultural differences between nations are identified as an

important influencing factor on reporting and disclosure behaviour with regard to financial statements. (E.g. individualism versus collectivism, strong versus weak uncertainty avoidance, professionalism versus statutory control, uniformity versus flexibility, secrecy versus transparency.)

Recent Empirical Evidence

As the business community becomes more and more internationalised it might seem that the differences play a less significant role in financial reporting. For large companies the location of the company is no longer the sole influencing factor on the reporting behaviour of the company. However, this is not the case. The variables pointed out by researchers in the 1970s and 1980s as causes which might explain differences in national accounting systems and national GAAPs are used in empirical comparative studies where different aspects of financial reporting practices are researched, e.g. value relevance of accounting information, earnings management practices, characteristics of the audit market and process.

For illustration: Ali and Hwang (2000) researched the value relevance of accounting information and found that it is less relevant in bank oriented financial systems.

Ball, Kothari and Robin (2000) investigated two properties of accounting income – conservatism and timeliness. Conservatism was for the first time researched by Basu (1997) and it is defined as the extent to which current period income asymmetrically incorporates economic losses relative to economic gains. They found that in common law countries accounting income is significantly timelier than in code law countries. Guenther and Young (2000) investigated cross-country differences in legal systems, differences in legal protection for external shareholders, and differences in the degree of tax conformity and their impact on the relation between accounting earnings and the real economic value relevant events that underlie them. They found that there is a high association for the UK and the US and a lower one for the bank-oriented countries.

This paper strived to characterise from the normative standpoint the major features of international accounting regulation and explored the differences between the reporting styles of different nations growing from their traditions. The recent empirical evidence suggests that the differences in provision of finance, the legal system, the link between accounting and taxation and cultural values can explain the differences between the financial reporting, accounting and economic behaviour of companies around the world. A study taking a longitudinal approach to the development of differences after the institution of accounting harmonization could be an interesting topic for future research.

Accounting provides a critical service to society, and in the wake of the recent accounting scandals, where billions of dollars of investment and retirement wealth evaporated for millions of investors and employees, the very integrity and survivability of this service have been called into question.

The globalization of international trade has had and continues to have a profound effect on the way business is conducted. It has not only turned companies into global institutions, but it has also challenged daily economic life, national identity, and created a persistent movement towards cultural and business homogenization. Being a product of the environment in which it operates, international accounting has been caught in this maelstrom of change.

The international accounting community has heard the clarion call for a set of universally accepted set of accounting standards to facilitate understandability of financial information across borders. Accounting diversity among societies is reflected in financial statements prepared under different accounting standards. If investors and creditors encounter difficulties in understanding financial statements, they would be reluctant to invest or lend funds to such companies. Therefore, it is imperative for financial reports to be written in a common accounting language that is understood globally.

In addition, globalization of business, foreign currency exchanges, and the need for consolidated financial statements are exerting tremendous pressure on the internationalization of accounting standards. Anderson (1993) stated that "An international set of accounting standards would allow a more level playing field because income statements and balance sheet ratios would become more consistent between competing companies." Against the backdrop of globalization several pertinent questions need to be asked.

How does accounting differ in various countries? Does this diversity create problems? What are the causes of such diversity? What efforts are being made to meet the problems of that diversity and with what success or failure are they being met? What are the emerging issues with which the accounting profession will have to deal? What will be the future of international accounting?

The purpose of this manuscript is to synthesize into a coherent conceptual model diverse literatures describing antecedents, processes and outcomes relating to the degree of international accounting diversity and favors the adoption of a universally accepted set of accounting standards.

Historical Perspective

The very first steps towards international accounting standards date back to 1959, when a founding partner of a major European firm of independent accountants urged that work begin on this subject. Since then, the work of accounting and non-accounting organizations culminated in the setting up of the International Accounting Standards Committee (IASC) in 1973. In 1997 the IASC changed its structure to "bring about convergence between national accounting standards and practices and high quality global accounting standards."

In July 2000 the IASC was renamed the International Accounting Standards Board (IASB), and in April of the following year, the IASB assumed the responsibility for promulgating international accounting standards. The Asian crises of 1997-1998 marked an impetus for supporting international accounting standards, where many countries either adopted international accounting standards in their entirety, or with minor changes.

Several companies in countries that did not implement international accounting standards, adopted international accounting standards nonetheless for their own financial statements in order to be able to compete in international markets.

Similar accounting adoption steps have been taken by Australia, Canada, and Russia, as well as in several countries in the Middle East and North Africa.

Conceptual Framework of Adoption

The model presented in this manuscript synthesizes information reported in diverse sources and literatures pertaining to antecedents of accounting standardization, the processes that facilitate/moderate adoption of common practices and the actual/expected outcomes of such processes.

The conceptual foundations and presentation of this model are intended as a stimulus to generate academic and practitioner discussion and refinements on defining and measuring relationships among constructs.

Antecedents

Adhikari and Tondkar (1992) reported that financial "accounting reporting and disclosure standards and practices do not develop in a vacuum but reflect the particular environment in which they are developed". Accounting principles and practices are generally influenced not only by environmental factors such as history, values and culture, but also by the stage of that society's economic development and accounting system. If accounting is the language of business, then this language becomes relevant when it is easily understood and satisfies users and decision makers.

Several studies have been conducted to identify the reasons explaining accounting diversity. Meek and Saudagaran (1990) and Iqbal (2002) identified five key major environmental influences relating to the economic system, the political system, the legal system, the educational system, and religion. In particular, the level of inflation, sources of finance, the stage of economic development, financial markets, and managerial development or sophistication, accounting education, and culture affect accounting practices.

Iqbal (2002) argues that the "degree of economic risk exposure to the investors and creditors in a country is directly related to the degree of economic instability of the country." In countries characterized by an unstable economy, economic forecasts are very difficult and require constant, if not drastic, changes leading to questionable accounting practices. Therefore, a stable economy facilitates the development of a conceptually sound accounting system.

A country's level of inflation is another determinant that shapes accounting systems and causes accounting diversity, in most countries, the historical cost concept is used for initially recording transactions.

In times of generally rising prices, inflation exerts an enormous pressure on historical cost accounting and attracts a great deal of attention in reporting the effects of changing prices as it happened in the late 1970s and early 1980s in the U.S. and the U.K..

A country's stage of economic development is a reflection of the business transactions that are prevalent in that country. As Choi, Frost and Meek (1999) suggest, types of economic transactions determine the accounting issues that have to be addressed. The greater the complexity of business transactions, the more difficult the accounting issues.

Business ownership determines the extent to which financial disclosures are to be made. Thus, if business ownership is held by several investors, then a myriad of disclosures will be necessary to address the needs of such a diverse group of investors. If equity financing is the main source of an economy's source of capital, such as in the U.S. and the U.K., then financial reporting will be geared to equity holders.

Conversely, in countries where debt financing is the major source of capital, such as Germany, Japan, and Switzerland, accounting reporting focuses on creditor protection that is achieved through conservative accounting measurements. Consequently, since financial institutions have direct and immediate access to information, detailed and transparent public disclosure is limited.

Apart from the idiosyncratic sources of finance in a country, tax legislation has an impact on accounting. In many countries (e.g., Germany, Japan, France, and Sweden) tax law effectively determines accounting standards because firms are required to record revenues and expenses for tax purposes. In other instances such as the U.S., the U.K., and the Netherlands, financial and tax accounting are two separate and distinct disciplines.

Taxable income is simply financial accounting income adjusted for the effects of tax laws.

Inextricably bound to a country's economic system is a country's political system and philosophy. Political and economic stability go hand in hand. If economic stability were a prerequisite for the development of an accounting system, then that development would be facilitated by a country's political stability. An Ernst & Young survey of the Global 1000 companies, identified that apart from financial risk, legal infrastructure, bureaucracy, exchange controls, and commercial infrastructure, political instability was the major barrier to investment in a country.

Iqbal (2002) posits "the political instability of a country is often a result of the deterioration of economic conditions. The development of a comprehensive and sophisticated accounting system is difficult under such a set of circumstances."

Perhaps no other factor causes more diversity in accounting than the legal system that typically prescribes accounting rules and regulations. In certain countries, the private sector is entrusted with setting accounting standards and policies.

Gernon and Meek (2001) discussed the dichotomization of the accounting world into those countries with a legalistic (code-law countries) orientation incorporating most of continental Europe and South America, and those countries with a non-legalistic (common-law countries) orientation such as the U.K. and the U.S.

Prior studies have shown that whereas "common law"

countries tend to be innovative and open to new business ideas, "code law" countries are likely to adhere to prescribed procedures. Doupnik and Salter (1995) found that the type of legal system (i.e., code versus common law) was the dominant explanatory variable and that the basic starting point lied in classifying accounting practices internationally.

Closely related to this issue is judicial corruption. Apart from undermining the integrity of a country's legal system, judicial corruption erodes the very fabric of a society's ethics and values. This state of affairs has an impact on accounting since the behaviour of a country's high institutions will trickle down and be emulated by all other institutions in that country.

Although the U.S. has played a leading role in curbing global bribery, other countries have been slowly following suit. For example, in 1997, Thailand formed an anti-corruption organization, the National Counter-Corruption Commission. This Commission was instrumental in removing the interior minister from office. Similar steps have been taken in Indonesia. The quality of accounting education plays a vital role in a country's accounting system. Saudagaran (2004) points out that there is an interaction between the quality of accounting education and a country's level of economic development, political and economic ties with other countries, and the reputation of that country's accounting profession. Iqbal (2002) surmises that whereas the economic, political, and legal systems are closely intertwined, the educational system can be a force to "counter, reinforce, or modify influences of the economic, political, and legal systems."

One key outcome of education is the accounting profession's values. Not surprisingly, the shared values of the members of the accounting profession in a country influence the accounting system of that country. Furthermore, information from a country's accounting system impacts the economic, political, legal, and educational systems.

One key factor that houses the development of an accounting system is culture. Hofstede (1980) defined culture as "the collective programming of the mind which distinguishes the members of one human group from another."

Culture in general is a very difficult construct to define and measure. Equally difficult is the relationship between cultural factors and accounting development. Several studies conducted by Hofstede (1980), and Gray (1988) have sought to examine such a link using traditional constructs of "individualism versus collectivism", "large versus small power distance", "strong versus weak uncertainty avoidance", "masculinity versus femininity", and "Confucian dynamism." Gray (1988) identified the four accounting values of "professionalism", "uniformity", "conservatism", and "secrecy" and argued that these values interact with the institutional consequences of culture such as capital markets in order to have a final set of accounting systems that include financial accounting reporting practices and professional structure. Salter and Niswander (1995) tested Gray's (1988) theory and found that uncertainty avoidance is most strongly associated with Gray's accounting values. Individualism, which Gray thought would have overall relative importance, was only related to secrecy.

Gray and Vint's (1995) study focused exclusively on the secrecy dimension and found that it was significantly related to uncertainty avoidance and individualism. Salter and Niswander (1995) also found that power distance had no relationship to Gray's (1998) four accounting values. They also concluded that masculinity was more strongly associated than Gray (1998) had actually hypothesized. Fechner Gustav Theodor 1801-1887.

German psychologist and physicist who studied the relationship between strength of stimulus and intensity of sensation, thereby founding psychophysics. And Kilgore (1994) asserted Hofstede's (1980) finding that uncertainty avoidance is the only dimension that significantly correlated with his other three cultural dimensions.

Saudagaran and Meek (1997) concluded that the probable reason that uncertainty avoidance dominates the other three culture dimensions is because it is a "summary index for the other three cultural dimensions." It has also been argued, that culture has a more important bearing on disclosure—the secrecy dimension, than on measurement—the conservatism dimension. Therefore, cultural factors directly influence disclosure whereas economic factors influence measurement.

Language could also be deemed to have a cultural impact on accounting diversity. Perera (1994) summarized comments made by Gerhard G. Mueller that accounting seems to flourish in English speaking countries and languish in others, particularly Romance language countries. However, as with most elements of culture, it should be noted that language is not a causal factor per se but a correlate of other factors too.

One cultural variable that affects all others, as well as basic accounting concepts, is religion. Religion is a question of faith and plays a very important role in a global economic context. Apart from the fundamental beliefs in each religion, certain religions practices crossover from the sublime to the business world. For instance, Muslim law prohibits interest on loans among Muslims. In the Western world, interest plays such an integral part in daily transactions that in several countries, accounting or tax regulations require that interest be imputed even on non-interest bearing loans.

In summary, regarding culture, Saudagaran and Meek (1997) admit that it remains an elusive construct since it is very difficult to operationalize. Some researchers have even argued that culture has become "... a residue for everything that cannot be explained by other factors..." and went even further by questioning whether culture is really a "homogenous phenomenon within countries".

Processes Due to Diversity

Saudagaran and Meek (1997) conjecture that pressure from international capital markets is likely to be one of the main reasons for moderating accounting diversity in the future. There are two main avenues of achieving accounting compatibility. The first is through standardization and the second is through harmonization.

By its very definition, standardization is the imposition of a rigid and narrow set of rules that in the case of international accounting standards would ensure full compatibility. On the other hand, accounting harmonization is the minimization of diversity with a view to increasing the comparability of financial information across borders.

The recent flurry of activity in the international accounting arena augers well for the future of international accounting. Against this background, accountability, transparency, and integrity are crucial issues in both developed and emerging markets. According to DiPiazza and Eccles, investors want greater transparency from companies, boards of directors, independent auditors, and from sell-side analysts. They argue that greater transparency begets higher standards of accountability.

Furthermore, principles based on global accounting standards should be pursued as keys to opening the door to the world's capital markets.

Without such global standards, access to capital markets will be expensive and difficult. Thus, international accounting will play a pivotal role in the global financial arena. Until fairly recently, no one would have thought that U.S. GAAP would be assailed by some principles-based approach as that advocated by the IASB.

The providers of capital in an economy play a crucial role in shaping that economy's accounting system by determining their own information needs. Thus, in countries where there is a multitude of individual and institutional providers of capital, financial reporting generally focuses on transparency, profitability, and stewardship. Conversely, in credit-based countries, in which banks are to sole providers of capital, financial reporting focuses on creditor protection with conservative measurement rules.

The degree of international accounting harmonization will also be strongly influenced by the use of the new Internet-based technology known as Extensible Business Reporting Language or XBRL. This technology uses accepted financial reporting standards to translate financial statements into information that users will be able to access and analyze immediately for their decision-making. DiPiazza and Eccles, agree that XBRL will play a two crucial roles; the first is in promoting financial reporting transparency, while the second involves the increased speed with which information can be obtained and analyzed.

Another important process is the dissemination of knowledge to domestic and foreign students of accounting alike. A large proportion of the student bodies on several U.S. campuses are made up of foreign students exposed to U.S. and international accounting standards, principles, and practices.

A significant majority of these students return home with terminal degrees in accounting and some of them even with professional designations such as the CPA and CMA. These highly U.S.-educated individuals play a crucial role in the development of accounting in their respective countries.

For example, the Taiwanese accounting standard setter, the Financial Accounting Standards Committee, relies heavily on accounting academics, the majority of which received their doctorate degrees from U.S. universities. As a result, Taiwanese accounting academics and practitioners are very familiar with the US rules-based approach to accounting standard setting.

Another key process affecting international accounting is the growth of emerging capital markets.

Apart from the fact that these emerging economies have their own unique needs, financial reporting is seen as the foundation for the infrastructure for the growth of these markets. Emerging markets are quite diverse in both size and history. For instance, the capital markets of Korea, Malaysia, Mexico, and South Africa have remarkably large market capitalization that even exceeds the market capitalization of shares traded on the stock exchanges of some developed economies.

Some emerging capital markets, such as India, Malaysia, South Africa, and Zimbabwe have existed since colonial times. Yet others, such as Botswana and Ecuador have been in existed since the 1990s.

Consequently, a well-functioning stock market in these emerging capital markets serves as a barometer for that country's economic well being specifying, to some extent, macroeconomic policy regarding growth and inflation. The World Bank pointed out that "... in developing countries, accounting and auditing practices are sometimes weak and financial laws and regulations do not demand accurate and timely reports. Developing an effective accounting and auditing profession is essential for building efficient capital markets".

Financial reporting in emerging capital markets should rest on a tripod. The first leg should ensure that accounting information is available, adequate, timely, and readily accessible. The second leg should ensure that financial reports are prepared on the basis of sound accounting requirements and be made to comply with those accounting requirements. The third leg should ensure that financial information is comparable. Achieving comparability encompasses specific accounting policies that are used to prepare financial statements and also the need to understand the contextual significance of the financial information.

A universally accepted set of accounting standards is well poised to address these concerns. In summary, as a result of the explosion of debt and equity placements in foreign capital markets and cross border transactions, the future of international accounting will see an increase in transparency and comparability among countries.

As Fletcher (2002) predicts, national standard setters, securities regulators, multinational corporations, audit firms, and also investors will have the same goal of using one set of high quality international accounting standards. Hensen Viktor 1835-1924. German physiologist noted for his research in embryology and his studies of the sense organs.

Points to the harmonization of accounting standards for ensuring long-term global financial stability, creating international capital markets, and ensuring full transparency. From the U.S. perspective, once it resolves its issues over adopting international accounting standards, the goal of having a set of global accounting standards will become a reality in the not too distant future.

The harmonization initiatives that have taken place of the

past few years have been aimed at reducing this diversity even though many, like Saudagaran (2004) opine that these have been very expensive initiatives. As a matter of fact, even the International Accounting Standards Board (IASB) has embarked on a standard-setter role rather than solidifying its role as a harmonizer.

Outcomes

Prior studies have shown that diversity in financial reporting practices around the world affects firms in many areas. For example, Biddle and Saudagaran (1991), Saudagaran and Biddle, and Cheung and Lee (1995) observed that differences in disclosure levels affect a firm's decision to list on a foreign stock exchange. Choi and Levich (1991) and Bhusan and Lessard (1992) studied the effects of regulatory differences on user groups and found that accounting differences are important and affect the capital market decisions of capital market participants, while the effects of differences in the treatment of goodwill on mergers and acquisitions was investigated by Choi and Lee (1991), Lee and Choi (1992), and Dunne and Ndubizu (1995).

Saudagaran and Biddle (1995) showed that the probability that a firm will list its securities on a foreign exchange is inversely related to the foreign exchange's disclosure level and directly related to that firm's exports to the foreign exchange's home country. Therefore, the less diversity in financial reporting across borders, the higher the probability that a firm will want to list its securities on a foreign exchange.

In 1990, Beresford, then chairman of the Financial Accounting Standards Board (FASB), expressed his concerns as follows: "It is widely reported that many foreign companies are reluctant to offer their securities in the U.S. public markets or list them on U.S. exchanges because they are unwilling to comply with the voluminous and detailed U.S. accounting and disclosure requirements or submit to the SEC's jurisdiction. This is said to put the U.S. exchanges and securities industry at a competitive disadvantage."

Differences in accounting practices affect users of financial information. Choi and Levich (1991) found that diversity in accounting affects capital market decisions (such as the geographic spread of investments, the types of securities selected, and information processing costs) of a significant number of market participants regardless of nationality, size, experience, scope of international activity, and organizational structure. Perhaps a quick solution to alleviate the problem of accounting diversity for users would be to restate foreign accounting information. However, according to Choi and Levich (1991), restatement alone is insufficient to do away with accounting diversity.

Choi and Levich (1991) likened the harmony and coordination of national accounting policies to "apple pie and motherhood" arguing that this promotes economic welfare. Of particular interest was the fact that in Choi and Levich's (1991) study, approximately 50 per cent of the companies surveyed felt that accounting diversity affected their capital market decisions.

The other 50 per cent responded that accounting diversity did not affect them either because they employed coping mechanisms or simply because they thought that accounting diversity was not an issue. Thus, because of the ambivalence found in these results, it can be argued that accounting diversity does have necessarily negative behavioural effects on a variety of users.

Choi and Levich (1990) also found that accounting differences significantly affect a firm's capital market decisions. According to them, nationality seemed to play an important role in issuer behaviour. They concluded that since U.S. and U.K. firms have to comply with fairly high disclosure standards at home, they appear to have greater flexibility in tapping international capital markets. This is in sharp contrast to German, Japanese, and other firms that provide less transparent financial statements.

Diversity of accounting practices also impacts international merger activity. For example, the accounting treatment of "goodwill" explains the premium firms place on acquiring target companies. Merger premiums offered by foreign companies based in countries that have a more favorable accounting and tax treatment for goodwill than the U.S., have been found to be higher than those offered by U.S. acquiring companies. Dunne and Ndubizu (1995) found that companies that write off goodwill against a reserve account, transfer more wealth to target shareholders that those that amortize goodwill against income.

In addition, foreign acquirers that deduct goodwill for tax purposes, transfer more wealth to the target shareholders at the acquisition announcement than other acquirers. Consequently, the more advantageous accounting and tax treatment for goodwill may leave U.S. bidders at a disadvantage when they compete with foreign bidders in the merger arena.

Economic principles rely on the idea that wider opportunities should make people better off. When trade barriers are removed, opportunities are created. Such opportunities for cross border transactions and the lure of international capital markets, are facilitated by a set of high quality accounting standards.

High quality necessarily implies comprehensiveness, rigorous implementation and application, clarity, comparability, and transparency. Regardless of the standing and endorsement of international accounting standards, the accounting profession is faced with challenges of substantial proportions. These global challenges include: global harmonization, the quality of financial reporting in developed and emerging markets, social and environmental reporting, financial reporting in the highly technological area, special purpose entities (the likes of which got ENRON into trouble), and revenue recognition.

Accounting diversity will probably be very difficult to eliminate completely. National sentiments and pride are embedded in the consciousness of every people. Such traits have existed for centuries and are passed on from one generation to the next. Indeed, the efforts to minimize diversity in accounting are laudable but perhaps the reality is that the international community will have to live with such accounting diversity. As Haskins, Ferris, and Selling (2000) state, " Never before has there been so much pressure on, and opportunity for, leaders of financial reporting thought to help shape the most useful "language" by which suppliers of capital and seekers of capital communicate across companies, industries, countries, and cultures".

Care must be taken because the forces behind global economic change exalt deregulation, cater to corporations, undermine social structures, and ignore popular concerns. It has also been argued that globalization is hurting many people while helping few.

In the words of John Gray, former advisor to Margaret Thatcher, the global market and free trade are not natural phenomena but creatures of state power, "an end product of social engineering and unyielding political will." Although there is a paucity of social and environmental disclosure requirements in both developed and emerging economies, socially conscious stakeholders are demanding that firms report on the social and environmental impact of their business decisions.

Thus, as Saudagaran (2004) forecasts, the growth in environmental consciousness and the increase in related legislation will make social and environmental reporting a crucial international accounting issue.

Clearly, a modus operandi would have to be found to continue to study the causes of international accounting diversity and to use the best global accounting practices. This will ensure that whichever body is responsible for promulgating international accounting standards will tackle future challenges with a global sense of purpose and equanimity of mind.

CONCEPTUAL FRAMEWORK

Economic

Stage of development, Inflation, Sources of finance, Financial markets, Managerial development, Accounting education, Stability, Complexity of transactions,

Political

System, Stability, Philosophy,

Legal

Type of system, Tax Legislation, System infrastructure, Rules, regulations, Contract law, Corruption.

Culture

History, Societal values/principles, Education system, Religion and Language.

Processes Accounting Practices

Transparency, Stewardship, Accountability, Disclosure, Integrity, Community, Speed of analysis, Dissemination of knowledge, Standardization, Harmonization, Exchange Controls, Bureaucracy, Emergent Market Response, Outcomes, Quality Of Financial Reporting Accounting Standards, Investments/Mergers/Acuisitions ,Global Compatibility, Access To Global Capital Markets, Universal Code Of Accounting Ethics, Listings In Foreign Stock Markets and Economic Welfare.

CORRUPTION CONTROL

The need for International Accounting Standards

There are several forces that are driving the need for international accounting standards. These forces include the ever increasing number of multinational corporations, as well as, the internationalization of the accounting discipline and profession.

The financial market is multinational. World markets have grown dramatically over the past ten years. The commercial unification of European countries, the emergence of Japan as the country having the largest value of securities traded and the fall of communism in portions of Europe and Asia are causes and symptoms of increased globalization of the capital market place.

There has been an explosive growth of cross border transactions and a rapid increase in companies trying to obtain capital in international markets, making international accounting issues a daily fact of life for people in business around the world. Multinational Corporations have played a significant part in the transfer of accounting technology from one country to another.

Currently, a great deal of world trade takes place within firms, as well as, between countries. A multinational firm raises capital where it is cheapest and usually produces goods where the costs are the lowest.

Firms wishing to reduce their risk exposure and widen their choices of funding sources are taking advantage of opportunities provided in the global market place. It is not unusual to see statements of financial position reporting short term to intermediate term loans from several different countries. Firms competing for international resources such as debt funding, include domestic corporations, multinational corporations, foreign corporations and joint ventures. This poses many problems for lenders in attempting to evaluate alternatives across international boundaries.

Multinational Corporations are obliged to satisfy many different requirements simultaneously in each country in which they operate. Accounting measurement rules and standards are currently not in sync with the needs and desires of worldwide Corporations.

The accounting profession has recognized a need for "harmonization ", by trying to increase the compatibility of accounting practices around the world. Harmonization focuses upon limiting the degree of variation in accounting standards. This is particularly true due to the ever increasing role that specialization plays in accounting. The International Accounting Standards Committee is trying to harmonize accounting among all countries and all companies.

International Accounting Standards

The International Accounting Standards Committee was formed in 1973 to develop world wide accounting standards.

Their objective is to harmonize the worlds' accounting standards and eliminate the difference that cannot be explained by legitimate environmental variables. The IASC has issued over 30 International Accounting Standards.

Compliance with the standards is voluntary. There is increased global support for the IASC as more and more countries are beginning to comply with their standards. The IASC is "letting the world know that its new set of global accounting rules is ready for companies around the world to use".

The new rules simplify bookkeeping for international companies, facilitate capital flows across borders, and pave the way for more international mergers.

The stated objectives of the International Accounting Standards Committee are:

- To formulate and publish in the public interest accounting standards to be observed in the presentation of financial statements.
- To promote their worldwide acceptance and observance.
- To work generally for the improvement and harmonization of regulations, accounting standards and procedures relating to the presentation of financial statements.

According to Choi and Mueller, the accounting profession has internationalized itself more slowly that the field of accounting. Tight national regulation and licensing may be contributing to the slow internationalization of the profession. Other barriers include a lack of mobility and outright protectionism. How can you hold a professional accountant responsible for an audit failure if he/she is licensed in a foreign country and permanently residing there?

The evolution of accounting has been an international exercise. In the fourteenth and fifteenth centuries the Italians developed double entry bookkeeping. Accounting terminology enjoys many words that are of Italian origin, such as debit, credit, folio, imprest, bank and capital. The British became the standard bearers of accounting in the nineteenth century, establishing English as the world's accounting language.

This led to the emergence of the organized public accounting profession in Scotland and England in the nineteenth century.

Most of the largest international accounting firms have British or American origins. The accounting standards and practices of every country are the result of a complex interaction of that country's culture, history, economy and institutions. There have been studies linking a nation's accounting practices and culture.

National accounting frameworks can be looked at in the following way: Most industrialized countries have organizations responsible for determining accounting and reporting standards. This maybe a private sector body similar to the FASB in the United States or a governmental body, such as in Germany.

Major Differences in Accounting Standards

The Income Statement

Around the world the presentation and content of the income statement, as well as the accounting methods used to measure income statement amounts vary. For example, there are differences in inventory measurement methods, the treatment of goodwill, and the valuation and depreciation methods for property and equipment. The U.K., Denmark, Norway, Belgium, Brazil and Japan have practices similar to the United States. The percentage of completion method is preferred and the completed contract method can be used only in unusual situations.

In Germany the completed contract method is most frequently used. The Germans rarely recognize gross profit prior to contract completion. In the Netherlands, the percentage of completion method can only be used when a separate identifiable portion of the work in progress is finished and payment has been made. Companies in Switzerland can use either the completed contract or the percentage of completion method. Many countries including the United States, recognize revenue on installment sales at the date of sale, unless the installment sale creates a situation where there is significant uncertainty concerning cash collection, in which case revenue and expense recognition are delayed.

However, the accounting procedures in Italy, Spain, Norway, the Netherlands, France and Belgium do not differentiate between installment and other credit sales. The Income Statement is called the "Group Profit and Loss Account" in the United Kingdom. Revenue is referred to as "turnover" in both the United Kingdom and Denmark.

In the Netherlands certain extraordinary gains and losses are not included in the income statement, but are shown as direct adjustments to shareholders' equity. In the U.K. extraordinary gains and losses are shown on the income statement at their gross amounts, not net of tax. In Korea, certain transactions such as casualty losses, gains and losses on the disposition of fixed assets and gains and losses on the disposition of investments are reported as extraordinary. In Australia a change in accounting principle is treated as an adjustment to retained earnings. No cumulative effect is shown on the income statement.

The Balance Sheet

Most countries classify assets and liabilities into current and noncurrent categories. Inventory is referred to as "stocks" in the United Kingdom. In the United States shareholders' equity includes paid-in capital and retained earnings. Many other countries describe this as "capital" and "reserves". In Germany equity includes "share capital", "capital reserves" and "revenue reserves". India defines liabilities whose existence is certain, but whose value must be estimated as "provisions". The "provisions" are listed separately.

The Statement of Cash Flows

Many countries, including Germany, Italy and Denmark, are not required to present either a statement of cash flows or a statement of funds flows. However, many large companies voluntarily provide either a cash flow or funds flow statement. The statement is required only for large firms in the United Kingdom. The international trend however is moving toward the U.S. practice of requiring cash flow statements.

Disclosure Practices

Most countries required specific disclosures by companies operating within their nation. There is some similarity in the disclosures required; however amounts and types of disclosure vary from country to country. Israel requires that all publicly traded companies disclose any receivable that is greater than 5% of total current assets. In Mexico long-term liabilities must be categorized as suppliers, affiliates income tax, employees' profit sharing and bank loans.

In France many companies are required to publish an annual social balance sheet covering such matters as employment, training, health and safety conditions, employee benefits and environmental issues. In general, European companies consider the full disclosure concept to include a broader set of information than do companies in the United States.

Receivables

Around the world, the practice of estimating bad debts is standard. Most countries have an allowance or reserve for bad debts, which reduces receivables to realizable value. There are some differences. In the United States Bad debts are estimated and the allowance for uncollectible accounts is deducted from the face of the receivables.

In Germany estimated bad debts are deducted directly from the receivables. The allowance for bad debts is recorded as a liability in Italy.

Inventories

There is significant variation in inventory measurement techniques around the world. In Germany both LIFO and FIFO are allowed as long as they correspond to the physical flow of goods. LIFO is not permitted or not often used for financial reporting in the United Kingdom, Norway, Denmark, Hong Kong, Israel and Australia. In the United States if LIFO is used for tax purposes then it must also be used for financial reporting. In Germany all financial accounting must be consistent with tax laws. Valuing inventories at the lower of cost or market is fairly standard internationally. The definition of "market" varies from country to country. Market in the United States means replacement cost, limited by the ceiling of net realizable value and the floor of net realizable value less a normal profit margin. The United Kingdom,

Denmark, Finland and New Zealand define market as net realizable value. Inventories in Sweden are carried at the lower of cost or real value. Real value is defined as net realizable value, but replacement cost is allowed for raw materials and semi-finished products.

Goodwill

In the United States, Australia, Japan and Sweden goodwill is capitalized and amortized over a period of time. Maximum amortization times vary from country to country. 40 years is the maximum in the United States whereas, the maximum is as little as five years.

Japan, France, Germany and Italy permit the immediate write off of goodwill against current earnings as an extraordinary or non-recurring item. In the United Kingdom goodwill is an immediate write off against shareholders equity. Switzerland is the only major industrialized country that permits companies to capitalize goodwill with no amortization.

Interest capitalization

Although some type of interest capitalization is common around the world there is a fair amount of variation. In Belgium and France interest can be capitalized on inventory routinely manufactured as long as the production cycle is greater than 12 months. In Argentina imputed interest on the company's equity may be capitalized. Japan and Brazil, however, do not permit interest capitalization.

Research and Development

The United States, Germany and Mexico expense all R & D cost in the period incurred. However, the capitalization of research and development cost as an intangible asset is permitted in most other industrialized countries.

Depreciation

In many countries around the world, such as Japan and Germany, depreciation rates for financial reporting must be the same as those used for income tax purposes. However, in the United States, income tax regulations allow companies to use different approaches to computing depreciation in their tax returns and financial statements.

Operational Assets

In the United States generally valuation is based on historical cost and generally reevaluations reflecting changes in market value, except in situations where the asset is impaired, is not permitted. Germany, Canada and Japan strictly adhere to historical cost.

However, Australia and France do allow for the periodic revaluation of property, plant and equipment to current market value. The International Accounting Standards Committee has issued IAS 16, Accounting for Property, Plant and Equipment. The requirements for the standard conform to U.S. GAAP except that a revaluation of property, plant and equipment is permitted.

Investments

The United States is unique in the way that investments are reported. Most countries report short term investments at the lower of cost or market. Argentina and Israel report investment at fair value, whereas, the United Kingdom uses "current cost" (usually current replacement cost). Noncurrent investments are generally reported at some variation of cost. However, methods vary. China uses unadjusted historical cost while New Zealand permits market value.

Liabilities

Foreign loans are frequently denominated in the currency of the lender. Loans from foreign banks that are denominated in dollars are called Eurodollar loans. When loans much be repaid in foreign currencies there is additional risks. Changes in exchange rates change the number of dollars that must be repaid.

Leases

Most industrialized countries distinguish between operating and nonoperating leases. However, the criteria for drawing the distinction varies dramatically from country to country. Japan and Italy have no accounting requirements for nonoperating leases. Capitalization is optional in Denmark and Sweden.

Deferred Taxes

Around the world there is a wide variation between accounting income and taxable income. In France and Germany financial accounting and tax accounting are the same. Finland does not defer income taxes. Tax expense is the actual tax paid. Under the standards of the International Accounting Standards Committee, income taxes are deferred, but if differences are not expected to reverse for at least three years, these amounts can be excluded from tax expense.

Pensions

The treatment of pension costs vary substantially around the world. Most large companies in Japan fund their pension plans through financial institutions. Contributions are tax deductible and most Japanese companies report annual pension expense equal to the cash contributions made to the pension fund.

Pension costs in Belgium, Finland, India and New Zealand are not covered by accounting standards. Pension accounting is irrelevant in Korea, Argentina and Brazil as pension plans in these countries are rare.

Currency Rates

The foreign operations of many U.S. firms are generally denominated in the currency of the foreign country. Currency rate changes that affect cash flows because they require settlement in a currency other than the firm's functional currency result in "transaction" adjustments. Currency rate changes that do not affect cash flow are "translation adjustments".

Translation adjustments are accumulated in a separate component of shareholders' equity called foreign currency translation adjustments.

Earnings per share

Earnings per share is a much more important concept in the United States than in most other countries. Requirements vary for countries that do require earnings per share disclosures. Basic and diluted EPS are reported in the United States. However, some countries require only one of the two calculations. Japan requires disclosure of only basic EPS. Calculations vary from country to country. Earnings for the numerator of the EPS calculation are defined as earnings available for common shareholders. Norway defines earnings as continuing income from operations only.

The move toward harmonization of accounting standards in the United States increased with the cooperation of FASB and IASC on the earnings per share issue. In 1994 the FASB and IASC began working on projects leading toward the issuance of new standards for calculating EPS. The purpose of the project was to issue an EPS standard that would be compatible with the new international standard and also simplify U.S. GAAP.

FASB has expressed some concern over the new international standards. The board had hoped that the international rules would be closer to U.S. standards, however, currently there are more than 200 key differences. FASB feels that the international standards lack clarity, provide too many alternatives, and are not comprehensive enough. There is some concern that there will be two sets of accounting standards, U.S. rules and the international ones.

DIFFERENCES AND SIMILARITIES

The Income Statement

There are significant differences from country to country in the presentation and content of the income statement as well as in the accounting methods used to measure income statement amounts. For example, differences in inventory measurement methods, differences in the treatment of goodwill, and the method used to value and depreciate property and equipment, are but three of several areas where global practices differ widely.

There are significant differences among countries in the method used to recognize profit on long-term contracts. Practices in many countries, such as the U.K., Denmark, Norway, Belgium, Brazil, and Japan are similar to the U.S.

The percentage-of-completion method is preferred and the completed contract method can be used only in unusual situations. In Germany, the completed contract method is used in almost all cases and recognizing gross profit prior to contract completion is rare. In the Netherlands, the percentage-of-completion method can only be used when a separate identifiable portion of the work in progress is finished and payment has been made. In Switzerland, companies can use either method. Many countries follow the U.S. practice of recognizing revenue on installment sales at date of sale, unless the installment sale creates a situation where there is significant uncertainty concerning cash collection, in which case revenue and expense recognition are delayed. There are, however, some countries where accounting procedures do not differentiate between installment and other credit sales. Italy, Spain, Norway, the Netherlands, France, and Belgium are examples of countries that fall into this category.

There also are many differences in the presentation and content of the income statement. Here are just a few examples:

- The title of the statement. For example, in the

United Kingdom (U.K.) it is called the "Group Profit and Loss Account."

- Revenue terminology. In a number of countries (e.g., the U.K. and Denmark), sales revenue is referred to as "turnover."
- The treatment of extraordinary gains and losses. In some countries, such as The Netherlands, certain extraordinary gains and losses are not included in the income statement, but are shown as direct adjustments to shareholders' equity. In other countries, such as the U.K., extraordinary gains and losses are shown on the income statement at their gross amounts, not net-of-tax. In Korea, accounting principles specify certain transactions that must be reported as extraordinary. These transactions include casualty losses, gains and losses on the disposition of fixed assets, and gains and losses on the disposition of investments.
- The treatment of a change in accounting principle. For example, in Australia, a change in accounting principle is treated as an adjustment to retained earnings. No cumulative effect is shown on the income statement.

The Statement of Cash Flows

In many countries, companies are not required to present either a statement of cash flows or a statement of funds flows. This is the case in Germany, Italy, and Denmark. In Germany, however, many large companies voluntarily provide either a cash flow or funds flow statement. In some countries, like the United Kingdom, it's required only for large firms. Many other countries also require either the presentation of a statement of cash flows or a similar statement based on funds flows (e.g., working capital). The international trend, however, is moving toward the U.S. practice of requiring cash flow statements.

Balance Sheet

In terms of balance sheet presentation, the classification

of assets and liabilities into current and noncurrent categories is prevalent globally. However, significant differences do exist, particularly with respect to terminology. In the U.K., the term "stocks" refers to inventory. A U.S. investor would interpret stocks to mean investments in equity securities of other companies. In the U.S., shareholders' equity is comprised of paid-in capital and retained earnings. In many other countries, shareholders' equity is divided into "capital" and "reserves."

For example, in Germany, equity is divided into share capital, capital reserves, and revenue reserves. In India, liabilities whose existence is certain, but whose value must be estimated, are called "provisions" and are listed separately. Balance sheet presentation differences also exist. For example, a typical U.K. balance sheet begins with non-current assets, called fixed assets. Current assets are listed next and current liabilities are subtracted to arrive at net current assets, which are added to fixed assets. Long-term debt is then subtracted from this subtotal to arrive at net assets. The net asset total agrees with shareholders' interest, which is reported last.

Disclosure Practices Around The World

Most countries require specific disclosures by companies operating within their borders. Many of these disclosures are similar. However, the amount and types of required and voluntary disclosures differ from country to country. For example, in Israel, companies whose securities are publicly traded are required to disclose any receivable that exceeds five percent of total current assets. In Mexico, a disclosure reports the separate identification of long-term liabilities into the following categories: suppliers, affiliates, income tax, employees' profit sharing, and bank loans.

Several supplemental disclosures are uniquely European. These include information about shares and shareholders, certain employee disclosures, and environmental disclosures. An example of an environmental disclosure would be a discussion of safety measures adopted by the company in their manufacturing plants.

In France, many enterprises are required to publish an

annual social balance sheet. This report covers matters such as employment, training, health and safety conditions, employee benefits, and environmental issues. In general, European companies consider the full disclosure concept to include a much broader set of information than do U.S. companies.

Reporting By Geographic Area

In today's global economy it is sometimes difficult to distinguish domestic and foreign companies. Most large U.S. firms conduct significant operations in other countries in addition to having substantial export sales from this country. Differing political and economic environments from country to country means risks and associated rewards sometimes vary greatly among the various operations of a single company. For instance, manufacturing facilities in a South American country embroiled in political unrest pose different risks from having a plant in Vermont, or even Canada. Without disaggregated financial information, these differences cause problems for analysts.

For operating segments not based on geography, information must be reported for the enterprise's country of domicile and in each other country from which the operating segment derives revenues and holds assets. However, some enterprise's activities are not organized on the basis of differences in geographic areas of operations. For each operating segment that has not been determined based on geography, the enterprise must report revenues from external customers, long-lived segment assets, and expenditures during the period for long-lived segment assets,

- In the enterprise's country of domicile and
- In each other country from which the operating segment derives revenues and holds assets.

There is more international uniformity regarding disaggregated disclosures than with many other accounting issues. More than 30 countries adopted International Accounting Standard No. 14, Reporting Financial Information by Segment issued in 1981 by the International Accounting

Standards Committee. Under this standard, companies report revenues, operating profit or loss, and identifiable assets for both industry segments and geographic segments. Recently, the FASB worked closely with the Accounting Standards Board of Canada and the International Accounting Standards Board (IASC) to develop similar new standards in this area.

Receivables

In the U.S., bad debts are estimated and the allowance for uncollectibles is deducted from the face amount of receivables. Globally, the practice of estimating bad debts is standard. Most countries also establish an allowance, or "reserve" for bad debts which reduces receivables to net realizable value. However, differences do exist. For example, in Germany estimated bad debts are deducted directly from the receivables, and in Italy the allowance for bad debts is recorded as a liability.

Inventories

Inventory measurement techniques vary widely across different countries. For example, in Germany both LIFO and FIFO are permitted if they correspond to the physical flow of goods. In the United Kingdom, Norway, Denmark, Hong Kong, Israel, and Australia LIFO is either not permitted or not commonly used for financial reporting purposes. In Japan and Mexico an acceptable technique is to use the latest purchase price to measure ending inventory.

In the United States, if a company uses LIFO for tax purposes, the same method must be used for financial reporting, but differences might exist for other accounting choices. Other countries require much closer conformity of accounting practice and tax laws. In fact, in Germany all financial accounting must be consistent with tax laws. The technique of valuing inventories at the lower-of-cost-or-market is fairly standard around the globe.

However, differences exist in the designation of "market." In the U.S., market is defined as replacement cost, constrained by the ceiling of net realizable value and the floor of net realizable value less a normal profit margin. In many other countries, for example the United Kingdom, Denmark, Finland, and New Zealand, market is defined as net realizable value. In Sweden, inventories are carried at the lower of cost or real value. Real value is defined as net realizable value, but replacement cost is permissible for raw materials and semi-finished products.

Goodwill

In the United States, goodwill is capitalized and amortized over a period of time no longer than 40 years. Under new standards being considered by the FASB the amortization period may change. Internationally, the treatment of goodwill varies widely. Countries such as Australia, Japan, and Sweden also capitalize and amortize goodwill, but the maximum amortization periods vary from 5 to 20 years.

Other countries, such as Japan, France, Germany, and Italy permit the immediate write-off of goodwill against current earnings, but as an extraordinary or non-recurring item. The United Kingdom permits the immediate write-off of goodwill against shareholders' equity. Switzerland is the only major industrialized country which allows companies to capitalize goodwill without amortization.

Interest Capitalization and R&D

The accounting principles of most countries permit some form of interest capitalization; Japan and Brazil are exceptions. However, differences do exist as to the situations when interest can be capitalized. For example, in Belgium and France interest can be capitalized on inventory routinely manufactured as long as the production cycle exceeds 12 months. Differences also exist as to the amount of interest to be capitalized. For example, in Argentina imputed interest on the company's equity may be capitalized. Unlike the United States, the capitalization of research and development costs as an intangible asset is permitted in most other industrialized countries. Germany and Mexico are two countries which do follow the U.S. treatment of expensing all R & D costs in the period incurred.

Depreciation

In the United States, income tax regulations allow firms to use different approaches to computing depreciation in their tax returns and financial statements. Internationally, in a number of countries, such as Japan and Germany, depreciation rates for financial reporting must be the same as those used for income tax purposes.

Operational Assets

In the United States, accounting for operational assets subsequent to initial acquisition is based on the historical cost of the asset, and revaluations to reflect changes in market values, other than in asset impairment situations, generally are not permitted. Internationally, the International Accounting Standards Committee has issued IAS 16, Accounting for Property, Plant and Equipment.

The requirements of IAS 16 conform to U.S. GAAP except that a revaluation of property, plant, and equipment is permitted. Countries such as Germany, Canada, and Japan adhere strictly to historical cost valuation. However, other countries, including Australia and France allow the periodic revaluation of property, plant, and equipment to current market value.

Investments

No other country reports its investments exactly like we do in the U.S. Most countries report short-term investments at lower of cost or market. Some, including Argentina and Israel, report at fair value. They are reported at "current cost" (usually replacement cost) in the United Kingdom. Most countries report noncurrent investments (other than equity method investees) at some variation of cost, but methods vary widely, ranging from unadjusted historical cost (China) to fair market value (New Zealand).

Liabilities

The financial market is becoming increasingly

multinational. World markets have grown dramatically in the last decade. The commercial unification of European countries, the emergence of Japan as the country having the largest value of securities traded, and the fall of communism in portions of Europe and Asia are both causes and symptoms of the heightened globalization of the capital marketplace.

Companies wishing to reduce their exposure to risk and to widen their choices of funding sources are taking advantage of the broader opportunities the global environment provides. Increasingly, U.S. corporate debt is displaying a multinational dimension, with statements of financial position often reporting short-term to intermediate-term loans in several different countries. Loans from foreign banks that are denominated in dollars are called Eurodollar loans. Also, foreign loans frequently are denominated in the currency of the lender (Swiss franc, German mark, and so on). When loans must be repaid in foreign currencies a new element of risk is introduced. This is because if exchange rates change, the number of dollars representing the foreign currency that must be repaid differs from the number of dollars representing the foreign currency borrowed. Firms competing for international resources, such as debt funding, include domestic corporations, multinational corporations, as well as foreign corporations and joint ventures. This poses several problems for lenders and other resource providers attempting to evaluate alternatives across international boundaries.

Leases

In Japan and Italy, there are no accounting requirements regarding non-operating leases. All leases in those countries are accounted for as operating leases by both lessees and lessors. Most other industrial nations differentiate between operating and non-operating leases. The criteria for drawing the distinction, though, vary widely from country to country. In Denmark and Sweden, capitalizing is optional.

Deferred Taxes

The extent of differences between accounting income and

taxable income varies widely from country to country. In fact, in France and Germany financial accounting and tax accounting must coincide. There also is little uniformity as to how to handle these differences. In many countries, Finland for instance, income taxes are not deferred. Instead, tax expense is simply the actual tax paid.

Under standards of the International Accounting Standards Committee (IASC), income taxes are deferred, but if differences are not expected to reverse for at least three years, these amounts can be excluded from tax expense. The United Kingdom, among others, subscribes to this approach.

Pensions and Other Postretirement Benefits

Most large companies in Japan sponsor pension plans that are funded through financial institutions. Contributions to pension funds are tax deductible. Because the taxes levied by the government is the amount reported as income tax expense on the income statement, most Japanese companies report annual pension expense equal to cash contributions to the pension fund. In other countries, such as Belgium, Finland, India, and New Zealand, pension costs are not covered by accounting standards. In still other countries pension accounting is irrelevant because the occurrence of pension plans is rare (Korea, Argentina, and Brazil are examples).

In the United States, postretirement benefits are accrued in a manner similar to pensions. In Canada, where benefits are commonly provided, three alternatives are permitted:

- Accrual,
- Pay-as-you-go, and
- Accrual only when employees retire.

Disclosure of the method used is required. In the United Kingdom, accounting is similar to the United States. In most other countries, little official guidance is offered. In many countries, postretirement benefits other than pensions are rare. In Japan, for instance, the prevalence of government-sponsored plans has caused most Japanese companies not to provide separate benefits.

Currency Rates

Ours is truly a global economy. Most large "U.S." companies are, in fact, multinational companies that may derive only a fraction of their revenues in this country. As a result, many operations are located abroad and foreign operations frequently are denominated in the currency of the foreign country (Japanese yen, Swiss franc, German mark, and so on). When exchange rates change, the dollar equivalent of the foreign currency changes.

Currency rate changes that affect cash flows because they require settlement in a currency other than the entity's functional currency result in "transaction" adjustments. These are reported as gains and losses in the earnings of the period the changes occur. Those that do not require settlement and thus don't affect cash flows are "translation adjustments." These are accumulated in a separate component of shareholders' equity: Foreign currency translation adjustments.

Earnings Per Share

The International Accounting Standards Committee (IASC) has as a stated objective to narrow worldwide differences in accounting practices and the presentation of financial information. The IASC has worked toward uniformity since 1973, but harmonization has by no means been achieved. The EPS requirements are a result of cooperation between the FASB and the IASC to develop common requirements for earnings per share. Still significant differences exist among countries that do not choose to follow the international standards in this area.

Earnings per share receives more attention in the United States than in most other countries. In countries that do require EPS disclosures, requirements differ widely. For instance, earnings for the numerator of the EPS calculation are defined in the United States as earnings available for common shareholders, and separate calculations are required for ordinary income and net income when differences exist. In some countries, though, earnings is defined as continuing income from operations only. In the United States, basic and diluted EPS are reported. Other countries have similar requirements but define the two calculations differently from the US (that is, the potentially dilutive securities included are different).

Some countries require only one of the two calculations. (Japan requires basic only, for example.) Some (Spain, Switzerland, and Germany for instance) require no EPS disclosure at all, but disclosure may be provided anyway. Some countries require disclosures not provided by US companies. Japan, for instance, also discloses net assets per share.

Accounting Changes

Accounting changes occur in all countries. The way those changes are accounted for, though, varies from country to country. For example, firms in many countries (Ireland, Netherlands, South Africa, and the United Kingdom, for instance) account for all changes in accounting principle retroactively. In the United States, most changes are reported as an adjustment to current period income and only a few exceptions are reported retroactively. In many countries all are reported currently, none retroactively.

INTERNATIONAL ACCOUNTING STANDARD BOARDS

The International Accounting Standards Board (IASB) founded on April 1, 2001 is the successor of the International Accounting Standards Committee (IASC) founded in June 1973 in London. It is responsible for developing the International Financial Reporting Standards (new name for the International Accounting Standards issued after 2001), and promoting the use and application of these standards. The International Accounting Standards Board is an independent, privately-funded accounting standard-setter based in London, UK.

Foundation of the IASB

In March 2001, the International Accounting Standards

Committee Foundation (IASCF) was formed as a not-for-profit corporation incorporated in the State of Delaware, US. The IASC Foundation is the parent entity of the International Accounting Standards Board, an independent accounting standard-setter based in London, UK.

On 1 April 2001, the International Accounting Standards Board (IASB) assumed accounting standard-setting responsibilities from its predecessor body, the International Accounting Standards Committee. This was the culmination of a restructuring based on the recommendations of the report Recommendations on Shaping IASC for the Future.

The IASB structure has the following main features: the IASC Foundation is an independent organization having two main bodies, the Trustees and the IASB, as well as a Standards Advisory Council and the International Financial Reporting Interpretations Committee. The IASC Foundation Trustees appoint the IASB members, exercise oversight and raise the funds needed, but the IASB has sole responsibility for setting International Financial Reporting Standards (international accounting standards).

IASB Members

The IASB has 14 Board members, each with one vote. The members are selected chiefly upon their professional competence and practical experience. A unanimous vote is not necessary in order for the publication of a Standard, exposure draft, or final IFRIC Interpretation. The approval by nine of the IASB's fourteen members is however required. At 28/01/2008 the IASB Chairman was Professor Sir David Tweedie. The Vice-Chairman was Thomas E Jones.

About the IASB

The International Accounting Standards Board is an independent, privately-funded accounting standard-setter based in London, UK. The Board members come from nine countries and have a variety of functional backgrounds. The IASB is committed to developing, in the public interest, a single set of high quality.

Understandable and enforceable global accounting standards that require transparent and comparable information in general purpose financial statements. In addition, the IASB co-operates with national accounting standard-setters to achieve convergence in accounting standards around the world.

There are 14 Board members, each with one vote. The Trustees appoint the Board members. The IASC Foundation Constitution provides that the Trustees shall: "select members of the IASB so that it will comprise a group of people representing, within that group, the best available combination of technical skills and background experience of relevant international business and market conditions in order to contribute to the development of high quality, global accounting standards".

As it develops International Financial Reporting Standards, the IASB follows a rigorous, open due process.

About the IASC Foundation Constitution

IASC Foundation Constitution

This Constitution was approved in its original form by the Board of the former International Accounting Standards Committee (IASC) in March 2000 and by the members of IASC at a meeting in Edinburgh on 24 May 2000. At its meeting in December 1999, the IASC Board had appointed a Nominating Committee to select the first Trustees.

These Trustees were nominated on 22 May 2000 and took office on 24 May 2000 as a result of the approval of the Constitution. In execution of their duties under the Constitution, the Trustees formed the International Accounting Standards Committee Foundation on 6 February 2001. As a consequence of a resolution by the Trustees, Part C of the revised Constitution approved on 24 May 2000 ceased to have effect.

Reflecting the Trustees' decision to create the International Financial Reporting Interpretations Committee, and following public consultation, the Constitution was revised on 5 March 2002. Subsequently the Trustees amended the Constitution, with effect from 8 July 2002, to reflect other changes that had taken place since the formation of the IASC Foundation. The Constitution requires the Trustees to review the Constitution every five years.

The Trustees initiated the first review in November 2003 and following extensive consultation completed the review in June 2005. This version reflects changes adopted and approved by the Trustees on 21 June 2005 for effect on 1 July 2005 and further amendments adopted and approved by the Trustees on 31 October 2007 for immediate effect.

IASC Foundation Constitution (approved by the Members of IASC at a meeting in Edinburgh, Scotland on 24 May 2000 and revised by the IASC Foundation Trustees on 5 March and 8 July 2002, 21 June 2005 and 31 October 2007). This Constitution consists of Part A and Part B. Part A deals with the organisation's name and objectives, and the membership and appointment of Trustees. Part B sets out the provisions that came into effect when the Trustees formed the International Accounting Standards Committee Foundation on 6 February 2001, following a Trustees' Resolution. In accordance with the Trustees' decision, Part C of the Constitution approved on 24 May 2000 no longer pertains

Part A

Name and objectives

- The name of the organisation shall be the International Accounting Standards Committee Foundation (abbreviated as "IASC Foundation"). The International Accounting Standards Board (abbreviated as "IASB"), whose structure and functions are laid out in Sections 18–32, shall be the standard-setting body of the IASC Foundation.
- The objectives of the IASC Foundation are:
- To develop, in the public interest, a single set of high quality, understandable and enforceable global accounting standards that require high quality, transparent and comparable information in financial

statements and other financial reporting to help participants in the world's capital markets and other users make economic decisions;

- To promote the use and rigorous application of those standards;
- In fulfilling the objectives associated with (a) and (b), to take account of, as appropriate, the special needs of small and medium-sized entities and emerging economies; and
- To bring about convergence of national accounting standards and International Accounting Standards and International Financial Reporting Standards to high quality solutions.

Governance of the IASC Foundation

- The governance of the IASC Foundation shall rest with the Trustees and such other governing organs as may be appointed by the Trustees in accordance with the provisions of this Constitution. The Trustees shall use their best endeavours to ensure that the requirements of this Constitution are observed; however, they are empowered to make minor variations in the interest of feasibility of operation if such variations are agreed by 75% of all the Trustees.

  This Constitution consists of Part A and Part B. Part A deals with the organisation's name and objectives, and the membership and appointment of Trustees. Part B sets out the provisions that came into effect when the Trustees formed the International Accounting Standards Committee Foundation on 6 February 2001, following a Trustees' Resolution. In accordance with the Trustees' decision, Part C of the Constitution approved on 24 May 2000 no longer pertains.

Trustees

- The Trustees shall comprise twenty-two individuals.

- The Trustees shall be responsible for the selection of all subsequent Trustees to fill vacancies caused by routine retirement or other reason. In making such selection, the Trustees shall be bound by the criteria set forth in Sections 6 and 7 and in particular shall undertake mutual consultation with international organisations as set out in Section 7, for the purpose of selecting an individual with a similar background to that of the retiring Trustee, where the retiring Trustee was selected through a process of mutual consultation with one or more international organisations.
- All Trustees shall be required to show a firm commitment to the IASC Foundation and the IASB as a high quality global standard-setter, to be financially knowledgeable, and to have an ability to meet the time commitment. Each Trustee shall have an understanding of, and be sensitive to the challenges associated with the adoption and application of high quality global accounting standards developed for use in the world's capital markets and by other users. The mix of Trustees shall broadly reflect the world's capital markets and a diversity of geographical and professional backgrounds. The Trustees shall be required to commit themselves formally to acting in the public interest in all matters. In order to ensure a broad international basis, there shall be:
  - Six Trustees appointed from North America;
  - Six Trustees appointed from Europe;
  - Six Trustees appointed from the Asia/Oceania region; and
  - Four Trustees appointed from any area, subject to establishing overall geographical balance.
- The Trustees shall comprise individuals that as a group provide an appropriate balance of professional backgrounds, including auditors, preparers, users, academics, and other officials

serving the public interest. Two of the Trustees shall normally be senior partners of prominent international accounting firms. To achieve such a balance, Trustees should be selected after consultation with national and international organisations of auditors (including the International Federation of Accountants), preparers, users and academics. The Trustees shall establish procedures for inviting suggestions for appointments from these relevant organisations and for allowing individuals to put forward their own names, including advertising vacant positions.

- Trustees shall normally be appointed for a term of three years, renewable once: in order to provide continuity, some of the initial Trustees will serve staggered terms so as to retire after four or five years.
- Subject to the voting requirements in Section 14, the Trustees may terminate the appointment of an individual as a Trustee on grounds of poor performance, mis behaviour or incapacity.
- The Chairman of the Trustees shall be appointed by the Trustees from among their own number. With the agreement of the Trustees, regardless of prior service as a Trustee, the appointee may serve as the Chairman for a term of three years, renewable once, from the date of appointment as Chairman.
- The Trustees shall meet at least twice each year and shall be remunerated by the IASC Foundation with an annual fee and a per-meeting fee, commensurate with the responsibilities assumed, such fees to be determined by the Trustees. Expenses of travel on IASC Foundation business shall be met by the IASC Foundation.
- In addition to the powers and duties set out in Section 13, the Trustees may make such operational commitments and other arrangements as they deem necessary to achieve the organisation's objectives,

including, but without limitation, leasing premises and agreeing contracts of employment with IASB members.

- The Trustees shall:
  - Assume responsibility for establishing and maintaining appropriate financing arrangements;
  - Establish or amend operating procedures for the Trustees;
  - Determine the legal entity under which the IASC Foundation shall operate, provided always that such legal entity shall be a Foundation or other body corporate conferring limited liability on its members and that the legal documents establishing such legal entity shall incorporate provisions to achieve the same requirements as the provisions contained in this Constitution;
  - Review in due course the location of the IASC Foundation, both as regards its legal base and its operating location;
  - Investigate the possibility of seeking charitable or similar status for the IASC Foundation in those countries where such status would assist fundraising;
  - Open their meetings to the public but may, at their discretion, hold certain discussions (normally only about selection, appointment and other personnel issues, and funding) in private; and
  - Publish an annual report on the IASC Foundation's activities, including audited financial statements and priorities for the coming year.
- There shall be a quorum for meetings of the Trustees if 60% of the Trustees are present in person or by telecommunications: Trustees shall not be represented by alternates. Each Trustee shall have

one vote and a simple majority of those voting shall be required to take decisions on matters other than termination of the appointment of a Trustee, amendments to the Constitution, or minor variations made in the interest of feasibility of operations, in which cases a 75% majority of all Trustees shall be required; voting by proxy shall not be permitted on any issue. In the event of a tied vote, the Chairman shall have an additional casting vote.

Part B

Trustees

- In addition to the duties set out in Part A, the Trustees shall:
  - Appoint the members of the IASB and establish their contracts of service and performance criteria.
  - Appoint the members of the International Financial Reporting Interpretations Committee and the Standards Advisory Council.
  - Review annually the strategy of the IASC Foundation and the IASB and its effectiveness, including consideration, but not determination, of the IASB's agenda.
  - Approve annually the budget of the IASC Foundation and determine the basis for funding.
  - Review broad strategic issues affecting accounting standards, promote the IASC Foundation and its work and promote the objective of rigorous application of International Accounting Standards and International Financial Reporting Standards, provided that the Trustees shall be excluded from involvement in technical matters relating to accounting standards.

- Establish and amend operating procedures, consultative arrangements and due process for the IASB, the International Financial Reporting Interpretations Committee and the Standards Advisory Council.
- Review compliance with the operating procedures, consultative arrangements and due process as described in (f).
- Approve amendments to this Constitution after following a due process, including consultation with the Standards Advisory Council and publication of an Exposure Draft for public comment and subject to the voting requirements given in Section 14.
- Exercise all powers of the IASC Foundation except for those expressly reserved to the IASB, the International Financial Reporting Interpretations Committee and the Standards Advisory Council.
- Foster and review the development of educational programmes and materials that are consistent with the IASC Foundation's objectives.

• The Trustees may terminate the appointment of a member of the IASB, the International Financial Reporting Interpretations Committee or the Standards Advisory Council, on grounds of poor performance, misbehaviour, incapacity or other failure to comply with contractual requirements, and the Trustees shall develop procedures for such termination.

• The accountability of the Trustees shall be ensured inter alia through:
  - A commitment made by each Trustee to act in the public interest.
  - Their undertaking a review of the entire structure of the IASC Foundation and its effectiveness, such review to include consideration of changing the geographical

distribution of Trustees in response to changing global economic conditions, and publishing the proposals of that review for public comment, the review commencing three years after the coming into force of this Constitution, with the objective of implementing any agreed changes five years after the coming into force of this Constitution (6 February 2006, five years after the date of the incorporation of the IASC Foundation).

– Their undertaking a similar review subsequently every five years.

IASB

- The IASB shall comprise fourteen members, appointed by the Trustees under Section 15(a), of whom twelve shall be full-time members (the expression 'full-time' meaning that the members concerned commit all of their time in paid employment to the IASC Foundation). The remaining two members shall be part-time members (the expression 'part-time' meaning that the members concerned commit most of their time in paid employment to the IASC Foundation) and shall meet appropriate guidelines of independence, established by the Trustees. The work of the IASB shall not be invalidated by its failure at any time to have a full complement of fourteen members, although the Trustees shall use their best endeavours to achieve a full complement.
- The main qualifications for membership of the IASB shall be professional competence and practical experience. The Trustees shall select members of the IASB so that it will comprise a group of people representing, within that group, the best available combination of technical expertise and diversity of international business and market experience in order to contribute to the development of high

quality, global accounting standards. No individual shall be both a Trustee and an IASB member at the same time.

- The selection of members of the IASB shall not be based on geographical criteria, but the Trustees shall ensure that the IASB is not dominated by any particular constituency or geographical interest. In particular, the Trustees shall observe the general parameters set out in the Criteria for IASB Members which are attached to this Constitution.
- The Trustees shall select IASB members so that the IASB as a group provides an appropriate mix of recent practical experience among auditors, preparers, users and academics.
- The IASB will, in consultation with the Trustees, be expected to establish and maintain liaison with national standard-setters and other official bodies concerned with standard-setting in order to promote the convergence of national accounting standards and International Accounting Standards and International Financial Reporting Standards.
- Each full-time and part-time member of the IASB shall agree contractually to act in the public interest and to have regard to the IASB Framework (as amended from time to time) in deciding on and revising standards.
- The Trustees shall appoint one of the full-time members as Chairman of the IASB, who shall also be the Chief Executive of the IASC Foundation. One of the full-time members of the IASB shall also be designated by the Trustees as Vice-Chairman, whose role shall be to chair meetings of the IASB in the absence of the Chairman in unusual circumstances (such as illness). The appointment of the Chairman and the designation as Vice-Chairman shall be for such term as the Trustees decide. The title of Vice-Chairman would not imply that the individual concerned is the Chairman-elect.

- Members of the IASB shall be appointed for a term of up to five years, renewable once. The Trustees shall develop rules and procedures to ensure that the IASB is, and is seen to be, independent, and, in particular, on appointment, full-time members of the IASB shall sever all employment relationships with current employers and shall not hold any position giving rise to economic incentives which might call into question their independence of judgement in setting accounting standards. Secondments and any rights to return to an employer would therefore not be permitted. Part-time members of the IASB would not be expected to sever all other employment arrangements.
- The terms of appointment of members of the IASB shall be staggered so that not all members retire at once. To accomplish this, the Trustees shall consider initial terms of three years for some members, four years for others and a full five years for the remaining initial members.
- Full-time and part-time members of the IASB shall be remunerated at rates commensurate with the respective responsibilities assumed: such rates shall be determined by the Trustees. Expenses of travel on IASB business shall be met by the IASC Foundation.
- The IASB shall meet at such times and locations as it determines: meetings of the IASB shall be open to the public, but certain discussions (normally only about selection, appointment and other personnel issues) may be held in private at the discretion of the IASB.
- Each member of the IASB shall have one vote. On both technical and other matters, proxy voting shall not be permitted nor shall members of the IASB be entitled to appoint alternates to attend meetings. In the event of a tied vote, on a decision that is to be made by a simple majority of the members of the

IASB present at a meeting in person or by telecommunications, the Chairman shall have an additional casting vote.

- The publication of an Exposure Draft, International Accounting Standard, International Financial Reporting Standard, or final Interpretation of the International Financial Reporting Interpretations Committee shall require approval by nine of the fourteen members of the IASB. Other decisions of the IASB, including the publication of a discussion paper, shall require a simple majority of the members of the IASB present at a meeting that is attended by at least 60% of the members of the IASB, in person or by telecommunications.
- The IASB shall:
  - Have complete responsibility for all IASB technical matters including the preparation and issuing of International Accounting Standards, International Financial Reporting Standards and Exposure Drafts, each of which shall include any dissenting opinions, and final approval of Interpretations by the International Financial Reporting Interpretations Committee.
  - Publish an Exposure Draft on all projects and normally publish a discussion document for public comment on major projects.
  - Have full discretion in developing and pursuing the technical agenda of the IASB and over project assignments on technical matters: in organising the conduct of its work, the IASB may outsource detailed research or other work to national standard-setters or other organisations.
  - Establish procedures for reviewing comments made within a reasonable period on documents published for comment.
  - Normally form working groups or other types

of specialist advisory groups to give advice on major projects.
- Consult the Standards Advisory Council on major projects, agenda decisions and work priorities.
- Normally issue bases for conclusions with International Accounting Standards, International Financial Reporting Standards, and Exposure Drafts.
- Consider holding public hearings to discuss proposed standards, although there is no requirement to hold public hearings for every project.
- Consider undertaking field tests (both in developed countries and in emerging markets) to ensure that proposed standards are practical and workable in all environments, although there is no requirement to undertake field tests for every project.
- Give reasons if it does not follow any of the non mandatory procedures set out in (b), (d) (ii), d(iv), (e) and (f).

- The authoritative text of any Exposure Draft or International Accounting Standard or International Financial Reporting Standard or Draft or final Interpretation shall be that published by the IASB in the English language. The IASB may publish authorised translations or give authority to others to publish translations of the authoritative text of Exposure Drafts and International Accounting Standards and International Financial Reporting Standards and Draft and final Interpretations.

International Financial Reporting Interpretations Committee

- The International Financial Reporting Interpretations Committee shall comprise fourteen voting members, appointed by the Trustees under Section 15(b) for renewable terms of three years. The

Trustees shall select members of the Committee so that it comprises a group of people representing, within that group, the best available combination of technical expertise and diversity of international business and market experience in the practical application of International Financial Reporting Standards (IFRSs) and analysis of financial statements prepared in accordance with IFRSs. Expenses of travel on Committee business shall be met by the IASC Foundation.

- The Trustees shall appoint a member of the IASB, the Director of Technical Activities or another senior member of the IASB staff, or another appropriately qualified individual, to chair the Committee. The Chair has the right to speak to the technical issues being considered but not to vote. The Trustees, as they deem necessary, shall appoint as non-voting observers representatives of regulatory organisations, who shall have the right to attend and speak at meetings.
- The Committee shall meet as and when required and ten voting members present in person or by telecommunications shall constitute a quorum: one or two IASB members shall be designated by the IASB and shall attend meetings as non-voting observers; other members of the IASB may attend and speak at the meetings.

  On exceptional occasions, members of the Committee may be allowed to send non-voting alternates, at the discretion of the Chair of the Committee. Members wishing to nominate an alternate should seek the consent of the Chair in advance of the meeting concerned. Meetings of the Committee shall be open to the public, but certain discussions (normally only about selection, appointment and other personnel issues) may be held in private at the Committee's discretion.
- Each member of the Committee shall have one vote.

Members vote in accordance with their own independent views, not as representatives voting according to the views of any firm, organisation or constituency with which they may be associated. Proxy voting shall not be permitted. Approval of Draft or final Interpretations shall require that not more than four voting members vote against the Draft or final Interpretation.

- The Committee shall:
  - Interpret the application of International Accounting Standards (IASs) and International Financial Reporting Standards (IFRSs) and provide timely guidance on financial reporting issues not specifically addressed in IASs and IFRSs, in the context of the IASB Framework, and undertake other tasks at the request of the IASB.
  - In carrying out its work under (a) above, have regard to the IASB's objective of working actively with national standard-setters to bring about convergence of national accounting standards and IASs and IFRSs to high quality solutions.
  - Publish after clearance by the IASB Draft Interpretations for public comment and consider comments made within a reasonable period before finalising an Interpretation.
  - Report to the IASB and obtain the approval of nine of its members for final Interpretations.

Standards Advisory Council

- The Standards Advisory Council, whose members shall be appointed by the Trustees under Section 15(b), provides a forum for participation by organisations and individuals, with an interest in international financial reporting, having diverse geographical and functional backgrounds, with the objective of:

  - Giving advice to the IASB on agenda decisions and priorities in the IASB's work.
  - Informing the IASB of the views of the organisations and individuals on the Council on major standard-setting projects.
- Giving other advice to the IASB or the Trustees.
- The Council shall comprise thirty or more members, having a diversity of geographical and professional backgrounds, appointed for renewable terms of three years. The Chairman of the Council shall be appointed by the Trustees, and shall not be a member of the IASB or a member of its staff. The Trustees shall invite the Chairman of the Council to attend and participate in the Trustees' meetings, as appropriate.
- The Council shall normally meet at least three times a year. Meetings shall be open to the public. The Council shall be consulted by the IASB in advance of IASB decisions on major projects and by the Trustees in advance of any proposed changes to this Constitution.

Chief Executive and Staff

- As provided under Section 24, the Chairman of the IASB shall also be the Chief Executive of the IASC Foundation, and shall be subject to supervision by the Trustees.
- The Chief Executive shall be responsible for the staffing of the IASB, which shall include a Director of Technical Activities appointed by the Chief Executive in consultation with the Trustees: the Director of Technical Activities, while not a member of the IASB, shall be entitled to participate in the debate but not to vote at meetings of the IASB and the International Financial Reporting Interpretations Committee.
- A Director of Operations and a Commercial Director shall also be appointed by the Chief Executive in

consultation with the Trustees. They shall have responsibility for publications and copyright, communications, administration, and finance under the supervision of the Chief Executive and for fundraising under the supervision of the Trustees.

Administration

- The administrative office of the IASC Foundation shall be located in such location as may be determined by the Trustees in accordance with Section 13(d).
- The IASC Foundation shall be a legal entity as determined by the Trustees and shall be governed by this Constitution and by any laws which apply to such legal entity, including, if appropriate, laws applicable because of the location of its registered office.
- The IASC Foundation shall be bound by the signature(s) of such person or persons as may be duly authorised by the Trustees.

ANNEX

International Accounting Standards Committee Foundation Criteria for IASB Members

The following would represent criteria for IASB membership:

- Demonstrated Technical Competency and Knowledge of Financial Accounting and Reporting. All members of the IASB, regardless of whether they are from the accounting profession, preparers, users, or academics, should have demonstrated a high level of knowledge and technical competency in financial accounting and reporting. The credibility of the IASB and its individual members and the effectiveness and efficiency of the organisation will be enhanced with members who have such knowledge and skills.

- Ability to Analyse. IASB members should have demonstrated the ability to analyse issues and consider the implications of that analysis for the decision-making process.
- Communication Skills. Effective oral nd written communication skills are ecessary. These skills include the ability to communicate effectively in private meetings with IASB members, in public meetings, and in written mterials such as accounting standards, speeches, articles, memos and correspondence with constituents. Communication skills also include the ability to listen to and consider the views of others. While a working knowledge of English is necessary, there should not be discrimination in selection against those for whom English is not their first language.
- Judicious Decision-making. IASB members should be capable of considering varied viewpoints, weighing the evidence presented in an impartial fashion, and reaching well-reasoned and supportable decisions in a timely fashion.
- Awareness of the Financial Reporting Environment. High quality financial reporting will be affected by the financial, business and economic environment. IASB members should have an understanding of the global economic environment in which the IASB operates.

  This global awareness should include awareness of business and financial reporting issues that are relevant to, and affect the quality of, transparent financial reporting and disclosure in the various capital markets worldwide, including those using International Financial Reporting Standards.
- Ability to Work in a Collegial Atmosphere. Members should be able to show respect, tact and consideration for one another's and constituents' views. Members must be able to work with one another in reaching consensus views based on the

IASB's objective of developing high quality and transparent financial reporting. Members must be able to put the objective of the IASB above individual philosophies and interests. Constitution

Memorandum of Understanding with the FASB

After their joint meeting in September 2002, the US Financial Accounting Standards Board (FASB) and the International Accounting Standards Board (IASB) issued their Norwalk Agreement in which they 'each acknowledged their commitment to the development of high quality, compatible accounting standards that could be used for both domestic and cross-border financial reporting.

At that meeting, the FASB and the IASB pledged to use their best efforts:

- To make their existing financial reporting standards fully compatible as soon as is practicable and
- To co-ordinate their future work programmes to ensure that once achieved, compatibility is maintained.

At their meetings in April and October 2005, the FASB and the IASB reaffirmed their commitment to the convergence of US generally accepted accounting principles (US GAAP) and International Financial Reporting Standards (IFRSs).

A common set of high quality global standards remains the long-term strategic priority of both the FASB and the IASB. The FASB and the IASB recognise the relevance of the roadmap for the removal of the need for the reconciliation requirement for non-US companies that use IFRSs and are registered in the United States.

It has been noted that the removal of this reconciliation requirement would depend on, among other things, the effective implementation of IFRSs in financial statements across companies and jurisdictions, and measurable progress in addressing priority issues on the IASB-FASB convergence programme.

Therefore, the ability to meet the objective set out by the roadmap depends upon the efforts and actions of many parties

- including companies, auditors, investors, standard-setters and regulators.

IASB Due Process

IASB's Due Process Handbook

The Handbook describes the consultative arrangements of the International Accounting Standards Board (IASB). It is based on the existing framework of the due process laid out in the Constitution of the International Accounting Standards Committee (IASC) Foundation and the Preface to International Financial Reporting Standards (IFRSs) issued by the IASB. It reflects the public consultation conducted by the IASB in 2004 and 2005.

The Trustees of the IASC Foundation have set up a committee—the Trustees' Procedures Committee—with the task of regularly reviewing and, if necessary, amending the procedures of due process in the light of experience and comments from the IASB and constituents. The Committee reviews proposed procedures for the IASB's due process on new projects and the composition of working groups and ensures that their membership reflects a diversity of views and expertise. The Trustees approved this Handbook on 23 March 2006, following two rounds of public consultations, review by the Standards Advisory Council, and public debate by the Trustees.

Working Relationships with Domestic Standard Setters

This Statement records an understanding between the International Accounting Standards Board (IASB) and other accounting standard-setters. It is particularly relevant to standard-setters in jurisdictions that have adopted or converged with International Financial Reporting Standards (IFRSs), or are in the process of adopting or converging with IFRSs.

The Statement identifies a range of activities that the IASB and other accounting standard-setters believe should be undertaken by them in the interests of facilitating the ongoing adoption of or convergence with IFRSs. Some accounting standard-setters may find it difficult to undertake certain of those activities with the resources at their disposal, but will use their best endeavours to do so. Some of the activities are new or different from the way in which the IASB and other accounting standard-setters have operated in the past.

Others are a confirmation of practices that are already being undertaken. This Statement assumes that the ultimate aims of the IASB and other accounting standard-setters are:

- To develop, in the public interest, a single set of high quality, understandable and enforceable global accounting standards that require high quality, transparent and comparable information in financial statements and other financial reporting to help participants in the world's capital markets and other users make economic decisions;
- To promote the use and rigorous application of those standards;
- In fulfilling the objectives associated with (a) and (b), to take account of, as appropriate, the special needs of small and medium-sized entities and emerging economies; and
- To bring about convergence of national accounting standards and IFRSs to high quality solutions.

This Statement is based on the premise that, in order to achieve the above aims for the benefit of constituents, it is essential that the IASB and other accounting standard-setters work together in a spirit of openness and close co-operation. The activities identified in this Statement are important in building and maintaining the relationship between the IASB and other accounting standard-setters.

OBJECTIVES AND FUNCTIONS

The following are the objectives of the Accounting Standards Board:

- To conceive of and suggest areas in which Accounting Standards need to be developed.

- To formulate Accounting Standards with a view to assisting the Council of the ICAI in evolving and establishing Accounting Standards in India.
- To examine how far the relevant International Accounting Standard/International Financial Reporting Standard can be adapted while formulating the Accounting Standard and to adapt the same.
- To review, at regular intervals, the Accounting Standards from the point of view of acceptance or changed conditions, and, if necessary, revise the same.
- To provide, from time to time, interpretations and guidance on Accounting Standards.
- To carry out such other functions relating to Accounting Standards.

The main function of the ASB is to formulate Accounting Standards so that such standards may be established by the ICAI in India. While formulating the Accounting Standards, the ASB will take into consideration the applicable laws, customs, usages and business environment prevailing in India. The ICAI, being a full-fledged member of the International Federation of Accountants (IFAC), is expected, inter alia, to actively promote the International Accounting Standards Board's (IASB) pronouncements in the country with a view to facilitate global harmonisation of accounting standards.

Accordingly, while formulating the Accounting Standards, the ASB will give due consideration to International Accounting Standards (IASs) issued by the International Accounting Standards Committee (predecessor body to IASB) or International Financial Reporting Standards (IFRSs) issued by the IASB, as the case may be, and try to integrate them, to the extent possible, in the light of the conditions and practices prevailing in India

The Accounting Standards are issued under the authority of the Council of the ICAI. The ASB has also been entrusted with the responsibility of propagating the Accounting Standards and of persuading the concerned parties to adopt them in the preparation and presentation of financial statements. The ASB will provide interpretations and guidance on issues arising from Accounting Standards. The ASB will also review the Accounting Standards at periodical intervals and, if necessary, revise the same.

The IASB Structure

The Old Structure: 1973-2000

The International Accounting Standards Committee (IASC) was formed in 1973 through an agreement made by professional accountancy bodies from Australia, Canada, France, Germany, Japan, Mexico, the Netherlands, the United Kingdom and Ireland, and the United States of America. Additional sponsoring members were added in subsequent years, and in 1982 the sponsoring "members" of the IASC comprised all of the professional accountancy bodies that were members of the International Federation of Accountants (IFAC). Accounting standards were set by a part-time, volunteer IASC Board that had 13 country members and up to 3 additional organisational members. Each member was generally represented by two "representatives" and one "technical advisor".

The individuals came from a wide range of backgrounds – accounting practice, business (particularly multinational businesses), financial analysis, accounting education, and national accounting standard-setting. The Board also had a number of observer members (including representatives of IOSCO, FASB, and the European Commission) who participated in the debate but did not vote.

Major components of the old IASC structure were:

- IASC Board – described above.
- Consultative Group – an advisory body representing a wide range of international organisations with an interest in accounting.
- Standing Interpretations Committee (SIC) – developed and invited public comment on interpretations of IASC Standards, subject to final approval by the IASC Board.

- Advisory Council – oversight body (despite its name, the Advisory Council functioned more like the Board of Trustees of the new IASC Foundation, described below).
- Steering Committees – expert task forces for individual agenda projects.

The International Accounting Standards Committee was essentially the structure, rather than a committee in the traditional sense of a group of people. The New Structure: Background and Chronology. After nearly 25 years of achievement, IASC concluded in 1997 that to continue to perform its role effectively, it must find a way to bring about convergence between national accounting standards and practices and high-quality globalaccounting standards. To do that, IASC saw a need to change its structure.

In late 1997 IASC formed a Strategy Working Party to re-examine its structure and strategy. (Jacques Manardo, Deloitte Touche Tohmatsu Global Managing Partner-Strategic Clients, was a member of that group.) The Strategy Working Party published its Report, in the form of a Discussion Paper, in December 1998. After soliciting comments, the Working Party published its Final Recommendations in November 1999.

The IASC Board approved the proposals unanimously in December 1999, and the IASC member bodies did the same in May 2000. A new IASB Constitution took effect 1 July 2000. The standards-setting body was renamed the International Accounting Standards Board (IASB). It would operate under a new International Accounting Standards Committee Foundation (IASCF).

On 1 April 2001, the new IASB took over from the IASC the responsibility for setting International Accounting Standards. In June 2005, the Trustees of the IASC Foundation completed their 2003-2005 Constitution Review and approved a broad range of Changes to the Constitution that went into effect on 1 July 2005. This web page reflects those changes.

Overview of the Restructured IASB

he IASB is organised under an independent Foundation

named the International Accounting Standards Committee Foundation (IASCF). That Foundation is a not-for-profit corporation created under the laws of the State of Delaware, United States of America, on 8 March 2001. Components of the new structure:

- International Accounting Standards Board – has sole responsibility for establishing International Financial Reporting Standards (IFRSs).
- IASC Foundation – oversees the work of the IASB, the structure, and strategy, and has fundraising responsibility.
- International Financial Reporting Interpretations Committee (IFRIC) – develops interpretations for approval by the IASB.
- Standards Advisory Council (SAC) – advises the IASB and the IASCF.
- Working Groups – expert task forces for individual agenda projects.

Trustees of the IASC Foundation

The following reflects revisions to the IASC Foundation Constitution that were approved by the Trustees in June 2005, effective 1 July 2005:

- Number of trustees. 22 Trustees. (Initially, the IASC Foundation Board of Trustees had 19 Trustees.)
- Geographical balance of trustees.
  - Six from North America.
  - Six from Europe.
  - Six from the Asia/Oceania region
  - Four from any area, subject to establishing overall geographical balance.
- Backgrounds of trustees. The constitution requires an appropriate balance of professional backgrounds, including auditors, preparers, users, academics, and other officials serving the public interest. Two will normally be senior partners of prominent international accounting firms.
- Selection of trustees. Trustees are appointed by the

Board of Trustees itself (self-perpetuating board). Trustees adopt their own procedures for appointing trustees.

Those procedures must include consultation with national and international organisations of auditors (including IFAC), preparers, users, and academics and public solicitation of nominees including self-nominations.

To achieve this objective, the trustees have established a Trustee Appointments Advisory Group. The trustees will consult that body before making decisions on trustee appointments.

- Responsibilities of the Trustees. The Trustees of the IASC Foundation have responsibility to:
  - Appoint the members of the Board, including those who will serve in liaison capacities with national standard setters, and establish their contracts of service and performance criteria.
  - Appoint the members of the Standing Interpreta-tions Committee and the Standards Advisory Council.
  - Review annually the strategy of IASB and its effectiveness.
  - Approve annually the budget of IASB and determine the basis for funding.
  - Review broad strategic issues affecting accounting standards, promote IASB and its work and promote the objective of rigorous application of International Accounting Standards, provided that the Trustees shall be excluded from involvement in technical matters relating to accounting standards.
  - Establish and amend operating procedures for the Board, the Standing Interpretations Committee and the Standards Advisory Council.
  - Approve amendments to this Constitution after following a due process, including consultation with the Standards Advisory Council and

publication of an Exposure Draft for public comment.

- Trustee voting. The Trustees act by simple majo-rity vote except for amendments to the Consti-tution, which require a three-fourths majority.
- Initial Trustees. The initial Trustees were chosen in 2000 by a Nominating Committee.

International Accounting Standards Board

IASB's responsibilities. The principal responsibilities of the IASB are to:

l competency and knowledge of financial accounting and reporting.

- Ability to analyse.
- Communication skills.
- Judicious decision-making.
- Awareness of the financial reporting environment.
- Ability to work in a collegial atmosphere.
- Integrity, objectivity, and discipline.
- Commitment to the IASC Foundation's mission and public interest.
- Geographical mix of IASB members. "Trustees shall ensure that the IASB is not dominated by any particular constituency or geographical interest".
- Background mix of IASB members. "Appropriate mix of recent practical experience among auditors, preparers, users and academics".
- Due process steps. Formal due process for projects normally, but not necessarily, involves the following steps. The steps that are required under the terms of the IASC Foundation Constitution are indicated by an asterisk.
- The staff are asked to identify and review the issues associated with the topic and to consider the application of the Framework to the issues;
- Study national accounting requirements and

practice and an exchange of views about the issues with national standard-setters.

- Consult the Standards Advisory Council about the advisability of adding the topic to the IASB's agenda.
- Form an advisory group (generally called a 'working group') to advise the IASB and its staff on the project.
- Publish for public comment a discussion document.
- Publish for public comment an exposure draft approved by at least nine votes of the IASB, including any dissenting opinions held by IASB.
- Members (in exposure drafts, dissenting opinions are referred to as 'alternative views').
- Publish within an exposure draft a basis for conclusions.
- Consider all comments received within the comment period on discussion documents and exposure drafts.
- Consider the desirability of holding a public hearing and of the desirability of conducting field tests and, if considered desirable, holding such hearings and conducting such tests.
- Approve of a standard by at least nine votes of the IASB and inclusion in the published standard of any dissenting opinions.
- Publish within a standard a basis for conclusions, explaining, among other things, the steps in the IASB's due process and how the IASB dealt with public comments on the exposure draft.

The IASB is required to explain its reasons if it decides not to follow any of the non-mandatory due process steps. Such non-mandatory steps are:

- Publishing a discussion document before an exposure draft.
- Forming working groups.
- Publishing a basis for conclusions.
- Holding public hearings.

- Conducting field tests.

  In March 2006, the Trustees of the IASCF published a new Due Process Handbook for the IASB. The Handbook describes the IASB's consultative procedures.

- IASB agenda. The IASB has full discretion over developing and pursuing its technical agenda. The trustees' annual review of the strategy of the IASC Foundation and the IASB and its effectiveness includes "consideration, but not determination, of the IASB's agenda".
- IASB voting. The publication of a Standard, Exposure Draft, or final SIC Interpretation requires approval by 9 of the Board's 14 members. (From the IASB's inception in 2001 to 30 June 2005, the required vote was 8 out of 14.)
- IASB working groups. The Board will normally form Working Groups or other types of specialist advisory groups to give advice on major projects. The IASCF Trustees' Procedures Committee reviews the proposed composition of each group to ensure that there is a satisfactory balance of perspectives.
- IASB Chairman. Appointed by the Trustees. In late June 2000, the Trustees announced the appointment of Sir David Tweedie as the first Chairman of the restructured IASB. Sir David continues today as IASB Chairman.
- Board meetings. The new IASB held its first official meeting in London in April 2001. The Board meets monthly (except August) for approximately one week. Board meetings are normally held at the IASB's office in London. Twice each year, the IASB and the US Financial Accounting Standards Board (FASB) hold a joint meeting (usually April and October). The April meeting is normally held at the FASB's office in the Unted States.

Standards Advisory Council

SAC role. The Standards Advisory Council (SAC) provides a forum for participation by organisations and individuals, with an interest in international financial reporting, having diverse geographical and functional backgrounds, with the objective of:

- Advising the IASB on agenda decisions and priorities in the IASB's work,
- Informing the IASB of the views of the organisations and individuals on the Council on major standard-setting projects, and
- Giving other advice to the IASB or the Trustees.

SAC members. Under the IASC Foundation Constitution, SAC has 30 or more members. The number is currently around 40. Members are appointed by the Trustees for a renewable term of three years. They have diverse geographic and functional backgrounds.

SAC chairman. SAC has an independent chairman appointed by the Trustees. SAC meetings. The SAC normally meets three times each year at meetings open to the public.

International Financial Reporting Interpretations Committee

The International Financial Reporting Interpretations Committee (until 2002 known as the Standing Interpretations Committee) has 14 members* appointed by the Trustees for terms of three years. IFRIC members are not salaried but their expenses are reimbursed. IFRIC meets approximately every other month at meetings that are open to public observation. Approval of Draft or final Interpretations requires that not more than three voting members vote against the Draft or final Interpretation. IFRIC is chaired by a non-voting chair who can be one of the members of the IASB, the Director of Technical Activities, or a member of the IASB's senior technical staff.

IFRIC's Responsibilities:

- Interpret the application of International Financial Reporting Standards (IFRSs) and provide timely guidance on financial reporting issues not specifically addressed in IFRSs or IASs, in the context of the IASB's framework, and undertake other tasks at the request of the Board.

- Publish Draft Interpretations for public comment and consider comments made within a reasonable period before finalising an Interpretation.
- Report to the Board and obtain Board approval for final Interpretations.

IFRIC Members: In November 2007, the IASC Foundation Trustees voted to enlarge IFRIC to 14 members from its original 12 members.

IASC Foundation Constitution

Current Constitution

- On 24 May 2000, the first IASC Foundation Constitution was approved by the Members of IASC. (Members of the IASC were the professional accounting organisations that were also IFAC members).
- On 5 March 2002, certain paragraphs were revised by the Trustees of the IASC Foundation, effective on that date. Those revisions were necessary to implement certain aspects of the IASB's Preface to IFRS relating to the Standing Interpretations Committee.
- In November 2003, the trustees of the IASC Foundation announced the appointment of a committee to Review the IASB's Constitution.
- On 21 June 2005, the Trustees of the IASC Foundation gave final approval to a broad range of changes to the Constitution, effective 1 July 2005.
- On 31 October 2007, the Trustees of the IASC Foundation revised the Constitution to reflect the expansion of IFRIC to 14 members, effective immediately. At their 31 October 2007 meeting, the Trustees Announced (PDF 55k) that a

comprehensive Constitution Review would be undertaken in 2008

Key Groups

Certain groups have been closely involved with the development of IASC Standards during the 1990s as participating observers at every IASC Board meeting and nearly all IASC steering committee meetings. Those groups continue to be closely involved with the work of the IASB. They are:

- European Commission.
- European Financial Reporting Advisory Group (EFRAG).
- International Organization of Securities Commissions (IOSCO).
- International Federation of Accountants (IFAC).
- US Financial Accounting Standards Board (FASB).
- United States Public Company Accounting Oversight Board (PCAOB).
- United States Securities and Exchange Commission (SEC).

Because they are important to the success of the IASB, we have provided separate pages of information about the involvement of these key groups with IASB.

IASC Board Statement December 2000

At its December 2000 meeting, the IASC Board approved a statement to be transmitted to the new International Accounting Standards Board. The Statement comments on current work in progress and expresses some of Board's current thinking based on its work on these items and other discussions. The Board expressed a hope that its successor would continue work on the projects on:

- Business combinations,
- Present value,
- Reporting financial performance,
- Insurance,
- Extractive industries, and

- Financial instruments.

In addition, the Statement suggests the following new projects:

- A project on convergence of national and international standards.
- A new 'improvements project' to deal with relatively minor matters in the existing IASC Standards.
- Share-based payment.
- Intangible assets.
- Narrative reporting outside the notes.
- Update the Framework and Preface to IAS.
- Special version of IAS for small enterprises.
- Review of IAS provisions relating to inflation accounting.
- Accounting in United States

Accounting: Historical Perspectives

With the establishment of the first English colonies in America, accounting or bookkeeping, as the discipline was referred to then, quickly assumed an important role in the development of American commerce. Two hundred years, however, would pass before accounting would separate from bookkeeping, and nearly three hundred years would pass before the profession of accounting, as it is now practiced, would emerge.

For individuals and businesses, accounting records in Colonial America often were very elementary. Most records of this period relied on the single-entry method or were simply narrative accounts of transactions. As rudimentary as they were, these records were important because the colonial economy was largely barter and credit system with substantial time passing before payments were made. Accounting records were often the only reliable records of such historical transactions.

The Emergence of Accounting

Prior to the late 1800s, the terms bookkeeping and

accounting were often used interchangeably because the recording/posting process was central to both activities. There was little need for financial statements (e.g., income statements) because most owners had direct knowledge of their businesses and, therefore, could rely on elementary bookkeeping procedures for information.

Although corporations (e.g., banks, canal companies) were present in the United States prior to the early 1800s, their numbers were few. Beginning in the late 1820s, however, the number of corporations rapidly increased with the creation and expansion of the railroads. To operate successfully, the railroads needed cost reports, production reports, financial statements, and operating ratios that were more complex than simple recording procedures could provide.

Alfred D. Chandler, Jr. (1977), noted the impact of the railroads on the development of accounting in his classic work, "The Visible Hand", when he stated "after 1850, the railroad was central in the development of the accounting profession in the United States".

With the increase in the number of corporations, there also arose a demand for additional financial information that A.C. Littleton (1933/1988) in his landmark book, "The Rise of the Accounting Profession", called "figure" knowledge. With no direct knowledge of a business, investors had to rely on financial statements for information, and to create those statements, more complex accounting methods were required.

The accountant's responsibility, therefore, expanded beyond simply recording entries to include the preparation, classification, and analysis of financial statements. As John L. Carey (1969) wrote in The Rise of the Accounting Profession, "the nineteenth century saw bookkeeping expanded into accounting".

Additionally, as the development of the corporation created a greater need for the services of accountants, the study of commerce and accounting became more important. Although there had been trade business schools and published texts on accounting/bookkeeping, traditional colleges had largely ignored the study of business and accounting.

In 1881, however, the Wharton School of Finance and Economy was founded, and two years later, the school added accounting to its curriculum. As other major universities created schools of commerce, accounting secured a significant place in the curriculum.

With a separation of management and ownership in corporations, there also arose a need for an independent party to review the financial statements. Someone was needed to represent the owners' interest and to verify that the statements accurately presented the financial conditions of the company.

Moreover, there was often an expectation that an independent review would discover whether managers were violating their fiduciary duties to the owners. Additionally, because the late nineteenth century was a period of major industrial mergers, someone was needed to verify the reported values of the companies. The independent public accountant, a person whose obligation was not to the managers of a company but to its shareholders and potential investors, provided the knowledge and skills to meet these needs.

In 1913, the responsibilities of and job opportunities for accountants again expanded with the ratification of the Sixteenth Amendment to the Constitution, which allowed a federal income tax. Accountants had become somewhat familiar with implementing a national tax with the earlier passage of the Corporation Excise Tax Law.

Despite the earlier law, however, many companies had not set up proper systems to determine taxable income and few were familiar with concepts such as depreciation and accrual accounting. As tax rates increased, tax services became even more important to accounting firms and often opened the door to providing other services to a client. Accounting firms, therefore, were often engaged to establish a proper accounting system and audit financial statements as well as prepare the required tax return.

Thus, in contrast to bookkeeping which often had been considered a trade, the responsibilities of accounting had expanded by the early twentieth century to such an extent that it now sought professional status.

One foundation of the established professions (e.g., medicine, law) was professional certification, which accounting did not have. In 1896, with the support of several accounting organizations, New York State passed a law restricting the title certified public account ant (CPA) to those who had passed a state examination and had acquired at least three years of accounting experience. Similar laws were soon passed in several states.

Professional Organization

Throughout the history of accounting, professional organizations have made major contributions to the development of the profession. For example, in 1882, the Institute of Accountants and Bookkeepers of New York (IABNY) was organized with the primary aim of increasing the level of educational resources available for accountants.

In 1886, the IABNY became the Institute of Accounts, and it continued to be active in promoting accounting education for nearly twenty years. Meanwhile, the first national organization for accounting educators, the American Association of University Instructors in Accounting (AAUIP), was organized in 1916. In 1935, the AAUIP was reorganized as the American Accounting Association.

The national public accounting organization, the American Association of Public Accountants (AAPA), was incorporated in 1887. Reflecting the need of most professions for a code of ethics, the AAPA added a professional ethics section to its bylaws in 1907.

The AAPA was reorganized as the American Institute of Accountants in the United States of America and then later as the American Institute of Accountants (AIA). In 1921, the American Society of Certified Public Accountants (ASCPA) was established and became a rival to the AIA for leadership in the public accounting area. The rivalry continued until 1937, when the ASCPA merged with the AIA. In 1957, the AIA became the American Institute of Certified Public Accountants (AICPA).

In contrast to the public accounting emphasis of the AIA

and ASCPA, the National Association of Cost Accountants (NACA) was founded in 1919. The NACA placed an emphasis on the development of cost controls and proper reporting within companies. In 1957, the NACA changed its name to the National Association of Accountants (NAA) in recognition of the expansion of managerial accounting beyond traditional cost accounting. Then, in 1991, recognizing its emphasis on the managerial aspects of accounting, the NAA became the Institute of Management Accountants.

External and Internal Regulation

During the nineteenth century, the federal government generally allowed accounting to regulate itself. Then, in 1913, Congress established the Federal Reserve System and, one year later, the Federal Trade Commission (FTC). From this date forward, federal agencies have had an increasing impact on the profession of accounting.

The government's first major attempt at the formalization of authoritative reporting standards was in 1917 with the Federal Reserve Board's publication of Uniform Accounting. In 1918, the bulletin was reissued as Approved Methods for the Preparation of Balance Sheet Statements.

Although directed toward auditing the balance sheet, the report presented model income and balance sheet statements. Because the proposal was only a recommendation, however, its acceptance was limited. The impetus for stricter financial reporting was provided by the collapse of the securities market in 1929 and the revelation of massive fraud in a company listed on the New York Stock Exchange (NYSE).

In 1933, the NYSE announced that companies applying for a listing on the exchange must have their financial statements audited by an independent public accountant. The scope of these audits had to follow the revised guidelines set forth by the Federal Reserve in 1929. Another major innovation in the regulation of accounting was the passage of the Securities Act of 1933 and the Securities and Exchange Act of 1934. The 1933 act conferred upon the FTC the authority to prescribe the accounting methods for companies to follow.

Under this act, accountants could be held liable for losses that resulted from material omissions or misstatements in registration statements they had certified. The 1934 act transferred the authority to prescribe accounting methods to the newly established Securities and Exchange Commission (SEC) and required that financial statements filed with the SEC be certified by an independent public accountant.

With the creation of the SEC and the passage of new securities laws, the federal government assumed a central role in the establishment of basic requirements for the issuance and auditing of financial reports. Additionally, these acts increased the importance of accountants and enlarged the accountant's responsibility to the general public. Under these acts, not only did accountants have a responsibility to the public, they were now potentially liable for their actions.

In 1938, the SEC delegated much of its authority to prescribe accounting practices to the AIA and its Committee on Accounting Procedures (CAP). In 1939, CAP issued its first of fifty-one Accounting Research Bulletins. Responding to criticism of CAP, the AICPA (formerly the AIA) in 1959 replaced the CAP with the Accounting Principles Board (APB). The APB was designed to issue accounting opinions after it had considered previous research studies, and in 1962, the APB issued its first of thirty-one opinions.

Although the SEC had delegated much of its standard-setting authority to the AICPA, the commission exercised its right to approve all standards when it declared that companies did not have to follow the rules set forth in APB No. 2, The Investment Credit.

Responding to criticism of the APB, a study group chaired by Francis M. Wheat was established to review the board structure and the rule-making process. The committee recommended that an independent, full time, more diverse standards board replace the APB. Following the recommendations, the Financial Accounting Standards Board (FASB) was established in 1973. This board is independent of the AICPA and issued its first statement in 1973.

The Changing Genderization of the Work Force

With the separation of bookkeeping from accounting, the demand for women bookkeepers dramatically increased, and by 1930, over 60 percent of all bookkeepers were women. A similar increase in the demand for women accountants, however, did not occur. Although World War II created some opportunities for women in accounting, at the start of the second half of the twentieth century, accounting still was not considered an appropriate career for most women.

In fact, in 1950, only 15 percent of the more than 300,000 accountants in the United States were women. Moreover, less than 4 percent of college students majoring in accounting then were women.

In the 1960s, social and legal events began that ultimately provided opportunities for women in the profession of accounting. As these events occurred, the overall demand for accounting services and accountants also greatly increased. This demand became so large that the traditional labour pool of men was not sufficient to maintain the accounting work force. Concurrently, women majoring in accounting increased dramatically from less than 5 percent of all accounting majors in 1960 to over 50 percent in 1985.

Given the increase of women accounting majors and the inability of the traditional labour pool to meet the work force demand, accounting (especially public accounting) increased the hiring of women. By 1990, women comprised a majority of the accounting work force. It would be the turn of the twenty-first century, however, before women began to obtain a significant number of upper-level management positions in accounting.

The Twenty-First Century

The accountant, the accounting firm, and the accounting profession of the twenty-first century are quite different from what existed at the beginning of the twentieth century. In contrast to a bookkeeper manually recording entries in a large bound volume, an accountant is now responsible for information concerning all facets of a business and is dependent on the latest technology for processing that information. In contrast to small local firms, accounting firms now can be large international organizations with reported revenues of billions of dollars.

In addition to the traditional audit/attest information, accounting firms provide their clients with tax services, financial planning, system analysis, consulting, and legal services. At the beginning of the twentieth century, the accounting profession was just emerging. Today, the profession is comprised of thousands of men and women working in public and private firms as well as profit and nonprofit organizations as members of management teams or as valued consultants.

Generally Accepted Accounting Principles (United States)

In the U.S., generally accepted accounting principles, commonly abbreviated as US GAAP or simply GAAP, are accounting rules used to prepare, present, and report financial statements for a wide variety of entities, including publicly-traded and privately-held companies, non-profit organizations, and governments. Generally GAAP includes local applicable Accounting Framework, related accounting law, rules and Accounting Standard.

Similar to many other countries practicing under the common law system, the United States government does not directly set accounting standards, in the belief that the private sector has better knowledge and resources. US GAAP is not written in law, although the U.S. Securities and Exchange Commission (SEC) requires that it be followed in financial reporting by publicly-traded companies. Currently, the Financial Accounting Standards Board (FASB) is the highest authority in establishing generally accepted accounting principles for public and private companies, as well as non-profit entities.

For local and state governments, GAAP is determined by the Governmental Accounting Standards Board (GASB), which operates under a set of assumptions, principles, and constraints, different from those of standard private-sector GAAP. Financial reporting in federal government entities is regulated by the Federal Accounting Standards Advisory Board (FASAB).

The US GAAP provisions differ somewhat from International Financial Reporting Standards, though efforts are underway to reconcile differences in principles so that financial statements created under international standards will be considered acceptable within the United States, and US GAAP financial statements will be acceptable internationally.

History

Auditors took the leading role in developing GAAP for business enterprises. Circa 2008, the FASB issued the FASB Accounting Standards Codification, which reorganized the thousands of US GAAP pronouncements into roughly 90 accounting topics.

Basic Objectives

Financial reporting should provide information that is:

- Useful to present to potential investors and creditors and other users in making rational investment, credit, and other financial decisions.
- Helpful to present to potential investors and creditors and other users in assessing the amounts, timing, and uncertainty of prospective cash receipts.
- About economic resources, the claims to those resources, and the changes in them.

Basic Concepts

To achieve basic objectives and implement fundamental qualities GAAP has four basic assumptions, four basic principles, and four basic constraints.

Assumptions

Business Entity: assumes that the business is separate from its owners or other businesses. Revenues and expenses should be kept separate from personal expenses.Going Concern: assumes that the business will be in operation indefinetly. This validates the methods of asset capitalization, depreciation, and amortization.Only when liquidation is certain this assumption is not applicable.

Monetary Unit principle: assumes a stable currency is going to be the unit of record. The FASB accepts the nominal value of the US Dollar as the monetary unit of record unadjusted for inflation.

Its the accounting table top

- The Time-period principle implies that the economic activities of an enterprise can be divided into artificial time periods.

Principles

Cost Principle

It requires companies to account and report based on acquisition costs rather than fair market value for most assets and liabilities. This principle provides information that is reliable (removing opportunity to provide subjective and potentially biased market values), but not very relevant. Thus there is a trend to use fair values. Most debts and securities are now reported at market values.

Revenue Principle

It requires companies to record when revenue is

- Realized or realizable and
- Earned, not when cash is received. This way of accounting is called accrual basis accounting.

Matching Principle

Expenses have to be matched with revenues as long as it is reasonable to do so. Expenses are recognized not when the work is performed, or when a product is produced, but when the work or the product actually makes its contribution to revenue. Only if no connection with revenue can be established, may cost be charged as expenses to the current period (e.g. office salaries and other administrative expenses). This principle allows greater evaluation of actual profitability and performance (shows how much was spent to earn revenue). Depreciation and Cost of Goods Sold are good examples of application of this principle.

Disclosure Principle

Amount and kinds of information disclosed should be decided based on trade-off analysis as a larger amount of information costs more to prepare and use. Information disclosed should be enough to make a judgment while keeping costs reasonable. Information is presented in the main body of financial statements, in the notes or as supplementary information

Constraints

- Objectivity principle: the company financial statements provided by the accountants should base on objective evidence
- Materiality principle: the significance of an item should be considered when it is reported. An item is considered significant when it would affect the decision of a reasonable individual.
- Consistency principle: accounting procedures should follow industry practices.
- Prudent principle: when choosing between two solutions, the one that will be least likely to overstate assets and income should be picked.

Required Departures from Gaap

Under the AICPA's Code of Professional Ethics under Rule 203 - Accounting Principles, a member must depart from GAAP if following it would lead to a material misstatement on the financial statements, or otherwise be misleading. In the departure the member must disclose, if practicable, the reasons why compliance with the accounting principle would result in a misleading financial statement.

Under Rule 203-1-Departures from Established Accounting Principles, the departures are rare, and usually take place when there is new legislation, the evolution of new forms of business transactions, an unusual degree of materiality, or the existence of conflicting industry practices.

Setting Gaap

These organizations influence the development of GAAP in the United States.

United States Securities and Exchange Commission (SEC)

The SEC was created as a result of the Great Depression. At that time there was no structure setting accounting standards. The SEC encouraged the establishment of private standard-setting bodies through the AICPA and later the FASB, believing that the private sector had the proper knowledge, resources, and talents. The SEC works closely with various private organizations setting GAAP, but does not set GAAP itself.

American Institute of Certified Public Accountants (AICPA)

In 1939, urged by the SEC, the AICPA appointed the Committee on Accounting Procedure (CAP). During the years 1939 to 1959 CAP issued 51 Accounting Research Bulletins that dealt with a variety of timely accounting problems. However, this problem-by-problem approach failed to develop the much needed structured body of accounting principles.

Thus, in 1959, the AICPA created the Accounting Principles Board (APB), whose mission it was to develop an overall conceptual framework. It issued 31 opinions and was dissolved in 1973 for lack of productivity and failure to act promptly. After the creation of the FASB, the AICPA established the Accounting Standards Executive Committee (AcSEC). It publishes:

- Audit and Accounting Guidelines, which summarizes the accounting practices of specific industries (e.g. casinos, colleges, airlines, etc.) and provides specific guidance on matters not addressed by FASB or GASB.
- Statements of Position, which provides guidance on financial reporting topics until the FASB or GASB sets standards on the issue.

- Practice Bulletins, which indicate the AcSEC's views on narrow financial reporting issues not considered by the FASB or the GASB.

Financial Accounting Standards Board (FASB)

Realizing the need to reform the APB, leaders in the accounting profession appointed a Study Group on the Establishment of Accounting Principles (commonly known as the Wheat Committee for its chair Francis Wheat). This group determined that the APB must be dissolved and a new standard-setting structure be created.

This structure is composed of three organizations: the Financial Accounting Foundation (FAF, it selects members of the FASB, funds and oversees their activities), the Financial Accounting Standards Advisory Council (FASAC), and the major operating organization in this structure the Financial Accounting Standards Board (FASB). FASB has 4 major types of publications:

- Statements of Financial Accounting Standards - the most authoritative GAAP setting publications. More than 150 have been issued to date.
- Statements of Financial Accounting Concepts - first issued in 1978. They are part of the FASB's conceptual framework project and set forth fundamental objectives and concepts that the FASB use in developing future standards. However, they are not a part of GAAP. There have been 7 concepts published to date.
- Interpretations - modify or extend existing standards. There have been around 50 interpretations published to date.
- Technical Bulletins– guidelines on applying standards, interpretations, and opinions. Usually solves some very specific accounting issue that will not have a significant, lasting effect.

In 1984 the FASB created the Emerging Issues Task Force (EITF) which deals with new and unusual financial transactions that have the potential to become common (e.g. accounting for Internet based companies).

It acts more like a problem filter for the FASB - the EITF deals with short-term, quickly resolvable issues, leaving long-term, more pervasive problems for the FASB.

Governmental Accounting Standards Board (GASB)

Created in 1984, the GASB addresses state and local government reporting issues. Its structure is similar to that of the FASB's. Other influential organizations (e.g. American Accounting Association, Institute of Management Accountants, Financial Executives Institute)

Precedence of GAAP-setting authorities

In the United States, GAAP derives, in order of importance, from:

- Issuances from an authoritative body designated by the American Institute of Certified Public Accountants (AICPA) Council (for example, the Financial Accounting Standards Board Statements, AICPA Accounting Principles Board Options, and AICPA Accounting Research Bulletins).
- Other AICPA issuances such as AICPA Industry Guides.
- Industry practice.
- Into para-accounting literature in the form of books and articles.

Other Accounting Standard Authorities

Institute of Chartered Accountants of India is empowered for issuance of Accounting Standard in India. So far ICAI has issued 31 Accounting Standards and AS-32 is under preparation. CBDT is also empowered to issue AS for appropriate accounting method for taxation. Central Government is in line of thinking to create separate Accounting Standard body for government accounting.

House of GAAP

The term "House of GAAP concept" derives from an article by Steven Rubin in the Journal of Accountancy June 1984 issue, and is commonly used to illustrate the hierarchy of pronouncements, standards, and similar literature which establish US GAAP.

About GAO

The U.S. Government Accountability Office (GAO) is an independent, nonpartisan agency that works for Congress. Often called the "congressional watchdog," GAO investigates how the federal government spends taxpayer dollars. The head of GAO, the Comptroller General of the United States, is appointed to a 15-year term by the President from a slate of candidates Congress proposes. Gene L. Dodaro became Acting Comptroller General on March 13, 2008, succeeding David M. Walker, who appointed him upon resigning. Mr. Dodaro will serve in this position until the President nominates and the Senate confirms a successor from a list of candidates proposed by the Congress.

Our Mission is to support the Congress in meeting its constitutional responsibilities and to help improve the performance and ensure the accountability of the federal government for the benefit of the American people.

We provide Congress with timely information that is objective, fact-based, nonpartisan, nonideological, fair, and balanced.

Our Core Values of accountability, integrity, and reliability are reflected in all of the work we do. We operate under strict professional standards of review and referencing; all facts and analyses in our work are thoroughly checked for accuracy.

Our Work is done at the request of congressional committees or subcommittees or is mandated by public laws or committee reports. We also undertake research under the authority of the Comptroller General. We support congressional oversight by:

- Auditing agency operations to determine whether federal funds are being spent efficiently and effectively;
- Investigating allegations of illegal and improper activities;
- Reporting on how well government programmes and policies are meeting their objectives;
- Performing policy analyses and outlining options for congressional consideration;
- Issuing legal decisions and opinions, such as bid protest rulings and reports on agency rules.

We advise Congress and the heads of executive agencies about ways to make government more efficient, effective, ethical, equitable and responsive. Our work leads to laws and acts that improve government operations, saving the government and taxpayers billions of dollars.

The GAO Human Capital Reform Act of 2004

Effective July 7, 2004, the GAO's legal name became the Government Accountability Office. The change, which better reflects the modern professional services organization GAO has become, is the most visible provision of the GAO Human Capital Reform Act of 2004, Pub. L. 108-271, 118 Stat. 811 (2004).

Besides the name change, the law:

- Decouples GAO from the federal employee pay system.
- Establishes a compensation system that places greater emphasis on job performance while protecting the purchasing power of employees who are performing acceptably.
- Gives GAO permanent authority to offer voluntary early retirement opportunities and voluntary separation payments (buy-outs).
- Provides greater flexibility for reimbursing employees for relocation benefits.
- Allows certain employees and officers with less than three years of federal service to earn increased amounts of annual leave.

- Authorizes an exchange programme with private sector organizations.

Opinion On The Financial Statements

We have audited the accompanying consolidated balance sheet of the U. S. Patent and Trademark Office as of September 30, 2003, and the related consolidated statements of net cost, changes in net position, financing, and cash flows, and the combined statement of budgetary resources for the year then ended.

The accompanying financial statements as of and for the year ended September 30, 2002, were audited by other auditors whose unqualified opinion thereon was dated December 13, 2002.

In our opinion, the financial statements referred to above present fairly, in all material respects, the financial position of the USPTO as of September 30, 2003, and its net costs, changes in net position, budgetary resources, reconciliation of net costs to budgetary obligations, and cash flows for the year then ended, in conformity with accounting principles generally accepted in the United States of America.

The information in the Management Discussion and Analysis section and the Required Supplemental Information presented on pages 81 through 86 are not a required part of the financial statements, but are supplementary information required by accounting principles generally accepted in the United States of America or OMB Bulletin No. 01-09, Form and Content of Agency Financial Statements. We have applied certain limited procedures, which consisted principally of inquiries of management regarding the methods of measurement and presentation of this information. However, we did not audit this information and, accordingly, we express no opinion on it.

Our audits were conducted for the purpose of forming an opinion on the financial statements taken as a whole. The Management and Performance Challenges Identified by the Inspector General and Other Accompanying Information presented on pages 93 through 136 are presented for purposes of additional analysis and are not a required part of the financial statements. This information has not been subjected to the auditing procedures applied in the audit of the basic financial statements and, accordingly, we express no opinion on it.

INTERNAL CONTROL OVER FINANCIAL REPORTING

Our consideration of internal control over financial reporing would not necessarily disclose all matters in the internal control over financial reporting that might be material weaknesses under standards issued by the American Institute of Certified Public Accountants.

Material weaknesses are conditions in which the design or operation of one or more of the internal control components does not reduce to a relatively low level the risk that misstatements caused by error or fraud, in amounts that would be material in relation to the financial statements being audited, may occur and not be detected within a timely period by employees in the normal course of performing their assigned functions.

However, we noted no matters involving the internal control and its operation that we considered to be material weaknesses as defined above. However, we noted other matters involving internal control over financial reporting and its operation that we have reported to the management of USPTO in a separate restricted use and distribution IT report dated November 3, 2003.

Compliance with Laws and Regulations

The results of our tests of compliance with other laws and regulations, exclusive of the Federal Financial Management Improvement Act (FFMIA), disclosed no instances of noncompliance that are required to be reported under Government Auditing Standards or OMB Bulletin No. 01-02. The results of our tests of FFMIA disclosed no instances in which the USPTO's financial management systems did not substantially comply with the three requirements discussed in the Responsibilities section of this report.

RESPONSIBILITIES

Management's Responsibilities

The Government Management Reform Act of 1994 (GMRA) requires each federal agency to report annually to Congress on its financial status and any other information needed to fairly present its financial position and results of operations. To meet the GMRA reporting requirements, the USPTO prepares annual financial statements.

Management is responsible for the financial statements, including:

- Preparing the financial statements in conformity with accounting principles generally accepted in the United States of America.
- Establishing and maintaining internal controls over financial reporting, and preparation of the Management Discussion and Analysis (including the performance measures) and required supplemental information.
- Complying with laws and regulations, including FFMIA.

In fulfilling this responsibility, estimates and judgments by management are required to assess the expected benefits and related costs of internal control policies. Because of inherent limitations in internal control, misstatements, due to error or fraud may nevertheless occur and not be detected.

Auditors' Responsibilities

Our responsibility is to express an opinion on the fiscal year 2003 financial statements of the USPTO based on our audit. We conducted our audit in accordance with auditing standards generally accepted in the United States of America, the standards applicable to financial audits contained in Government Auditing Standards, and OMB Bulletin No. 01-02. Those standards and OMB Bulletin No. 01-02 require that we plan and perform the audit to obtain reasonable assurance about whether the financial statements are free of material misstatement.

An audit includes:

- Examining, on a test basis, evidence supporting the amounts and disclosures in the financial statements.
- Assessing the accounting principles used and significant estimates made by management.
- Evaluating the overall financial statement presentation.

We believe that our audit provides a reasonable basis for our opinion. In planning and performing our fiscal year 2003 audit, we considered the USPTO's internal control over financial reporting by obtaining an understanding of the USPTO's internal control, determining whether internal controls had been placed in operation, assessing control risk, and performing tests of controls in order to determine our auditing procedures for the purpose of expressing our opinion on the financial statements.

We limited our internal control testing to those controls necessary to achieve the objectives described in OMB Bulletin No. 01-02 and Government Auditing Standards. We did not test all internal controls relevant to operating objectives as broadly defined by the Federal Managers' Financial Integrity Act of 1982. The objective of our audit was not to provide assurance on internal control over financial reporting. Consequently, we do not provide an opinion thereon.

As required by OMB Bulletin No. 01-02, with respect to internal control related to performance measures determined by management to be key and reported in the Management Discussion and Analysis, we obtained an understanding of the design of significant internal controls relating to the existence and completeness assertions. Our procedures were not designed to provide assurance on internal control over performance measures and, accordingly, we do not provide an opinion thereon.

As part of obtaining reasonable assurance about whether the USPTO's fiscal year 2003 financial statements are free of material misstatement, we performed tests of the USPTO's compliance with certain provisions of laws and regulations, noncompliance with which could have a direct and material effect on the determination of financial statement amounts, and certain provisions of other laws and regulations specified in OMB Bulletin No. 01-02, including certain provisions referred to in ffmia. We limited our tests of compliance to the provisions described in the preceding sentence, and we did not test compliance with all laws and regulations applicable to the USPTO. Providing an opinion on compliance with laws and regulations was not an objective of our audit and, accordingly, we do not express such an opinion.

Under OMB Bulletin No 01-02 and Ffima, we are required to report whether the USPTO's financial management systems substantially comply with. Federal financial management systems requirements, applicable Federal accounting standards, and the United States Government Standard General Ledger at the transaction level. To meet this requirement, we performed tests of compliance with FFMIA Section 803 requirements.

Distribution

This report is intended solely for the information and use of USPTO's management, the Department of Commerce's Office of the Inspector General, OMB, the U.S. General Accounting Office, and the U.S. Congress, and is not intended to be and should not be used by anyone other than these specified parties.

Audited Financial Statements

Audits are conducted in accordance with generally accepted auditing standards (GAAS). Those standards require that the audit is planned and performed to obtain reasonable assurance about whether the financial statements are free of material misstatement. An audit includes examining, on a test basis, evidence supporting the amounts and disclosures in the financial statements.

An audit also includes assessing the accounting principles used and significant estimates made by management, as well as evaluating the overall financial statement presentation. An audit must provide a reasonable basis for the opinion rendered. The two most common opinions are the unqualified and the qualified opinion.

A qualified opinion is rendered when there is a lack of sufficient competent evidential matter or restrictions on the scope of the auditor's examination due to one of the following:

- The financial statements contain a departure from generally accepted accounting principles (GAAP), the effect of which is material.
- There has been a material change between periods in accounting principles or in the method of their application.
- There are significant uncertainties affecting the financial statements.

A Review is a second level of attestation. A review consists primarily of inquiries of the organization's personnel and analytical procedures applied to the financial data. It is substantially less in scope than an audit in accordance with generally. Accepted auditing standards, the objective of which is the expression of an opinion on the financial statements taken as a whole. Accordingly, such an opinion is not rendered.

Statement of Financial Position

The primary purpose of the statement of financial position is to help donors, members, creditors, and others to identify the organization's financial strengths and weaknesses, evaluate its performance during the period, and assess its ability to continue to render services. This statement focuses on the organization as a whole and reports the amounts of its total assets, liabilities, and net assets.

A statement of financial position provided by a not-for-profit organization reports the amounts of each of three classes of nets assets—permanently restricted net assets, temporarily restricted net assets, and unrestricted net assets—based on the existence or absence of donor-imposed restrictions.

Information about the nature and amounts of different types of permanent restrictions or temporary restrictions shall be provided either by reporting their amounts on the face of the statement or by including relevant details in notes to the financial statements. Similarly, separate line items may be reported within temporarily restricted net assets or in notes to the financial statements to distinguish between temporary restrictions.

An organization reports gifts of cash and other assets as restricted support if they are received with donor stipulations that limit the use of the donated assets. When a donor restriction expires, that is, when the stipulated time restriction ends or purpose restriction is accomplished, temporarily restricted net assets are reclassified to unrestricted net assets and reported in the statement of activities as net assets released from restrictions.

Donor-restricted contributions whose restrictions are met in the same reporting period may be reported as unrestricted support provided that an organization reports consistently from period to period and discloses its accounting policy. Contributions without donor-imposed restrictions are reported as unrestricted support that increases unrestricted net assets.

Statement of Activities (and Changes in Net Assets)

The primary purpose of the statement of activities is to provide relevant information about:

- The effects of transactions and other events and circumstances that change the amount and nature of net assets.
- The relationships of those transactions and other events and circumstances to each other.
- How the organization's resources are used in providing various programmes or services. This statement helps donors, creditors, and others to:
- Evaluate the organization's performance during a period.
- Assess an organization's service efforts and its ability to continue to provide services.
- Assess how an organization's managers have discharged their stewardship responsibilities and

other aspects of their performance. This statement focuses on the organization as a whole and reports the amount of the change in net assets for the period.

To help donors, creditors, and others in assessing an organization's service efforts, including the costs of its services and how it uses resources, a statement of activities or notes to the financial statements provide information about expenses reported by their functional classification such as major classes of programme services and supporting activities.

Not-for-profit organizations (other than voluntary health and welfare organizations for which it is required) are encouraged, but not required, to provide information about expenses by their natural classification (i.e., salaries, consultants, rent, electricity, interest expense) in a matrix format in a separate financial statement (the Statement of Functional Expenses).

Programme services are the activities that result in goods and services being distributed to beneficiaries, customers, or members that fulfill the purposes or mission for which the organization exists. Those services are the major purpose for and the major output of the organization and often relate to several major programmes.

Supporting activities are all activities of a not-for-profit organization other than programme services. Generally, they include management and general, fundraising, and membership-development activities.

Management and general activities include oversight, business management, general record keeping, budgeting, financing, and related administrative activities, and all management and administration except for direct conduct of programme services or fundraising activities.

Fundraising activities include publicizing and conducting fundraising campaigns; maintaining donor mailing lists; conducting special fundraising events; preparing and distributing fundraising manuals, instructions, and other materials; and conducting other activities involved with soliciting contributions from individuals, foundations, government agencies, and others.

Membership-development activities include soliciting for prospective members and membership dues, membership relations, and similar activities.

Statement of Cash Flows

The primary purpose of the statement of cash flows is to provide relevant information about the cash receipts and cash payments of an organization during a period.

Chapter 6

Accounting Standards

INDIAN SCENARIO

The paradigm shift in the economic environment in India during last few years has led to increasing attention being devoted to accounting standards as a means towards ensuring potent and transparent financial reporting by corporates. Further, cross-border raising of huge amounts of capital has also generated considerable interest in the generally accepted accounting principles in advanced countries such as USA.

Recent initiatives taken by International Organisation Securi-ties Commission (IOSCO) towards propagating International Financial Reporting Standards (IFRSs)/ International Accoun-ting Standards (IASs), issued by the International Accounting Standards Committee, as the uniform language of business to protect the interests of international investors have brought into focus the FRSs/IASs.

The Institute of Chartered Accountants of India, being the premier accounting body in the country, took upon itself the leadership role by establishing Accounting Standards Board, more than twenty five years back, to fall in line with the international and national expectations. Today, accoun-ting standards issued by the Institute have come a long way. Presented hereinafter are some salient features of the accounting standard setting endeavours in India.

RATIONALE OF ACCOUNTING STANDARDS

Accounting Standards are formulated with a view to harmonise different accounting policies and practices in use in a country. The objective of Accounting Standards is, therefore, to reduce the accounting alternatives in the preparation of financial statements within the bounds of rationality, thereby ensuring comparability of financial statements of different enterprises with a view to provide meaningful information to various users of financial statements to enable them to make informed economic decisions.

International Harmonisation of Accounting Standards

Recognising the need for international harmonisation of accounting standards, in 1973, the International Accounting Standards Committee (IASC) was established. The IASC has been restructured as International Accounting Standards Board (IASB).

The objectives of IASC include promotion of the International Accounting Standards for worldwide acceptance and observance so that the accounting standards in different countries are harmonised. In recent years, need for international harmonisation of Accounting Standards followed in different countries has grown considerably as the cross-border transfers of capital are becoming increasingly common.

Accounting Standards-setting in India

The Institute of Chartered Accountants of India (ICAI) being a member body of the then IASC, constituted the Accounting Standards Board (ASB) on 21st April, 1977, with a view to harmonise the diverse accounting policies and practices in use in India. After the avowed adoption of liberalisation and globalisation as the corner stones of Indian economic policies in early '90s, the Accounting Standards have increasingly assumed importance.

While formulating accounting standards, the ASB takes into consideration the applicable laws, customs, usages and business environment prevailing in the country. The ASB also gives due consideration to International Financial Reporting Standards/ International Accounting Standards issued by IASB and tries to integrate them, to the extent possible, in the light of conditions and practices prevailing in India. Although the Accounting Standards Board is a body constituted by the Council of the Institute of Chartered Accountants of India, it is independent in the formulation of accounting standards since in case the Council considers it necessary that certain modifications be made in the draft accounting standards formulated by the ASB, it can only be done in consultation with the ASB.

Composition of the Accounting Standards Board

The composition of the ASB is broad-based with a view to ensuring participation of all interest-groups in the standard-setting process. These interest groups include industry, representatives of various departments of government and regulatory authorities, financial institutions and academic and professional bodies. Industry is represented on the ASB by their apex level associations, viz., Associated Chambers of Commerce (ASSOCHAM), Federation of Indian Chambers of Commerce and Industry (FICCI) and Confederation of Indian Industries (CII).

As regards government departments and regulatory authorities, Reserve Bank of India, Ministry of Company Affairs, Central Board of Direct Taxes, Comptroller & Auditor General of India, Controller General of Accounts, Securities and Exchange Board of India and Central Board of Excise and Customs are represented on the ASB.

Besides these interest-groups, representatives of academic and professional institutions such as Universities, Indian Institutes of Management, Institute of Cost and Works Accountants of India and Institute of Company Secretaries of India are also represented on the ASB. Apart from these interest-groups, members of the Central Council of ICAI are also on the ASB.

The Accounting Standards-setting Process

The accounting standard setting, by its very nature, involves reaching an optimal balance of the requirements of financial information for various interest groups having a stake in financial reporting. With a view to reach consensus, to the extent possible, as to the requirements of the relevant interest-groups and thereby bringing about general acceptance of the Accounting Standards among such groups, considerable research, consultations and discussions with the representatives of the relevant interest-groups at different stages of standard formulation becomes necessary. The standard-setting procedure of the ASB, as briefly outlined below, is designed in such a way so as to ensure such consultation and discussions:

- Identification of the broad areas by the ASB for formulating the Accounting Standards.
- Constitution of the study groups by the ASB for preparing the preliminary drafts of the proposed Accounting Standards.
- Consideration of the preliminary draft prepared by the study group by the ASB and revision, if any, of the draft on the basis of deliberations at the ASB.
- Circulation of the draft, so revised, among the Council members of the ICAI and 12 specified outside bodies such as Standing Conference of Public Enterprises (SCOPE), Indian Banks' Association, Confederation of Indian Industry (CII), Securities and Exchange Board of India (SEBI), Comptroller and Auditor General of India (C& AG), and Ministry of Company Affairs, for comments.
- Meeting with the representatives of specified outside bodies to ascertain their views on the draft of the proposed Accounting Standard.
- Finalisation of the Exposure Draft of the proposed Accounting Standard on the basis of comments received and discussion with the representatives of specified outside bodies.
- Issuance of the Exposure Draft inviting public comments.
- Consideration of the comments received on the Exposure Draft and finalisation of the draft Accounting Standard by the ASB for submission to

the Council of the ICAI for its consideration and approval for issuance.

- Consideration of the draft Accounting Standard by the Council of the Institute, and if found necessary, modification of the draft in consultation with the ASB.
- The Accounting Standard, so finalised, is issued under the authority of the Council.

Present Status of Accounting Standards in India in harmonisation with theInternational Accounting Standards

So far, 29 Indian Accounting Standards on the following subjects have been issued by the Institute:

AS 1 Disclosure of Accounting Policies
AS 2 Valuation of Inventories
AS 3 Cash Flow Statements
AS 4 Contingencies and Events Occurring after the Balance Sheet Date
AS 5 Net Profit or Loss for the Period, Prior Period Items and Changes in Accounting Policies
AS 6 Depreciation Accounting
AS 7 Construction Contracts (revised 2002)
AS 8 Accounting for Research and Development (withdrawn pursuant to the issuance of AS 26)
AS 9 Revenue Recognition
AS 10 Accounting for Fixed Assets
AS 11 The Effects of Changes in Foreign Exchange Rates (revised 2003)
AS 12 Accounting for Government Grants
AS 13 Accounting for Investments
AS 14 Accounting for Amalgamations
AS 15 Accounting for Retirement Benefits in the Financial Statements of Employers (recently revised and titled as Employee Benefits)
AS 16 Borrowing Costs
AS 17 Segment Reporting
AS 18 Related Party Disclosures

AS 19	Leases
AS 20	Earnings Per Share
AS 21	Consolidated Financial Statements
AS 22	Accounting for Taxes on Income
AS 23	Accounting for Investments in Associates in Consolidated Financial Statements
AS 24	Discontinuing Operations
AS 25	Interim Financial Reporting
AS 26	Intangible Assets
AS 27	Financial Reporting of Interests in Joint Ventures
AS 28	Impairment of Assets
AS 29	Provisions, Contingent Liabilities and Contingent Assets

Compliance with Accounting Standards

Accounting Standards issued by the ICAI had got legal recognition through insertion of sections 211(3A), (3B) and (3C) in the Companies Act, 1956, which may be prescribed by the Central Government in consultation with the National Advisory Committee on Accounting Standards.

Recent development in this regard is Accounting Standards 1to 7 and 9 to 29 as recommended by the ICAI, have been prescribed by Ministry of Company Affairs, Government of India vide its notification dated December, 7, 2006, in the Gazette of India. This notification provides that every company and its auditor(s) shall comply with the notified Accounting Standards.

The Securities and Exchange Board of India (SEBI) through the listing agreement requires that listed companies shall mandatorily comply with all the Accounting Standards issued by ICAI from time to time. Also, the Insurance Regulatory and Development Authority (IRDA) requires insurance companies to follow the Accounting Standards issued by the ICAI.

Apart from the corporate bodies, the Council of the Institute of Chartered Accountants of India has made various accounting standards mandatory in respect of certain non-corporate entities such as partnership firms, sole-proprietary concerns/individuals, societies registered under the Societies Registration Act, trusts, associations of persons, and Hindu Undivided Families, where financial statements of such entities are statutorily required to be audited, for example, under Section 44AB of the Income-tax, 1961.

The Council has cast a duty on its members to examine compliance with the Accounting Standards in the financial statements covered by their audit in the event of any deviations therefrom, to make adequate disclosures in their audit reports so that the users of the financial statements may be aware of such deviations.

Respected members on the Dias, distinguished delegates, distinguished Ladies, Gentlemen and friends. Good Afternoon. It is a great pleasure for being invited for discussion on 2006 Policy Dialogue on Corporate Governance in India. For a person like me, in the presence of such eminent and knowledgeable persons who are probably more qualified, more experienced in these fields.

Here, I may add that by temperament I believe to listen than to speak because I know that by listening, you will get better knowledge than by speaking, however, I am associated with B. K. Birla Group, which is one of the pioneers in bringing and upholding the ethical value and good corporate governance practices in India.

Moreover, having spent more than forty years in industry and being a professional accountant and Compliance Officer of Kesoram Industries Ltd., a listed company of the group, I would like to share my views, which can broadly be categorized in three parts. Ladies and Gentlemen, as a Chief Accountant and Company of said company, now I deal with the past, going through a copy of 46th Annual Accounts for the year ended 31st March 1965 of the above referred company,

I observed that during those days, the Managing Agency system was prevalent, the disclosure was made then to the shareholders, being a listed company and the explanatory statement to the proposed regulation and the annual report of that year may not reflect, in terms of all regulations and disclosure that are required today but the basic principles of disclosure, whether statutory or not were made by our company and I feel also by other companies, even forty years ago, as well as, which to summarize, may be as follows.

In the said annual accounts, we had disclosed the name of selling agents and commission paid to each and sole agent, the name of distributors of the company and the commission that they were entitled to, whether there has been any change in the commission, structure for the agents, distributors during the year, under review.

The remuneration paid to the management agents, disclosure in terms of purchases, sales and exports, disclosure in terms of operation of each unit and plants that the company was operating at that point of time. Also, there was relevant information, which the company's board felt desirable to disclose for the benefit of the shareholders.

If we go towards the annual report, the annual report also contained the summarized financial performance of the company for last five years. The auditor's report, we get the same today, the report for that year, contained the following observation on the main audit report itself by Price water house, our auditors – 'certain detailed records of the textile factory are not available for our inspection as the same, we are informed, were destroyed in a recent fire'.

If we go through the present scenario, it is even after forty years, similar disclosures are being made by the auditors. On the face of audit report, for example, in the year 2004-05, it was like this –'on the basis of examination of the inventory record, in our opinion, the company has maintained proper records for inventory other than 'work in progress'.

My only intention by referring the above is to bring to your knowledge that disclosure norms prevalent at those years hold good even today and I am now, under circumstances, trying to glorify the past of the company, therefore now let us come to the present. The Accounting Standard Board in India was constituted and it has come with 29 standards so far as they are necessary, keeping in view, liberalization, globalization trend in our country and which are being complied with by Indian corporate world generally.

In the meantime, to improve the existing non-financial disclosure on the basis of Kumar Mangalam Birla Committee, the first formal regulatory disclosure was listed for the listed companies, specifically for the corporate governance was established by SEBI in 2000 by directing the Stock Exchanges to incorporate a new clause 49 in the listing agreement. It is worth praising the SEBI for further periodical steps taken by it. In other words, tremendous changes have been taken place and specially, I will say, in the matter of the auditors, directors audit committee, I would term it as a regulation than to call it mere changes.

The development in computerization, information technology, networking, internet, e-business, outsourcing have affected the business world but sadly the world has also witnessed major financial disasters like South Asian financial crises, the collapse of Barrings Bank,

Enron, World Com, the collapse of one of the largest accounting firm in the world, financial inflow and outflow through electronic transfer resulting in ill-gotten money being diverted to terror medium and narcotics. Nude dimension of risk and fraud that have been detected on account of change in IT system, to only name a few.

Friends, all this has resulted in complicating the disclosure norms, corporate governance ethical business practices. In India, the standards of financial as well as non financial disclosures are prescribed by the Company Act, SEBI, ICAI, ICSI to serve the following purposes, to ensure that all the stakeholders get proper information about the working of their companies to ensure that the wealth of stakeholders invested in corporation is not wasted by the management, to ensure that all the statutory rules and regulations are being observed and followed by these corporations.

Moreover, the present era has also witnessed stock option, financial derivatives so without really going into details of comparing the international non financial disclosure with Indian non financial disclosure and how they are similar or different from one another, it is my personal opinion that today, in 2006, bearing the least developed nations that are still closed to the world, majority of the nations which probably comprises 70% or more of the total global trade have quiet similar non-financial disclosure and corporate governance norms at macro level except for the legal angle which varies from country to country.

The difference of legal system from country to country can easily be understood with the help of experts like you who are present in this august gathering and efficiently conduct gap studies, effectively report and disclosure norms between a financial statement of a country and another.

Resultingly, necessary standards could be formulated for the above gaps. Of course, keeping in view the applicability and desirability of the Indian business conditions. Challenge for future. Business is continuous process and any hindrance in the continuity affects its growth, which is undesirable. Now, I would like to share with you, some of the interesting issues relating to problems which a corporate company faces.

As you know, there are more and more requirement prescribed for compliance by the industry whereas the privileges are made available to the shareholders only. We have got 80,000 shareholders. Out of that, 70,000 or 65,000 hold only 10 shares. We make two time offer of buy-back because one folio costs 32 rupees, we offered them that you sell it, we will purchase it but no one came forward except 2 to 300 shareholders.

With this background, kindly take it, what I am saying now. Recently, more and more shareholders are taking the AGM as a profession by holding qualification shares, to earn a right to speak at the said meetings for unlimited time, aimlessly and the Chairman of the AGM has no right to stop them.

Further, management always informs the shareholder by way of notice to send their queries in advance but no compliance is made to that whereas they insist for information in the very said meeting or after the meeting is over.

The Company Act allows only availing of certain information and inspection of certain documents as prescribed in the Act like, inspection of charge register, shareholders debenture holder register, contract register, loan, guarantee and investment register, director's register and their shareholding register but it is silent on other financial statements of the company.

What information they are entitled to, what information the management should give? Although the shareholders have got every right to complain against the company with the Company law department but the management should also have similar right to complain against such professional shareholders who do not allow to

conduct the meeting in a graceful manner and prevent the genuine shareholders to speak and put forward their views for the benefit of the company and investor at large. These kind of professional shareholders do not have any obligation or accountability, whatsoever.

Unparliamentarily language is used in the speeches. Undesirable actions witnesses in the meetings and otherwise, which will be clear from the following example. A company 'A' receives a notice in December 2005, requesting the company to remove the Chairman, the allegation appeared to be only that, that reply to the shareholder letter is not signed by the Chairman but by some junior officer.

After that, one month, again a letter is received from the same shareholder, which reads as under 'please refer to my letter dated such and such, giving the notice under the Company's Act for removal of the Chairman of the company in the forthcoming Annual General meeting. I hereby withdraw the said notice unconditionally and request you, not to take any action in respect of said notice. I have full faith in the able leadership of Shri. so and so, the Chairman of the company.'

You can easily understand, what is the motto? It is not out of place to mention that company has not taken any action in respect of this episode. I think, most of the companies being represented here must be facing similar experience, so my humble suggestions are, why a code of conduct should not be prescribed for such professional shareholders? What about the code of conduct or behaviour of the shareholders at the AGM.

Further, I feel it, it is necessary that some norms should be laid down by ICSI, ICAI or any other authority for the AGM in respect of time a shareholder is entitled to speak, for supplying the information about the annual accounts, his right to get the information other than what is prescribed under the Company's Act after the shareholder meeting is over. Further, in order that the standards, non financial disclosure, corporate governance are implemented in substance, a more proactive role of ICAI, ICWAI and SEBI is necessary.

It is highly desirable that seminars, workshops, training programme are organized regularly so that Executives get opportunities to express clearly and practically difficulties and participate in the process to help to improve the quality of efficacy of such companies.

Some of the items of Section 49 on corporate governance still require immediate attention like, there is one provision, periodic reviews of the compliance report of all the laws applicable. So far, I have been able to identify 75 laws. How many are applicable, how many are not applicable, how to implement, what should be done?

Risk management and minimization procedures, basis on which CEO or CFO should rely while confirming to the Board that for necessary compliance and there must be some defined back to back comfort mechanism. The certificate was placed before the audit committee. Audit committee's question was, Mr. so and so how you have verified that these laws have been duly complied with. No reply.

Corporate India is in favour of transparency and implementation of all financial and non financial disclosures including Corporate governance norms that regulators desire. These corporations and business groups have always followed and have never objected to any legislation, which is practicable and for the benefit of stakeholders but always brought forward in front of relevant authorities, the difficulties faced for implementing their impractical, illogical legislature. The issues raised by me are being raised only on account of practical difficulties experienced by the industry and it is for the benefit for the entire industry.

Here I would also like to give an example. Our group had decided that audit committee meeting should also be held at plant level, at least two meetings in a year so that all the senior executives of the plant are present there, they give their views, the directors are able to take the round of the factory and they can give their suggestions and I inform you that, that experience is very well appreciated, that report we have shown to the bankers, that report we have shown to the other authorities and they have appreciated that independent directors have given their report about the working of the company.

It will be unfair on my part, if I don't put forward the problem of the industry before this august gathering. Wherever the eminent experts are present and many are presiding over their various technical sessions to substantiate my point of view barring a few 'fly by night' operators, a vast majority of industry has been in existence for business nearly a century now, so challenges are many in front of the learned audience but take it from me that an octogenarian like me,

I am a firm believer that the future is great, I am sure that the gatherings like this will bring forward and better and more transparent and practical norms, which must of course ensure that all stakeholders interest are protected and just do not remain as a legislation or guidance. The industry welcomes such new thought processes as it always has been open and acceptable to the changes, new ideas, which benefits all the stakeholders including regulators.

The first question is about the modus operandi as to the implementation from 01st April, since it is notified. In India, there will be no difficulty in such an implementation for the simple reason that all the standards have been in vogue, formulated from time to time since 1977. They were recommendatory, to begin with, even to the professionals. Then in 1991, we made them mandatory for the professionals, Chartered Accountants but it did not have statutory backing under any law. It was the Institute's formulation and imposing on the members who were reporting on the financial statements.

Then in 1999, the Ministry of Company Affairs amended the Company's Act and said, we will have to give the standards a statutory backing so that it is not only the professionals who will enforce these standards, even the corporates will follow the standards, will be mandated to follow the standards and since this process is bound to take time, to fine tune it, they said, for the time being, let the standards of the Institute of Chartered Accountants of India, which is already existing shall be applicable to the companies so in 1999 itself, the Ministry was gracious enough to say, let there be no void or a gap, let them be applicable so it gave a deeming statutory backing.

Now what is being done is, it is being formalized by clear vetting by an independent authority, National Committee for Accounting Standards Advisory Committee, so they have vetted it. Infact, when we formulate standards, we get views from various stakeholders and interest groups and fine tune it or modify it, same way, NCAS also has applied its mind, vetted it and suggested to us, certain fine tunings, certain modifications, which has been done.

So these standards as modified, which are the accounting standards applicable on the professionals, were also deemed to be applicable to companies now gets absolute statutory backing with the Government's notification, as it comes, so therefore, there is no additional cost of compliance because they are already being complied.

Now with more statutory backing, it will be monitored. Now, who will do this? Effective implementation is your supplementary question. As far as the professionals, Chartered Accountants who are attesting our concern, the Institute will monitor that any deviation from accounting standards are properly reported to the stakeholders by the members of our profession, failing which, we will take action against them. If corporates are not complying, the Ministry will take action against the corporates, so the responsibility is divided but joint and we ill do it in a cohesive manner.

Now, as per your second question, as to the rotation of auditors is concerned, here also the debate started five years ago as to the stand to be taken and after analyzing the pros and cons because rotation has certain advantages and it also has its disadvantages of destabilizing the firm, which has domain knowledge of that business and a newcomer taking time to get to know that business before he starts auditing and management, which is not comfortable with a good firm can destabilize that firm by using rotation, so there are pros and cons.

We thought, to begin with, we must consider only, rotation of partners, not rotation of firms. So this is the recommendation made by Naresh Chandra Committee to the Government also and the new Company Law bill is in the reformation stage, so this is the line of thinking at present.

No, just as I mentioned, rule-based has its disadvantages and I just gave an illustration. With reference to any philosophy, in any field, there may be certain strings attached. There may be certain inherent weaknesses attached but which one is capable of being monitored more effectively with lesser perils or lapses is the question so on a comparative analysis, I do not disagree with you that principle-based, there could be an element of, when I say, professional judgment, it is possible that somebody exercises that judgment with some amount of discretion and therefore he deviates and all that and still tries to justify but on a comparative basis, I am of the opinion that principle-based approach has less pitfalls as compared to rule-based approach.

Now as far as the convergence to be carried forward to its logical conclusion among the global nations, who will do it, who has to pioneer it, while all the agencies here will march towards that line of thinking, I think, the actual initiative has to be pushed by the IASB, International Accounting Standards Board, which is the standard setter for the IFRS.

As far as the auditing standards, it will be the IFAC, the International Federation of Accountants, which will have to get that accomplished through the mandate to be given to the member bodies because 163 accounting bodies are members of IFAC drawn from 122 countries and the Institute of Chartered Accountants of India is a founder member of IFAC and is in the governing body of the IFAC represented by Shri.

Kamlesh Vikamsey is IFAC Board member so IFAC is taking the initiative for the convergence of auditing Standards across the globe and I am sure, on the same lines, IASB also is, infact IASB is saying that we are having open mind as far as IFRS is concerned. If any national standard setting body is deviating from IFRS, we are open for a dialogue or a discussion. Either you convince us to modify IFRS or we will convince you to modify your standards at par with IFRS so with that mechanism of negotiation dialogue, I think, world over the community should march towards convergence.

Now, as far as the other aspect, you have also supplemented the earlier speaker saying that when it comes to certain transactions like related party transactions, maybe rule-based is simpler and all that. As I said, it is a matter of opinion as to which one is better but by historical experience, we find that principle-based gives room for evaluating it in an objective manner whereas rules might be simpler but they also become sometimes easy to overcome or difficult to exercise your judgment in an objective manner, that is where the itch arises but it is a debate, which has to continue. Infact the agreement entered by standard setters of US GAP with IASB, the clear indication is that, even the US GAP standard setters are moving towards principle-based.

They seemed to have realized that it may be in the larger interest on a holistic approach, principle-based is better than rule-based and they have given a road map by 2009, the US standards GAP also will move towards IFRS, the cost of compliance has gone up phenomenally making some of the corporates not to go for NASDAQ or New York Stock Exchange but to go to UK stock exchange or European markets, so these things must have made the US standard setters also that maybe it is in the larger interest better to have convergence and they also seem to be thinking of abandoning the rule based approach and moving towards the principle based approach.

You mentioned about the countries, which have now converged and you said that there is an inverse relationship of GDP with the countries which have adopted IASB but of course, the development of the European Union is a very significant development, which has accepted the IASB, the IFRS plus the Australian economy has accepted.

China, we are told, so David was here in India last month in one of the international conferences, which the ICAI had organized and he made a public statement that even China is willing to negotiate talk, Japan is willing to negotiate and talk,

India of course, we are open to the idea of a dialogue provided of course, there are some standards where we have our own opinions, which we are going to share with the IASB and of course, thereafter, the road map is there for convergence but of course, you would agree that the need for having a one global standard, it has become a compulsion in terms of how the businesses are operating now across the various borders and therefore there is definitely a need for one set of international standards, that cannot be wished away, with the kind of scenario in which we are living in today.

In developed countries, the XPRL is being implemented, Extend Civil Business Reporting Language is the software that has been developed whereby if the entity uploads its financial statements and other details into that reporting language, it automatically gets translated into the standardized format which is understandable to all stakeholders and users because that is the level and quality of the software that has been developed and now that is spreading across the globe to different countries so this XPRL is also taking.

Initiatives in India because what happens is, in every country, some authority, some agency, some body has to assume jurisdiction to monitor and implement XPRL so that the regulators also get the facility of that language so that the comparability becomes easier, the crucial data becomes readily traceable and acceptable by press of one button so that XPRL is already in vogue, what you have in mind, is already in vogue but the successful implementation of that is taking time because again the acceptability across the country has to take place and the implementation in terms of jurisdictional issues need to be addressed and I request Chairman to further elabourate.

Well, as far as the IT platform is concerned, you are right, most of the accounting is now done on IT platform. In fact, large companies, why talk of large companies, even SMEs are now going towards ERP packages, maybe not the large ones but smaller ones. Looking at the profession, let me just inform you that we also train our members to do auditing on the computers through various audit tools. In fact, we have introduced a specialized course, which is called the CAATs, computer aided audit techniques, whereby we train our members, how to do an audit on the computer straight instead of going around the computers and doing an audit.

We have also launched a course on *'Information Systems Audit'*, which is basically an audit of not necessarily financial statement but the systems as far as the IT environment is concerned, weaknesses and controls, how to plug those weaknesses so these kind of trainings are being imparted to our members, even at the student's level, we have now started imparting training on IT.

This is of course a very important question, which you have raised on the IT platform and yes, everything must move towards IT, that goes without saying and because the world is moving towards IT, world is digitizing and digitizing at a very fast pace, it is very important that we as a profession also keep track of things, what are happening, so of course, it is a very good suggestion, which you have given and we are alive to that. They are welcome. The question is, the question or the information, which they want should be of interest to all the shareholders, not to one and moreover the Act or the rules are silent that to which information they are entitled to.

Moreover, they put the question, gentleman, here the word *'Mr.'* has been used and somewhere *'Shri'* has been used so why the accounts should not be not passed, these type of things, to create the problem.

What happens Sir that those genuine stakeholder, they want to give their suggestion, they get only one time in the year, where they can put up their views before the directors that is lost. How long they can go on. One thing, they go on repeating, repeating. Only from that angle, if there can be a code of conduct for the Board, there is a code of conduct for the directors, there is a code of conduct for the senior executive, why not a code of conduct for shareholders.

I am only equalizing them. Someone put a question, how you can make a code of conduct for directors, you are under us. Still a code of conduct has to be prepared and that responsibility is there. Similarly, I say that some institution or Government or someone has to say that yes, this is the code of conduct for the shareholder, you can only ask for this information, you send a notice well in advance, that should be made available. If they are not satisfied, Company Law department is there to take the action.

The practical solution, which I have seen in such cases is that companies have their registered offices in remote locations so I know of a company where we had 80,000 shareholders and only 5 shareholders attended the AGM so all resolutions were passed without any objection. I think, that's not a very healthy kind of a thing because in a democracy, even when there are stakeholders, I mean, obviously, you must give them opportunity Do you think Sir, this will be fair in the interest of the shareholders.

My only question is, we want to follow a system which is fair to both, the management and the shareholder otherwise you can pass all the resolutions by ballot. It is a question of balancing. Let's not destroy the corporate democracy. In fact, corporate democracy must work in this country also it will be of interest to you. My Chairman has never missed Annual General meeting because the moment the people come to know that he is out of India, even if we have to defer the date because they say, it is only one occasion in a year that the shareholder who have faith in the board, they are able to meet him.

Question: While we are discussing convergence of IFRs with Indian standards, I have one or two very small doubts on which I need your clarifications since we have got the opportunity. What happens when there is a contradiction between IFRS and the corresponding Indian standard on a particular situation. The second is whether what happens when Indian standard is silent and there is a relevant IFRS available to meet a particular situation and the third and the last one is when both are silent. Is it a situation like, we have Articles of Association, we have some standard procedure to be followed to deal with the internal management situation vis-à-vis this Articles of Association and related question also. What about the qualitative aspects of certain activities of the corporate which cannot be quantified. Are their accounting standards or their proposals to have accounting standards, for example, comment of the auditor on the quality of manpower of the company, quality of the senior management of the company, which cannot be quantified.

Response: Standards are nothing but best accounting principles codified so these are codified best practices and therefore the process of codifying more and more best practices into standard is an ongoing process so where there are no standards, what ever is considered appropriate or best needs to be followed. Number two, where there is no accounting standard in India on a particular subject, then that particular industry is expected to follow, whatever is adoptable to that particular industry so as to present a true and fair view to the stakeholders.

It is not as if only the standards pronounce the best accounting principles, the accounting principle fundaments are already in place and they are also pronounced in the form of guidance notes, technical guides, which we come out from time to time. Infact, what I can say, what is initially bought out as a guidance only transforms into an accounting standard and wherever the industry is emerging newly into a stronger base of operation in the economy, we immediately come out with that kind of a guidance to the business entities and to the stakeholders.

You asked about a situation where it is conflict between international and Indian, it depends on the jurisdiction under which the corporate entity has to report or has to submit, so as far as the Indian jurisdiction is concerned, our standard is binding and operating and if they are reporting to regulatory authority in a nation where IFRS is binding, then they will have to translate the same accounts into IFRS mode, that is why you find some of the entities, like Infosys translating their financial statements into 18 accounting standards because they are governed by regulators in 18 different countries so this is how it operates. The scope of reporting by a professional is not all encompasse. It is with reference to the true and fair view of the statements. Now, therefore the scope of general audit is confined to the evaluation of the compliance of the standards visà- vis the disclosure presentation requirements. Now we are yet to come out with this human resources accounting or evaluation and so on and so forth, that is unknown.

Till such time, it is not yet evolved, that is not an area, which is commented upon but if it could be a special audit or an investigation audit, then the scope could be different and based on the terms of reference, the professional is expected his opinion or objective evaluation on those aspects also.

Just to supplement the reply to Mr. Parekh that the question, which was raised, the gentleman was out of context because he perhaps referred to the problem, which is about the professional shareholders. These are limited to very few numbers. In the AGM of 1500 shareholders who are attending, only 5 or 6 persons who are common to every AGMs are creating these kind of problems. This is reference to that particular shareholders only.

We have had a very healthy discussion on the international standards, on the Indian standards, Mr. Manoharan gave a very broad overview of the Indian standards, Mr. Parekh very nicely came out with the evolution of the disclosure and accounting principles over the last more than four decades, he has vast experience on the subject. I would only briefly make certain few comments and thereafter conclude the session. In an international conference it was mentioned that if anybody has understood IAS 39, he has not understood.

That is the statement which Sir David the Chairman of IASB made himself. He mentioned that these have been borrowed from the US rule-based kind of a thing and therefore, the standard is very lengthy and very complicated, the financial institutional standard, we are grappling with it. We want to bring it in India as soon as possible, we want to put it into place but we want to carry all the regulators, the Ministries into that particular exercise of adopting that particular standard. Now, as far as training is concerned, very important. The ICA Institute is taking it very seriously. Infact, we hold considerable amount of continuing professional educational programmes, as Mr.

Manoharan rightly pointed out, we have several publications of the Institute like guidance notes, the study on various standards where we try to explain the standards when we try to say, how the standards have to be applied but training of course, as far as the user point of view is concerned, also is very important.

Training inside the companies who actually do the accounting and training the auditors, who actually go and audit and see whether those standards have been followed or not. We take it up very seriously and we would see that we would enhance the levels of training, which are required to implement these standards.

Enforcement, most important because you may have the best of standard but if it is not enforced and nobody looks at it, it is not a very happy situation and therefore as far as the ICAI is concerned, we have taken it upon ourselves the fact that, number one, as I mentioned, peer review are very important exercise and FRRB, which are the most important, that statements in public domain which have several qualifications and we have seen several financial statements being qualified by auditors and of course a stage will come when the regulators and Ministry may say, no qualifications, one should go and explain the auditors, auditors will enforce whatever may, their professional judgment on the standards but this is a very important aspect, which we need to work on. Well, friends, we have had a very good discussion and I must thank the Ministry and OECD and National Foundation for Corporate Governance for organizing this programme and keeping this very important subject of financial reporting standards topic for discussion in this conference. What we would do is, we would send our feedback to the Ministry from the discussions, what we had with the participants.

Chapter 7

Monetary System

Historically, any commodity that was generally accepted as a medium of exchange could be used as money. Various objects have been used as money over time, including human skulls, cows, wine, shells, and mainly metals. Even today in the Yap island of the Pacific, large stones (*fei*) are used as money.

Cows were used as money in ancient Greece or Hellas, Egypt, China, Italy, and Britain. In Southern Sudan, even today, people use cattle and goats as a standard of value. Thus, "a reasonably sound wife costs about 40 head of cattle, with perhaps a few goats and chickens thrown in."

From recent discoveries in Dispilio, near Kastoria, Greece, the most ancient signs of written words, fishing and other instruments, and vases were dated back to 5260 B.C. Also, shapes of coins, similar to talents used in ancient Greece and Rome and existing now in the Museum of Heracleion, Crete, were found to belong to the same ancient times (7,260 years ago). Such discoveries put an end to the myths about the Phoenician alphabet and the Indo-European race.

INTERNATIONAL MONETARY FUND

The most effective international organizations, formed by agreements among a large number of nations, are the International Monetary Fund (IMF), the International Bank for Reconstruction and Development or World Bank, and the General Agreement on Tariffs and Trade (GATT), recently named the World Trade Organization (WTO). The IMF and the World Bank were established by forty-four countries at Bretton Woods, New Hampshire (United States), in July 1944, whereas the GATT was negotiated in Havana, Cuba, and established in Geneva in 1948.

The International Monetary Fund (IMF), which is a pool of central-bank reserves and national currencies, was established at Bretton Woods in 1944 under the auspices of the United Nations, but it actually started operations on March 1, 1947. In order to facilitate international finance and help correct fundamental balance-of-payments disequilibriums, it tied all currencies to gold and hence to each other.

The IMF, with headquarters in Washington, D.C., was created to help finance balance-of-payments deficits and to reform the international monetary system toward mutual cooperation and freely convertible currencies among the member nations.

The waves of devaluations in the currencies of a number of countries before World War II, mainly in 1931–1936, as a way to increase exports and reduce imports at the expense of their trading partners (beggar-thy-neighbour policies) was the rationale of the creation of the IMF. These policies resulted in frequent changes in exchange parities, economic instability, and high unemployment.

The IMF makes its own stock of currencies available (gives loans) to the members. It functions as a pool of currencies or an international clearing institution, using the assigned quotas of the member countries to arrange international payments. Also, it provides short-term loans and advice to member countries, primarily emerging nations, with balance-of-payments difficulties.

Member nations were committed to keep their currencies within plus or minus 1 percent of parity, although further changes in exchange rates were permitted if needed. From that standpoint, the system can be characterized as an "adjustable peg" exchange rate system. Moreover, because the dollar, being the key currency, was convertible into gold (1/35 ounce of gold), every currency had a gold value related to the dollar, which may be considered as a yardstick of value. The Bretton

Woods system then may also be characterized as a gold exchange standard system.

Each member nation was responsible to subscribe to the capital of the IMF, paying one fourth in gold and three fourths in its currency (in demand notes), depending mainly on its share of world trade. The member countries were responsible to sell their currencies to the IMF, which could also borrow currencies from its members above their subscribed quotas. Initially the IMF had a total quota of $8.8 billion, but that was increased gradually to about $260 billion (198 billion Special Drawing Rights or SDRs) and 182 members presently.

Immediately after World War II, the United States had about 33 percent of the voting power in the IMF and 35 percent in the World Bank, because of its dominant economic position. Thereafter, the U.S. voting power steadily declined to the current levels of less than 20 percent in the IMF and around 17 percent in the World Bank.

As we enter a new millennium, international institutions, mainly the IMF, are expected to play a more important role in regulating financial cooperation and reducing tensions among member nations, particularly between rich and poor nations, which have heavy debts.

Nevertheless, gold is an expensive reserve asset, as human resources are used to dig it in distant areas and bury it in heavily guarded places in central banks or in the IMF in Washington. That is why Professor Robert Triffin of Yale University suggested that central bank deposits with the IMF be denominated in a new international unit of account or a form of paper gold.

A similar system was proposed by John M. Keynes, as an alternative to the U.S. plan for the IMF at Bretton Woods in 1944. Moreover, the use of gold for the determination of money supply may lead to excessive liquidity and global inflationary pressures, when excessive amounts of gold are available, as well as to inadequate liquidity, when not enough gold is available, resulting in recessions or even depressions, as happened with the severe recession of 1907 (rich man's panic) and the Great Depression of the 1930s.

Although the Bretton Woods system performed well in the 1950s, the fact that the United States had large deficits in its balance of payments in the 1960s increased the dollar reserves of other countries and consequently the demand for gold, forcing the United States to apply first voluntary controls and then mandatory controls to capital outflows. At the same time, Japan, West Germany, and other European countries with surpluses refused to revalue their currencies, suggesting that the United States eliminate its balance-of-payments deficits.

In an attempt to further discourage European companies from raising capital in the United States, the interest-equalization tax was imposed in the mid-1960s to equalize the cost of raising funds in the United States, where interest rates were lower. Moreover, the U.S. Treasury issued medium-term bonds with an exchange-rate guarantee, known as Roosa bonds, to discourage foreign central banks from cashing their excess dollars for gold.

Also, U.S. short-term interest rates were raised to attract foreign funds, but long-term interest rates remained low to encourage domestic investments, a policy known as "operation twist." Nevertheless, the "dollar glut" continued in the 1960s, mainly because of the U.S. trade deficits, in contrast to the "dollar shortage" in the 1950s.

In 1969, a special quota (of $10 billion) was created by the IMF to be used for automatic drawings. They are Special Drawing Rights (SDRs), which are gradually replacing gold as a reserve asset. The acceptance of SDRs is an obligation for members, subject to some limitations. Each member can buy currencies directly from other countries up to the amount allocated by the IMF, without going through the regular Fund operations. In the case of SDRs the IMF acts as an intermediary or guarantor. Although large amounts of SDRs are allocated to developed countries, a growing number of emerging nations receive SDR allocations lately.

The IMF carries on its books $5 billion gold, but at market prices the gold the fund owns is worth more than $30 billion. Therefore, the fund can write off some $8 billion that forty poor countries owe it, but under conditions that would not give them incentives for further borrowing with the expectation of not paying back future loans.

Each member paid one fourth of its quota in gold or in dollars and the rest in its own currency. This pool may be considered as an extension of the central-bank reserves and aimed at stable exchange rates. It was accepted that drawings of member countries could be made on permission, as Harry D. White, the U.S. representative, insisted, and not automatically, as John M. Keynes, the British representative, suggested.

The quotas, which are revised every five years to reflect economic changes of members, determine the number of votes and the borrowing limits of the member countries. As mentioned previously, the United States has almost 20 percent of the total voting power, followed by Germany and Japan with 5.7 percent each, and then Britain and France with 5.1 percent each. These five developed countries with more than 40 percent voting power dominate the IMF, which operates as a central bank for central banks. Member governments select governors, who constitute the highest governing body of the Fund and meet every September in Washington, whereas power is vested in the Board of

Executive Directors (some twenty persons). A member of the Fund can borrow 25 percent of its quota without restrictions (gold tranche) and higher amounts with restrictions (credit tranches), but repayments are normally to be made within three to five years.

Approximately, the quotas (in billions of Special Drawing Rights or SDRs) (one SDR is equal to about $1.3) are: 27 for the United States; 8 each for Germany and Japan; 7 each for Britain and France; 5 for Saudi Arabia; 4 each for Canada, Italy, and Russia; 3 each for Belgium,

China, India, and Netherlands; 2 each for Australia and Brazil; and close to 2 each for Mexico, Spain, and Venezuela, and so on. The U.S. official reserve assets in March 1998 were $69.35 billion, $30.22 billion of which were foreign currencies, $11.05 billion gold, $10.11 billion holdings of IMF SDRs, and

$17.98 billion was the reserve position, that is, the U.S. ability to draw foreign currencies from the IMF.

As the cure for sick economies, the IMF usually prescribes tough austerity measures, which lead to deep cuts in public spending, tight credit, high unemployment, sharp currency depreciation, severe stock market decline, and even social unrest. Some of these symptoms occurred in Mexico and the Southeast Asian countries. Some countries blame Washington and other Western capitals for their strong influence on the IMF. Such austerity measures may result in high unemployment, and many people blame IMF for worsening their misery and for losing their jobs (arguing that IMF stands for I'M Fired?). Moreover, the loans from the IMF are relatively small compared to about $2 trillion traded daily in the international currency market.

Athough it provided more than $150 billion for the Asian and Mexican bailouts lately, as a lender of last resort, it is criticized that in its effort to save weak economies, it discourages the private sector and the related governments to take the necessary painful fiscal and monetary measures to correct the problems of crony capitalism. That is why the U.S. Congress is skeptical on providing additional financing for the IMF.

Hellenes (Greeks) were living in that area and the rest of Greece at that time. The research continues and is financed by the European Union (LIFE Programme), whereas a museum is under construction near the lake of Kastoria where such monuments and tools were found. Moreover, human fossil bones and tools were discovered by French and Greek archeologists in Triglia, Halkidikis (*homo erectus trigliensis*), as ancient as 11–12 million years old, compared to 2.5-million-year-old tools found in Africa.

Lending operations for commodities predates money itself, as for example during the Minoan (Cretan) and Mycenean civilizations (earlier than 3000 B.C.), when values were expressed in terms of cows and oxen. Also, the Code of Hammurabi (about 1800 B.C.) deals with mortgages and debts. However, the use of coins and other monetary units, away from the inefficient barter system, later necessitated the establishment of banks.

In addition to cattle, during the Homeric period (about 1200 B.C.), certain pieces of gold called talents were used as money. Recent research in Mycenae (Greece) discovered a copper ingot 2.5 feet long in a shape of ox-hide, dated around the fourteenth century B.C. Moreover, certain pieces of gold (talents) were in circulation but were expressed mainly in terms of cows. An alternative name to euro, suggested in the European Union (EU), was the talent, used in ancient Greece and classical Rome, which are considered as the common roots of the EU member states. It was considered as a hard currency with a value of 26 kg of silver.

In ancient Sparta, large iron disks were introduced by Lycurgus as money units (ninth century B.C.). The Spartan monetary units had a face value higher than the intrinsic or metal value. This system of debased money is used even today by advanced money societies. Later, gold and silver were deposited by the Lacedaemonians with the Arcadians for safekeeping.

Silver coins (drachmas) replaced previous tortoise-shell currency in Corinth, the island of Aegina, and mainly Athens (seventh–fifth century B.C.). They were stamped to indicate their value on the one side, and with an owl (the wisdom bird of Athens) on the other side. According to Aristotle, commodities have a use value and an exchange value measured in drachmas, which can be used for exchanges and storage of wealth.

Plato proposed, in the *Laws*, that token money be used for domestic transactions and gold and silver for transactions with foreigners. In that way, money was internationalized by the Hellenes at that time. However, Aristophanes noted in "The Frogs" (405 B.C.) that "in our Republic bad citizens are preferred to good, just as bad money circulates while good money disappears." This concept is very near to Gresham's law, after Sir Thomas Gresham, Queen Elizabeth's Chancellor of the Exchequer (A.D. 1559).

As domestic and foreign trade increased, mainly between

Athens-Piraeus and Phoenicia, Egypt, Sicily, and other neighboring countries, banking transactions developed. A number of arcades, the most famous called Degma, were used for exhibitions and exchanges of commodities from all the markets of the eastern Mediterranean and beyond. Moreover, regulations similar to our antitrust laws were enacted by the city government.

Other important monetary units used in ancient times were the Pu money, in the shape of a shirt, as well as knives and other metallic instruments, in China around 700 B.C. Also, the first paper or parchment money was issued in China in 140 B.C. In Egypt, the first coinage was established under the Ptolemies at the end of the fourth century B.C.

Roman Period

Money and credit opened new freedoms and opportunities during the period of the Roman Empire. Financiers and profiteers flourished while trade enterprises were growing, and money interest began to play an important role in trade and finance. The Romans used a common currency to help military cooperation and to stimulate free economic transactions with the regions under their domain. Such common currencies were used later by the United States (the dollar) and the European Union (the euro).

Copper bars or ingots were the first monetary units in ancient Rome. Silver coins, called denarii, similar to those previously used in Greece and mostly debased, were introduced after 269 B.C. Furthermore, with the use of gold later, three metals were used together and serious problems of trimetalism or bimetalism appeared as the relative values of the various metals (gold, silver, copper) changed over time.

During the Roman Empire (31 B.C. to A.D. 476), the creation of a new commercial class, the patricians, increased transactions in the cities and necessitated a body of laws that later had a profound influence on legal and economic institutions, including banks and other financial firms. The recognition of juristic or artificial persons by the Roman laws was important for the creation and expansion of the corporate form of modern enterprises. The Romans, with their efficient administration of justice and the security of life and property, created many trading, financial, and shipping centers in their dominion and promoted international transactions.

Nevertheless, Rome suffered at times from too little or too much gold and silver and the frequent debasement of its metal money. The rudimentary banking system was inadequate to deal with price changes in the absence of a paper or check system.

Middle Ages and Later

Moral corruption, slavery, and decline of the silver and gold mines of Spain and Greece were the main reasons for the fall of the Roman Empire. During the Byzantine Empire (330–1453) and the Middle Ages (476 to about 1500), gold was the main currency used, but there were problems of debasement of currencies and price fluctuations, mainly from changes in the supplies of gold and silver. Tax reductions and other administrative reforms stimulated trade and made Constantinople, the capital of Byzantium, a commercial and financial centre for southeastern Europe and the Middle East.

However, commercially minded Venetians, who were better organized in foreign trade and finance, managed to settle in a number of ports around the Balkan and other areas and to control customs revenue and banking activities. In competition with the Genoese, another commercial people, they exploited the lucrative trade and financial markets of the Golden Horn, the Black Sea, and other neighboring regions.

In the Middle Ages, early financial operations were carried on by monasteries, but any interest was considered immoral by Church law and was considered unnatural by Aristotle (two dimes cannot beget a baby dime).

After the Renaissance, modern banking activities were conducted at the old Fairs and monasteries and by the Lombard bankers in England, as well as by financial houses such as the Bardi, the Medici, the Peruzzi, and the Strozzi of Italy, based mainly in Florence, and the Fuggers and the Rothschilds in Germany.

They were exempted from the ban on usury and made loans to kings and even to the Pope. Goldsmiths or jewelers in Lombard Street (London) and other places accepted deposits for safekeeping, giving the proper receipts, which were payable to the bearer. The depositors could hand the receipts over to their creditors, performing the same functions as in modern banking. Thereafter, important banks appeared, such as the Bank of Sweden (1694), the Bank of France (1800), and the German Reichs Bank (1873).

The British silver coin initially was a pound of standard (sterling) silver (divided into 240 pennies). Also, the French livre was one pound of silver (ninth century A.D.), and both represented one of the early international monetary units. Other countries, mainly Mexico, China, and India, developed a silver standard.

During the period of Mercantilism (1550–1776), emphasis was given (1) on foreign trade as a means of accumulating precious metals, primarily gold and silver, as the most desirable form of national wealth, and (2) on the supremacy of the state over the individual. Gold and silver could be used to finance trade or pay large armies for foreign wars or be retained as luxuries. As Columbus said (1503), with gold one can get even souls into paradise. The state should support foreign trade and establish colonies to increase national wealth. Commercial expansion occurred by monopolies, such as the Merchant Adventurers, the Eastland Company, the Muscovy Company, and the East India Company.

Toward the end of the Mercantilistic period, the physiocratic school appeared (1756–1778) in France. The school was based on the natural order, which prevailed over all the economic activities in a harmonious way, similar to that of the planetary system. This laissez-faire system was further developed by Adam Smith (1776) and other classical economists and is considered as the basis of capitalism. Later, Eugen Von Böhm Bawerk (1891) and other Austrian economists stressed the justification of interest payment, based mainly on the productivity of capital, which helps the worker and the entrepreneur to increase production.

The gold standard, first introduced in Britain in 1821, was also adopted by Portugal (1854), Germany (1871), and other European countries later. Britain abandoned gold from 1914 to 1925 and permanently in 1931.

During the classical gold era, roughly from 1870 to 1914, there was a high capital mobility, mainly from Britain, France, and Germany (about 3–9 percent of the GDP) to Australia, Canada, New Zealand, and Sweden. Such capital flows were used primarily for investment but also as official reserves (gold and foreign exchange), mainly by the United States, Russia, India, Belgium, and Sweden. A similar phenomenon can be observed in our day with the capital flow in emerging nations, which is used primarily for reserve holdings. In all these cases, the role of investment banks in 1870–1914 was important in stimulating global capital flows, as it is now.

Monetary Systems in the Americas

In the Western Hemisphere, the Incas, covering most of the coast and Highlands of western South America, had no monetary system of any kind, whereas in the American colonies, coins brought over by European immigrants and Indian wampums (ornamental cloth) were initially used as money. Corn was mainly used as a medium of exchange (1631) in Massachusetts, whereas tobacco and rice were used in the south. In order to facilitate trade with the Spanish colonies, the Spanish silver dollars, or fractions of them, were also used in the Americas. After George Washington's inauguration (1789) as the first president of the United States, gold and silver full-bodied coins were used.

In the United States, for practical purposes, silver was used from 1792 to 1834 and primarily gold from 1834 on, although the Coinage Act of 1792 provided for a mint and stipulated that the principal coin would be the $10 Eagle (weighing 270 grains and containing 247.5 grains of pure gold out of 480 grains in a troy ounce). In 1837, the price of an ounce of gold was fixed by the U.S. Congress at $20.67.

In 1832 and later, Robert Owen of England introduced a paper money in "the Owenite communities in America," mainly in Cincinnati, Tennessee, and Ohio, with nominal values in labour hours. These labour notes entitled "National Equitable Labour Exchanges," based on the utopian teachings of Charles Fourier of France, were short-lived, primarily because of the difficulties in exchanges.

Nevertheless, bank notes and U.S. Treasury notes were mostly used because they were less costly and more convenient than gold. But, as David Ricardo mentioned, "In issuing paper money...it is only necessary that its quantity should be regulated." Moreover, international payments were made in bills of exchange, comparable to postdated checks. Thus, a U.S. exporter would receive gold or more usually bills of exchange from the importers of other countries and sell them for U.S. dollars in New York or other cities.

Because of the Civil War and the increase in prices, payments in gold in the United States were suspended in December 1861. The convertibility of gold for the dollar was restored at $20.67 in January 1879 and remained so until 1933. The pure gold standard system was introduced in 1900 in order to avoid relative price fluctuations in the prevailing bimetalic system of gold and silver. The United States managed to hang onto gold during World War I, but prices increased by more than double from 1914 to 1920, and then by 1932 they fell more than they had risen.

However, new discoveries of gold led to changes in prices and economic instability. Also, when a country had a deficit in the balance of payments, a net outflow of gold would take place, and under a gold standard system, money supply and eventually prices would be reduced, with the possibility of a recession or depression and unemployment. Ceteris paribus, lower prices would lead to more exports and less imports, thereby restoring the balance-of-payments equilibrium. The opposite is expected in countries with surplus in the balance of payments, which would lead to a net inflow of gold, an increase in money supply and prices, less exports and more imports until the balance-of-payments equilibrium is restored.

As mentioned earlier, metals, primarily gold and silver, were used as money mainly in international transactions by different societies. Metals are generally accepted as money because they are homogeneous commodities, easily portable, divisible, storable, and relatively scarce and have a cost to produce and a value in industrial use.

In 1933, the United States abandoned the pure gold standard system, in which anybody could get gold. In its place, the gold reserve system was introduced, in which a certain percentage of the money supply was kept in gold. The price of gold was determined at $35 per ounce in January 1934, but in practice, it was used only for the settlement of international transactions. In March 1973 the price of gold was left to the free market of supply and demand.

The Bank of North America, established by the Continental Congress in 1781, and the Bank of the United States, established by Alexander Hamilton in 1791, were the first U.S. banks. In order to manage money and credit more effectively, the Federal Reserve Bank ("Fed"), as an institution independent of the federal government.

THE WORLD BANK AND ITS AFFILIATES

Together with the IMF, the International Bank for Reconstruction and Development (World Bank) was created at Bretton Woods in 1944. The member nations must pay 10 percent of the subscription (1 percent in gold), and the rest is subject to call any time the bank needs it. Its main source of money, though, is borrowing from the free money market.

The World Bank and its affiliates—the International Finance Corporation (IFC), created in 1956, and the International Development Association (IDA), created in 1960—provide development assistance by extending loans to emerging nations. The IFC specializes mainly in promoting private enterprises through investment in indigenous and foreign sources, whereas the IDA makes long-term loans for housing, sanitation, irrigation, and other projects in poor member nations at subsidized rates.

Moreover, within the World Bank Group is a globally operating intergovernmental organization providing investment insurance against political risks, and the

International Centre for Settlement of Investment Disputes (ICSID), which provides facilities for arbitration of disputes between foreign investors and governments.

The authorized capital of the World Bank accounts for $171.4 billion, that of IFC for $1.3 billion, and that of MIGA for $1.1 billion. Also, the capital received by IDA in the form of pledged contributions totals $68.6 billion. Borrowing from the World Bank stands at about $12 billion per year and is expected to increase, as external financing remains essential for many emerging nations.

The World Bank, which lends money to emerging nations, issued $4 billion in dollar-denominated global bonds, the largest ever. It was priced to yield 5.703 percent for maturity in 2003, that is, 14 basis points above a similar Treasury security. A basis point is one one-hundredth of a percentage point (0.0001). For this issue, which was the largest of the 14 dollar-denominated bond issues by the World Bank, Europe subscribed for 45 percent, the United States for 35 percent, and Asia for 20 percent.

Some other regional development banks, with limited effectiveness, are the Inter-American Development Bank (IDB) created in 1959 mainly to promote the Alliance for Progress programme; the African Development Bank (AFDB), organized in 1964; and the Asian Development Bank (ADB), established in 1966.

GOVERNMENT FINANCIAL INSTITUTIONS

Other institutions dealing with international trade and investment financing, mainly through low-interest loans, are those created by the U.S. federal government to help exporters and investors. They include the Export-Import Bank (EXIMBANK), which was created in 1945 as an independent government institution to aid U.S. exporters and foreign importers through loans, guarantees, counseling, and training. When commercial banks hesitate to give loans to high-risk countries, the EXIMBANK may guarantee such loans, thereby helping poor nations and U.S. exporters to be able to compete with foreign receiving subsidies.

Moreover, the Commodity Credit Corporation (CCC) was created to support U.S. exports of agricultural products through long-term loans, mainly to poor nations, in competition with other countries providing similar loans.

Finally, the Overseas Private Investment Corporation (OPIC) was created to support U.S. investment in other countries, mainly friendly emerging nations. Other industrial countries provide export subsidies, mainly Japan and Europe, in many cases disguised, although this is unfair in international economics. For that reason, the United States raises, from time to time, serious complaints against other nations providing such concealed subsidies, which are financed by the governments involved.

BANKING OPERATIONS

Central banks control and regulate commercial banks, primarily through discount rates, reserve requirements, open market operations, and other monetary policy tools. In their efforts to manage money and credit, they influence trade financing, inflation, and exchange rates. They are lenders of the last resort. Also, they intervene in the financial markets in order to reduce volatility or influence exchange rate levels.

Commercial banks are middle-persons or agents of the public. They accept deposits from the entrusting public and lend them back to the public, charging a higher interest rate than they pay to depositors, who are the ultimate lenders. The amount of borrowers' demand for credit depends on the banks' propensity to lend and the rates they charge.

Although they do not create legal-tender money, they create money (or credit) in the form of bank notes. As it is usually said, "Money talks and banks command."

The creation of money depends on the reserve requirement and the money-supply multiplier. For example, if the reserve requirement (RR) on demand deposits (checking accounts) is 10 percent, the money-supply multiplier is 10 (or 1/RR = 1/0.10 = 10). This means that, assuming no leakage in loans and redeposits, a $100 demand deposit would create $1,000. From that standpoint, bankers are not only middle-persons but also "manufacturers" of money and may affect business cycles. This was the case with the policies of John Law in France in 1720 (the Mississippi Bubble), who was mistaking money for wealth or credit for capital, as well as in other inflationary policies in history that led to serious international financial crises.

In addition to commercial banks, credit unions are engaged in a wide range of banking activities. Thus, in the United States about 70 million people are members of credit unions, which maintain their cooperative structure and their tax-exempt status.

Banks are crucial to domestic and international economies, as they gather savings, make loans, and coordinate financial transactions. In the industrial countries they are the prime providers of financial services, and in the emerging nations they are the heart of the financial markets. However, over the past twenty years, about three fourths of the member countries of the International Monetary Fund have faced problems with bank failures, and many of them considered or adopted measures to protect their financial systems.

Thus, in its effort to reform the banking system, the government of Brazil decided to rescue the Banco de Brazil, the largest bank of Latin America, by buying risky bonds worth $3.4 billion. The same policy was used earlier with another bank, run by the federal government, Bovespa. However, sooner or later, both banks would follow the path of privatization implemented currently by Brazil.

Offshore Banking

The volatility of financial markets around the world makes it nearly impossible to discipline them without some form of coordination and regulation. National banking regulations are unable to keep pace with the rapid development of global financial markets. There is no international institution to initiate changes and play the role of an international regulator.

Even the International Monetary Fund (IMF) finds it difficult to convince member countries to take measures of exchange rate stabilization and other policies to avoid economic crises. Although more than 100 countries signed an agreement in December 1997 to dismantle national barriers and open their markets to foreign banks, insurance companies, and investment firms, such measures were largely ignored, and the financial turmoil in Asia,

Latin America, and other parts of the world continues. Bermuda is an attractive place for offshore banks and mutual funds. It is considered by affluent international investors as a lightly regulated tax sanctuary.

There are around 1,000 funds on the island, with more than $20 billion net assets, about 30 percent more than from last year. A recent law deals with money laundering and the formalization of mutual funds regulation. It requires approval for any money received, whereas the administrators must prove an acceptable source. Other Caribbean islands are also used for offshore banks and mutual funds as in Bermuda.

On the Cayman islands, which are a British dependency, there are 575 banks with about $500 billion deposits. More than 20,000 huge and small corporations, including hedge funds, are chartered on the Caymans, where there are financial secrecy laws and no income tax, no inheritance tax, no capital gains tax, no sales or other consumption taxes, and no tax treaties.

Other offshore sanctuaries, in addition to Bahamas and the Cayman islands, include the British Virgin Islands, Antigua, the Isle of Jersey, Panama, Liechtenstein, the Netherlands Antilles, Luxembourg, and Switzerland. Although the Group of Seven industrialized nations said that disclosure rules should prevail, it is difficult to implement such rules in practice.

Extensive controls on a global scale may be impossible or ineffective to slow the rapid growth of financial markets and the movement of capital and other banking services from one place to another. Such controls may be difficult to implement in today's advanced technology and may have negative effects on the economies involved, as they may lead to recessions or depressions. Probably the strengthening of the banking system in weak emerging and other economies will promote financial stability and global economic growth.

Also, a specialized international institution, possibly under the IMF, may solve the problem.

Intervention by Central Banks and Governments

If a country, say the United States, wants to defend its currency (the dollar) and keep a constant exchange rate with another currency, say the Japanese yen, and the value of the first currency (the dollar) is declining because of higher inflation or other reasons, then the central bank (the Federal Reserve Bank or Fed) would buy some of its currency in order to avoid a reduction in the market value and an expected depreciation. This is what happened in a number of cases when the value of the dollar gradually declined from more than 250 yen to less than 100 yen per dollar.

The demand for dollars is declining and the demand curve shifts from D to D1, then the Fed, which wants to defend the dollar, would buy ac dollars at a price (say 100 yen per dollar) determined by the equilibrium of supply (S) and demand (D), instead of letting it to drop to a lower price (say 80 yen). The opposite would occur when the price of the dollar is going up and the Fed wants to keep it down to the equilibrium point, in which case the Fed would sell dollars for yen.

In many cases, if commercial banks are in trouble, the government can spend money from the budget to bail them out, thereby avoiding a depreciation in its currency and possible decline in the stock market. Thus, in order to bring stability to its volatile financial system, the Japanese government decided to spend more than $500 billion to bail out banks. Such an action is expected to help dispel pessimism, calm the stock market, and support the currency.

As a result, the Nikkei index, which was fluctuating around 17,000 at the beginning of 1999, and the yen, which was quoted at around 120 yen to the dollar at the same time, began to improve. The hope was to help out banks, which had about $620 billion in bad loans, and avoid further credit squeeze and corporate bankruptcies.

Other measures were enacted to guarantee bank deposits and strengthen the Deposit Insurance Corporation (DIC), an institution similar to the U.S. Federal Deposit Insurance Corporation (FDIC). Also, the Japanese government decided to buy preferred shares in banks, as the U.S. government did in the 1930s to pull the country out of the Depression. However, it would be better to allow ailing banks to close down or be merged in order to avoid similar problems in the future. Japanese banks with bad loans include the big banks Daiwa Bank Ltd. and Sumitomo Bank Ltd., as well as Dai-Ichi Kangyo Bank Ltd.,

Industrial Bank of Japan Ltd., Sakura Bank Ltd., Sanwa Bank Ltd., and Tokai Bank Ltd. After foreign exchange controls were lifted in Japan in April 1998, large amounts of capital are flowing out of the country. Now, more and more Japanese retail and corporate clients are willing to take on foreign exchange risk to enjoy higher returns in stock exchanges. Moreover, the 10-year government bonds in Japan yield only 1.7 percent currently, which is far lower than in other countries.

Hoping to help restore worldwide confidence in the financial system and make it competitive internationally, the Japanese government, which decided to bail out weak banks, tries to imitate the American policy of bailing out banks by the Reconstruction Finance Corporation of the 1930s.

However, this is not well accepted by several Japanese banks, which are issuing preferred shares in New York to raise money on their own. In its effort to make the financial system more attractive, the Japanese government is also adopting international accounting standards, relaxing regulations on disclosure, and making the financial system free, fair, and global. Also, it is privatizing the huge Post Deposits with $2 trillion in deposits, which is offering better interest rates than the private sector and better services, as the mailman collects deposits from households every morning.

The once-mighty economy of Japan has been stalled in recent years, and severe fiscal measures are needed to reverse its economic decline and spur the economy, mainly through public works and tax cuts. However, the Organization of

Economic Cooperation and Development, a group of twenty-nine industrial countries based in Paris, and other nations in Asia and elsewhere criticized these measures as insufficient to uplift the Japanese economy as well as the other ailing trading partners in Asia.

Moreover, the feeling in the United States, which has been urging Japan for years to open its economy to more imports, is that Japan should spend more and save less than some 28 percent of its national income, thereby reducing its huge foreign trade surpluses.

In order to shore up its four gigantic state-owned commercial banks, with some $200 billion in bad loans, China floated a $32 billion bond issue in April 1998 and speeded up economic reforms through streamlining, downsizing, and privatizing public enterprises. This is in addition to the $32 billion the Chinese government pumped into these banks recently, including the Guangdong International Trust and Investment Company, also known as Gitic, for which the government assumed a large part of its $2.4 billion foreign debt after its recent closing.

Although China does not have a convertible currency and it is not immediately affected by the financial turmoil in other countries, it is expected to do that in the near future after privatizing state banks. The Chinese government is in the process of closing many debt-ridden trust and investment companies. Beijing plans to close some 200, out of a total 240, such companies with about $10 billion in foreign debt.

An important measure to counteract an economic downturn as a result of the Asian financial crisis is the plan of the Chinese government to spend $1 trillion in public works projects, thereby hoping to keep the 8 percent growth rate of the $900 billion GDP and avoid high unemployment. The financing of these projects would include domestic and foreign bonds and loans as well as allocations from central and provincial governments. With a relatively small foreign debt of $120 billion and about $140 billion in foreign exchange reserves, China is not expected to face serious problems to find international lenders.

Furthermore, in order to avoid the faltering of private banks, some nations resort to the nationalization of banks, a measure that might create more problems in the future. Thus, the Thai government, which shuttered fifty-six of fifty-eight nonbank finance companies and speculative lenders in the early 1990s, nationalized three large private banks (First Bangkok City Bank, Siam City Bank, and Bangkok Bank of Commerce) in February 1998.

This happened after the Thais failed to attract Western banks, such as Citibank (a unit of Citicorp of the United States) and the ING Bank of the Netherlands, to create alliances and bail them out. Neverthe-less, purging the financial system is a condition of the IMF's $17 billion bailout of the country. Although Thailand relaxed some strict regulations for foreign ownership, foreign banks cannot hold more than 50.1 percent stake and cannot increase shareholding in Thai banks, many of which are owned by powerful Thai and Thai-Chinese business families.

Another tool the government can use, through the central bank, is to raise interest rates so that private investors would be induced to increase their demand for its currency. The use of the interest rate as a tool of exchange rate stability is extensively used in our day. Recently, it was used by many emerging nations to avoid currency depreciation (devaluation) due to the Asian turmoil.

CONSOLIDATION OF BANKS AND OTHER FINANCIAL INSTITUTIONS

Cross-Atlantic Banking Mergers

Merger mania, which can be observed domestically, is gradually becoming an international phenomenon. The open and competitive world markets require large companies with global reach. Megamergers, such as the Travelers Group, which recently bought Salomon Brothers, intertwined with nine other firms around the world and merging with Citicorp later, are globalizing the financial markets.

In competition with other global heavyweights such as

Merrill Lynch & Company and Morgan Stanley, Dean Witter, Discover & Company, Salomon also acquired other firms around the world, including most of County NatWest brokerage businesses in Sydney, London, Tokyo, and other cities. Such acquisitions can exaggerate the volatility in world stock markets and currencies and create economic havoc. Nevertheless, such Goliaths usually introduce new technology, reduce cost, and facilitate capital investment worldwide.

The recent financial deregulations all over the world are allowing banks and other firms to operate internationally and to underwrite securities and distribute stock offerings. However, there are serious concerns regarding the public interest.

The ferocious competition of American, European, Japanese, and other financial giants may lead them to speculative trading in risky options and futures contracts. Although powerful financial firms would not be allowed to fall, as governments would shore them up, extensive risky operations may result in international crises. Perhaps this may invite commercial banks and other firms to merge and operate on a global scale.

The cross-border financial services of money management firms, including banks, mutual-funds, brokerage firms, and other investment companies, are rapidly growing. Such companies manage huge amounts of savings for pension funds, insurance firms, and ordinary investors in a global scale. Big American financial firms, such as Fidelity Investments, Merrill Lynch and Company, J. P.

Morgan and Company, and Citigroup, are accelerating their movements in other countries to become international money managers. Other big money firms eager to expand internationally include Deutsche Bank, the largest German bank, which acquired Bankers Trust, a big U.S. bank; AXA-UAP of France; the Swiss Bank Corporation; and the Zurich Group of Switzerland, which agreed to buy Scudder Stevens and Clark, the American mutual fund company.

Merrill Lynch, based in New York, agreed to acquire

Mercury Asset Management Group P.L.C., based in London. Merrill, with $272 billion of funds under management, 5,200 employees, and $22 billion market capitalization plans to finance the acquisition with preferred stock and long-term debt. The Bank of New York Company agreed to buy trust businesses from the British bank Coutts & Company, a unit of National Westminster Bank P.L.C., for an undisclosed amount. This will add some $15 billion to the about $400 billion business of the bank outside the United States.

Mercury, with assets of $177 billion under management and nineteen offices around the world, announced that there would be no layoffs among its 1,500 managers and employees. With $4 billion capitalization, it was spun off from S.G. Warburg and Company, a company that was acquired by the Swiss Bank Corporation in 1995. Mercury manages money for about half the companies in the Financial Times–Stock Exchange 100 index and handles funds for half of the largest fifty company pension funds in Japan.

In order for the countries of the world to trade, international financial institutions must exist to facilitate exchanges of different currencies and other transactions. The growing use of the flexible-exchange-rate system, compared to the old gold standard or the fixed-exchange-rate mechanism and the intermediate managed-exchange rate-regime, necessitates the development of sophisticated international banking.

As long as there are barriers to cross-border investment, international financial intermediary institutions are needed to deal with different national jurisdictions and investment diversification. From that standpoint, commercial banks play a vital role in dealing with direct and portfolio investment, private debt, different-country risks, and the associated cross-border fees or penalties.

Financial liberalization, diffusion of technology, competition, and trade and capital flows undermine political autonomy and reduce national divergence. Controls over allocation of credit, guided liberalization, and state financing gradually change toward private financing and self-financing on a global scale, as almost all countries try to attract foreign capital.

An important international banking market is the Eurocurrency market. In addition to the European countries, Eurocurrency banking centers include the Bahamas and other Caribbean islands, Canada, Japan, Singapore, Hong Kong, and the United States. The Eurocurrency market, which appeared in the 1950s, grew drastically thereafter to account now for about $4 trillion.

Deutsche Bank A.G., the biggest bank of Germany, agreed to acquire Bankers Trust Corporation, the eighth-largest American bank, for some $9 billion. Deutsche Bank had also acquired Morgan Grenfell of Britain in the early 1990s and lately 10 percent of the Eurobank of the Latsis group, which agreed to acquire the Bank of Athens. Recently, in order to focus more on international banking, Deutsche decided to spin off its industrial assets, worth $24 billion, in such companies as DaimlerChrysler, a car industry, and Allianz, the biggest insurer of Germany, where it holds large stakes.

Through banks and other financial institutions, large amounts of money from pension funds move to international stock markets. Thus, the U.S. Teachers Insurance and Annuity Association and College Retirement Equities Fund (TIAA-CREF), available to over 6,100 educational and research institutions with 1.8 million participants and more than $250 billion in assets, is moving aggressively to profitable European, emerging, and other well-established world stock markets.

On both sides of the Atlantic, merger fever continues. Recently, the U.S. Federal Reserve Bank approved the merger of the Swiss Bank Corporation, with operations in the United States, and the Union Bank of Switzerland. The new bank, named United Bank of Switzerland, is the biggest bank in the world, after the Bank of Tokyo-Mitsubishi, with some $706 billion assets.

United States Banking Mergers

Recently, many banks follow the general trend of mergers and acquisitions in order to reduce operational costs and be more efficient in the global financial markets. Also, severe competition from brokerage firms, mutual funds, and credit card firms forces them into the creation of mammoth banks with national and international aspirations.

The merger of Citicorp and the Travelers Group in 1998, worth $77.6 billion, formed Citigroup Inc., with a market capitalization of $153.9 billion. This merger created the largest financial service company in the world and deals with banking, securities (stocks and bonds), and insurance activities worldwide. The Citigroup is in fierce competition with Merrill Lynch, American Express, Goldman Sachs, American International Group, and Morgan Stanley, Dean Witter in the field of global investment banking. The Nationsbank Corporation and the BankAmerica Corporation agreed to merge to create the largest U.S. bank in terms of total branches and deposits and the second bank in total assets. The deal involves a stock-to-stock transaction worth more than $61.6 billion. Furthermore, the Bank One Corporation merged with the First Chicago NBD Corporation, creating the fifth-largest banking company by assets worth $30 billion. Their combined deposits are more than $340 billion, compared to about $200 billion each for Citicorp and Chase Manhattan and around $170 billion each for BankAmerica and Nationsbank.

Mainly because of the stock market exchange, the Corestates Financial Corporation accepted the merger deal with the First Union Corporation, which it had rejected some time before when the market prices were not favorable. First Union of Charlotte, North Carolina, and Corestates of Philadelphia (the first U.S. banking capital) have combined assets of about $204 billion and plan to reduce cost primarily by laying off a large number of the 11,000 employees of Corestates.

Wells Fargo & Company agreed with Norwest Corporation in a $31.4 billion merger to create a banking group with $191 billion assets, smaller than Citigroup (with $697 billion assets) and BankAmerica (with $571 billion assets), but bigger than Washington Mutual Inc. (with $144 billion assets). The new group, based in San Francisco, is named Wells Fargo Bank.

Other megamergers in the banking sector, in addition to the First Union's deal with Corestates for $17.1 billion, include the purchase of Barnett Banks by Nationalbank for $15.5 billion and that of the Washington Mutual Inc., a large savings and loans association in Seattle, and the H.F. Ahmanson & Company in Los Angeles, which agreed to merge in a $9.9 billion stock swap and create a new company with $149.2 billion assets, trailing the BankAmerica Corporation but surpassing Wells Fargo & Company.

Merrill Lynch, with some 18,000 retail brokers, is under consideration to be taken over by American International General for $30 billion. Also, Chase Manhattan and Bank of America are in negotiations to buy.

Merrill Lynch. The Bank of New York (BoNY) agreed to a friendly takeover of Mellon Bank Corporation for $24 billion, creating a large banking institution.

Mellon, which recently acquired a $7.9 billion serving portfolio from the Bankers Trust New York Corporation, expects to sell its commercial mortgage business, including $17 billion of servicing rights, and concentrate on residential mortgages. Moreover, Mellon, parent of the Dreyfus Corporation, agreed recently to buy the Denver-based Founders Funds.

Fleet Financial Group agreed to buy Bank Boston for $16 billion. The new Fleet Boston Corporation, based in Boston, has some $178 billion assets and is about half the size of Citigroup Moreover, Fidelity Investments and Lehman Brothers, both big investment companies, announced a broad alliance for distribution channels, research, and other activities.

It is expected that such deals would put pressure on other banks, mutual funds, and financial firms in general to merge so that they can compete internationally. More consolidations are expected after the United States changed, on November 12, 1999, the Glass–Steagel Act of 1993 and the Bank Holding Company Act of 1956, which did not permit banks to get into securities and insurance operations. Other goverments are expected to enact similar banking and other antitrust laws to encourage global competition.

Banking Mergers in Europe

Merger mania in the United States affected Europe as well. Thus, UBS merged with Swiss Banking Corporation, and Dresder Bank of Germany formed alliances with Commerzbank in other European countries.

Moreover, Banque Nationale de Paris increased its hostile takeover offer for Societe Generale and Paribas to $40 billion.

In order to gain approval by the European Union of a $16.6 billion government bailout of Credit Lyonnais, a state-owned bank with heavy losses, France decided to sell a large amount of assets, as well as half of the bank's "commercial presence" in other European countries. Such an action would increase competition in the banking sector of France, as well as among other members of the European Union.

In competition with Fortis, the Belgo-Dutch financial group, ABN Amro, the largest bank of the Netherlands, offered $12.3 billion for Generale de Banque of Belgium so that it can increase its international operations, mainly in Europe, which is expected to achieve a monetary union soon. Such a merger was necessary as other big banks in Belgium and other countries are involved in similar mergers and takeovers. At the same time, Fortis sold 624,000 shares it owns in Munich Re, a large reinsurance company, to Lehman Brothers, which then sold them to European and U.S. investors. Also, Fortis agreed to buy the American Bankers Insurance of Miami for $2.6 billion in cash.

Lloyds TSB P.L.C. acquired Scottish Widows for $11.1 billion to create Britain's biggest bank and insurance group. Expecting growth in the stock price of Assurances Generales de France S.A. on the Paris Stock Exchange, the Allianz A.G. of Germany agreed to buy 100 percent of the shares of the company, as the French law requires, with $10.4 billion, higher than the $9.5 billion offer by Assicurazioni Generali S.p.A. of Italy. As a result, Allianz shares rose in Frankfurt and Assicurazioni Generali fell in Milan.

The Lend Lease Corporation, with shares in the Sydney and London stock markets, in competition with the Latsis Group and a Portuguese firm, is interested in buying some 350 acres of land in Attica for construction development from the Mesogea A.E. Moreover, Lend Lease recently acquired the Equitable insurance company of the United States. The government of Poland, which is easing restrictions on foreign banks, sold a 37 percent stake in Bank Przemyslowo-Handlowy S.A. to Bayrische Hypo-und Vereinsbank A.G. of Germany, which is publicly traded for $607 million (1 billion DMs).

Unicredo Italiano, a large bank in Italy, agreed to buy Banca Commerciale Italiana (B.C.I.) for $16 billion, offering eight of its own shares for every five in B.C.I. The Deutsche Bank owns shares in both banks. Also, Unicredito agreed to be acquired by Credito Italiano S.p.A, the largest bank of Italy, for $10.7 billion, thereby creating a financial group with $168 billion in assets and about 3,000 branches.

It is expected that the new banking group would be able to compete with other European banks, not only in Italy but in other neighboring countries as well. Furthermore, the Instituto San Paolo di Torino, the largest commercial bank of Italy, and IMI, a banking group in Rome, plan to merge to create one of the largest EU banks.

The Bankgesellschaft Berlin A.G., which was formed through the merger of three state-owned banks in 1994, agreed to buy the Norddeutsche Landesbank Girozentrale for $3.54 billion in cash and stock. As the EU adopted a common currency, the euro, German states, which operated their own banks for two centuries, plan to keep 60 percent ownership of Bankgesellschaft and trade publicly the rest. As a result of this consolidation, the new bank moved to fourth place behind Dresdner Bank A.G.

Moreover, the Deutsche Bank A.G., with global investment banking business in North America and other places, plans to concentrate in Europe in order to be able to face the expected stiff competition into the European Union.

Expecting that the monetary union of Europe will shake out the banking sector, Banco Bilbao Vizcaya (BBZ) and Banco Santander, both in Spain, plan to cooperate and eventually to merge because banking concentration became inevitable in a wider Europe. Already, the group has cemented a partnership with the Royal Bank of Scotland, raised to 100 percent its stake in CC Bank of Germany, and is moving aggressively into Latin America, mainly Brazil and Chile. To make the banking sector more competitive with other international banks, mergers are sometimes encouraged. Thus, Spain approved the merging of Banco Espanol de Credito and Banco Central to create the biggest commercial bank in Spain and the twentieth in the world in capital and reserves. The combined profits of the two banks are more than 60 billion pesetas (120 pesetas to the U.S. dollar) per year.

Their total assets are more than 7 trillion pesetas, deposits about 5.5 trillion, and equity 530 billion pesetas. In competition with the Piraeus Bank S.A., the European Financial Group (EFG) owned by the Latsis family, which owns already a 15.6 percent stake in Ergo plus 5 percent owned by its parent Deutsche Bank, agreed to buy Ergo Bank S.A. for $5.2 billion. The new bank, with its subsidiaries, Hiosbank A.E. and Macedonia-Thrace Bank A.E., would have more than 250 branches. Such mergers are needed so that the Greek banks would be able to survive strong competition from EU banks before the adoption of the euro in 2001.

In the process of privatization and reorganization of state enterprises, the National Bank of Greece announced its merger with the National Mortgage Bank of Greece through the exchange of 1.9 shares of National Mortgage Bank for each share of the National Bank. The new financial institution, with more than 12.5 trillion drachmas assets and some 10 trillion drachmas deposits, has 605 branches in Greece and more than 100 branches abroad. Moreover, the Bank of Piraeus acquired 37 percent of the Bank of Macedonea-Thrace and 51 percent of the Marathon Bank, which is based in New York and has a number of branches. Other banks privatized or under privatization include Ionian Bank, Cretabank, Central Bank of Greece, and Commercial Bank of Greece.

UBS merged with Swiss Banking Corporation, and Dresdner Bank of Germany formed alliances with Commerzbank in other European Countries.

Other Banking Mergers

Consolidation and restructuring eliminate banks in almost all countries through acquisitions, mergers, and joint ventures. The rapid consolidation of banks became a worldwide phenomenon. In Canada, the Royal Bank of Canada and the Bank of Montreal announced their merger in early 1998 to create the largest bank of Canada with some $333 billion assets.

About three months later, the Canadian Imperial Bank of Commerce and the Toronto-Dominion Bank announced their merger to create the second-largest bank in Canada and the tenth in North America with assets of about $320 billion (United States) and 2,300 branches all over Canada. The market capitalization of the new bank, named ICBC, is estimated at $30 billion.

Moreover, there are expectations that the two remaining large banks that is, the Bank of Nova Scotia and the National Bank of Canada, with a market capitalization of about $18 billion, may merge in the near future.

In contrast to the U.S. unit-banking system, Canada has the branch-banking system, which is highly concentrated in four large banks, after these mergers, creating problems for government regulators and consumers regarding competition stifling. Such deals would also affect financial services in the United States, where Toronto-Dominion owns Waterhouse Securities and Waterhouse Bank, whereas Canadian Imperial owns CIBC Openheimer, a securities firm.

Under the $58 billion IMF rescue programme, Korea decided to sell two large banks to foreign investors. Thus, Newbridge Capital of the United States agreed to acquire Korea First Bank. Also, HSBC Holding, a British financial group, agreed to buy SeoulBank.

Barclays, an international bank, and Standard Chartered, which covers Africa, Asia, and the Middle East, are discussing the creation of a $60 billion international banking group.

Salomon Smith Barney, which is an investment banking arm of the Travelers group of the United States, agreed to buy the National Westminster's Australian and New Zealand banking firm, which makes sizable profits from flotation and privatization. This is the first international acquisition of Solomon since its merger with the Travelers group in November 1997, worth $9 billion, whereas plans exist for expansion in the Asian Pacific area. As a result of the relaxation of Australia's resistance to takeovers by foreign investment banks, other investment firms, such as Morgan Stanley, Goldman Sachs, and Credit Suisse First Boston, plan to move into Australia.

Garantia S.A., a big investment bank in Brazil, was purchased by Credit Suisse First Boston, a Swiss-American investment banking group, for $675 million in cash and stock. In competition with Merrill Lynch, which won a mandate to underwrite the $6 billion privatization of Petrobras, Brazil's national oil company, Credit Suisse Group, which paid $10 billion to buy the Winterthur Insurance Company of Switzerland in 1997, is making serious efforts to expand in Asia, Europe, and other areas.

Citibank, a unit of Citigroup, agreed to take over the Banca Confia SA of Mexico, after the government pays $1 billion for the bailout of the bank. Banco Bilbao Vizcaya S.A. reached an agreement to acquire, for $450 million, a 55 percent stake in Banco Excel Economico, which is based in São Paulo.

Chapter 8

Accounting Ethics

IMPLEMENTATION OF ETHICS IN ACCOUNTING

Codes of Ethics

One way of implementing ethics in accounting is to use the deontological view of ethics and use a code of ethics for each of the professions of accounting. Each of the main accounting professions in the United States has in fact a code of ethics. The codes of ethics for management accountants and internal auditors. In 1988 the AICPA issued a new code of professional conduct that has a more positive tone than the previous one.

It contains Principles of Professional Conducts that are enforceable through the Rules of Performance and Behaviour and through the interpretation of the various senior-level committees of the AICPA: Ethics, Accounting and Auditing, Accounting and Review Services, Taxes, and Management Advisory Services.The Principles cover the following areas:

- Responsibilities of Members: In carrying out their responsibilities as professionals, members should exercise sensitive professional and moral judgments in all their activities.
- The Public Interest: Members should accept the obligation to act in a way that will serve the public interest, honor the public trust, and demonstrate commitment to professionalism.
- Integrity: To maintain and broaden public confidence, members should perform all

professional responsibilities with the highest sense of integrity.

- Objectivity and Independence: A member should maintain objectivity and be free of conflicts of interest in discharging professional responsibilities. A member in public practice should be independent in fact and appearance when providing auditing and the other attestation services.
- Due Care. A member should observe the profession's technical and ethical standards, strive continually to improve competence and the quality of services, and discharge professional responsibility to the best of the member's ability.
- Scope and Nature of Services: A member in public practice should observe the Principles of the Code of Professional Conduct in determining the scope and the nature to be provided.

The focus on ethical modes for the implementation of ethics in accounting is strongly recommended by the profession and associated units. For example, the National Commission on Fraudulent Financial Reporting recommends that public companies develop and enforce written codes of corporate conduct.

This view of the strengths of ethical codes in implementing ethics is not shared by the academic literature. Various limitations are raised about codes of ethics:

- Codes of ethics make the rules the central focus of morality. Being ethical means simply following the rules rather than having a moral character.
- Ethical codes are either too vague or too detailed, making them difficult to apply.
- Ethical codes can make it easier for individual to hide behind rules as an excuse for making appropriate decisions.
- Ethical codes can be enforced by punitive and coercive actions because they are similar to laws and regulations rather than ethics.
- Ethical costs may be used by professions to limit

the supply of practitioners and to restrict competition.

In reality ethical codes in accounting have had limited effect in stemming the trade of white-collar crimes and serve mainly as a symbolic exercise. Witness the following comment:

The effects of ethics codes on accounting appear limited. Readers of AICPA and state society newsletters see periodic listings of code violators. Most appear to be CPAs in small firms, and their offenses seem to be rather unequivocal. Frequently, their membership or license is stripped following conviction in the courts for fraud or conspiracy.

The tougher, "borderline" cases appear less often, and large practitioners seem almost never to be involved in violations. It may be, then, that ethics codes play a minor role in structuring the limits of practice. They also lend themselves to violation in spirit because they are subject to broad interpretation. This, perhaps, explains why they are ineffective as enforcement devices for borderline cases.

General Forms of Discipline

The press has a tendency to emphasize the role of the accounting profession in some of the more flagrant and unethical business practices. Some may argue that the ethical standards in our society are relatively low, which should explain the role accountants have played in some business scandals. In addition, the profession's commitment to the general public and to the protection of the public interest is not exactly part of the accountant's environment. D. F. Linowes argues the same point as follows:

What is needed is an environment which establishes an attitude. on the part of the practitioner so that he personally practices his profession using his best technical judgment, supported by the counsel and guidance of his peers, and constantly striving toward his appropriate role in society.

Unfortunately, there are few guidelines in the accounting profession concerning which clients accountants are to serve or what services they are expected to render. In some cases, the government or the courts intervene to pinpoint the kinds of services expected. Due to this lack of identification of their role, accountants wind up serving various masters. One consequence has been the frequent use of footnotes to avoid making hard and fast professional judgments. One solution would be to define the mission of the accounting profession. Linowes offers some questions:

Are we experts in internal information systems? If so, should we be integral parts of the field of behavioral science? Are we solely independent verifiers of the results of an organization's activities? Are we market-research experts, systems designers, energy-utilization experts, tax advisers, or are we all of these things? If we are all of these things, is it reasonable to expect that one set of standards can serve so many diverse functionS?

Obviously, no one accountant or one set of standards can effectively serve all these functions. Some form of discipline is required. Several forms are possible:

- CPAs may need to develop adequate specialization in one or several areas before exercising any functions in those areas.
- Adequate literature could be developed to guide CPAs in all these functions.
- The AICPA could be reorganized into specialized sections that could serve as a forum for new ideas, creative thinking, and specific ethical guidelines.
- Continuing education by the profession and/or academia would be necessary to ensure the best performance of all specialized professional services.
- CPA firms could be organizationally restructured to differentiate and integrate various functions more efficiently.

  Each unit — whether an audit department, a tax department, or a management advisory services department — would be assured a minimum level of independence.
- The sanctions provided under the licensing laws are injunctive in nature because they are restricted to suspensions or revocations of rights to practice.

Stronger medicine may be needed, as the following remark suggests:

Redress for civil damages or punishments for criminal acts relating to malpractice must be sought under the civil liability and criminal laws that are designed for application to a much wider range of activities than that of professionals.

- Practitioners may have to be motivated to adhere to the high ideals of professionals. These ideals are best defined as follows:

Those who are inclined to ascribe a much higher level of altruism to the motives of professionals have long insisted that the essence of professionalism is to put the public's interest ahead of self interest. A dedication to serving others is regarded as essential to laying claim to being a professional, and a profession has an obligation to be concerned about substandard behaviour whether or not it is actionable under the law.

The question is: Would the threat of punishment for wrongdoing be necessary to motivate practitioners to adhere to the high ideals of professionals? Can morality and good behaviour be legislated? If so, how? These questions must be faced by the accounting profession. As a first step, two reports have been published by the United States and Canada, respectively: the Cohen Report and the Adams Report. Each is examined next.

The Cohen Report: United States

In 1974 the American Institute of Certified Public Accountants' Commission on Auditors' Responsibilities (usually known, from the name of its chairman, as the Cohen Commission) was established, with the following objective:

To develop conclusions and recommendations regarding the appropriate responsibilities of independent auditors. It should consider whether a gap may exist between what the public expects or needs and what auditors can and should reasonably expect to accomplish. If such a gap exists, it needs to be explored to determine how the disparity can be resolved.

The Commission eventually released its report, referred

to here as the Cohen Report, which concluded that there is a gap between the performance of auditors and the expectations that users of financial statements have of auditors. The Report proposed that this gap be narrowed by making fundamental changes in the auditor's role and by educating users about some of their unrealistic expectations.

It may be useful to examine some of the highlights of the Report as it speaks to each of the following technical issues: the independent auditor's role in society, forming an opinion about financial presentations, reporting on significant uncertainties in financial presentations, clarifying responsibility for the detection of fraud, corporate accountability and the law, the boundaries and extension of the auditor's role, and the auditor's communication with users.

The Independent Auditor's Role in Society

The *Cohen Report* describes the auditor as an intermediary in an accountability relationship and as the third party in the relationship between the issues covered in financial statements and users who rely on these statements. The auditor's primary responsibility is considered to be to the users of his or her work.

The Report attempts to correct the fallacious beliefs held by users that auditors are responsible for the actual preparation of financial statements or that a report prepared by an auditor indicates that a business is sound. The direct responsibility for financial statements is placed on management; the auditor's responsibility is to audit the information and to express an opinion about it.

Forming an Opinion about Financial Presentations

The Cohen Report considers the difficulties that arise when one is asked to analyze the meaning of the phrase in the auditor's report "present fairly... in conformity with generally accepted accounting principles." The Report suggests that the emphasis on "fairness" be removed. The essence of the auditor's responsibility is not to judge the fairness of the information that is presented but to determine whether the judgments made by management in the selection and application of accounting principles are appropriate or inappropriate. As a result, the Report calls for guidance for auditors in three areas:

- Evaluating the appropriateness of accounting in areas for which there are no detailed accounting principles;
- Evaluating the appropriateness of selection when alternative accounting principles are acceptable;
- Evaluating the cumulative effects of accounting principles.

Reporting on Significant Uncertainties in Financial Presentations

The Commission made two main recommendations: First, it proposed the elimination of the "subject to" qualification of the auditor's opinion. The "subject to" qualification is generally issued when a material uncertainty exists and its subsequent resolution may substantially affect the financial condition of the firm. Three reasons were given for the proposed elimination of the "subject to" qualification:

- It requires auditors to be both reporters and interpreters of uncertainties;
- The "subject to" concept is ambiguous;
- Its absence may be interpreted as meaning that the company faces no uncertainties. Following the Cohen Commission's recommendation, the Auditing Standards Board of the AICPA decided to retain the "subject to" qualification. However, in November 1980, the Canadian Institute of Chartered Accountants terminated the use of the "subject to" qualification. Second, the Commission proposed the addition of a new note on uncertainties to highlight significant uncertainties as well as to give users enough information to make their own evaluations of uncertainties and their potential effects on future operations.

Clarifying Responsibility for the Detection of Fraud.

Given that detection of fraud is ranked as the most important objective of an audit, the Commission stated that an audit should be designed to provide users of financial statements with reasonable assurance that the financial statements are not affected by fraud and that management is accountable for material amounts of corporate assets. To do so, the standards of professional skill and care should be:

- A systematic approach to investigating the reputation and integrity of a company and its management before accepting a new engagement or a continuing engagement.
- Approaching an audit with an open mind about the integrity and good faith of management — neither assuming that management is dishonest nor taking management's integrity and good faith for granted; if auditors have serious doubts about the management's honesty, integrity, or good faith that cannot be resolved satisfactorily, they should consider resigning.
- Taking into account unusual circumstances or relationships that may predispose management to commit frauds.
- Maintaining an understanding of a client's business and industry.
- Extending the study and evaluation of internal control beyond that now required.

Corporate Accountability and the Law.

The Cohen Commission suggested that the auditors must be able to approach the detection and disclosure of illegal or questionable acts by management within a defined and agreed-on-framework. Two recommendations form the basis of this framework:

- Companies should adopt a policy on corporate conduct and monitor compliance with such a policy.
- The auditor's report should review compliance with the corporate-conduct policy; the auditor's report

could include a conclusion about such compliance. When discovering illegal or questionable acts, the auditor should consider them without regard to the conventional concepts of materiality.

The Boundaries and Extension of the Auditor's Role.

The Cohen Commission suggested that the audit function should be broader than the traditional association of auditing with financial statements. The Commission recommended that the auditor's role be extended to permit the auditor to express an opinion on internal accounting control as part of the audit. It also recommended that the audit be viewed as a function to be performed during a particular set of financial statements.

Furthermore, the Commission recommended that the audit function should be expanded to cover information of an accounting and financial nature that management has a responsibility to report, provided that the auditor's competence is relevant to the verification of the information and that the information is produced by the accounting system. Three steps are deemed necessary to facilitate this extension of the role of auditors:

- The auditors' study and evaluation of the internal control over the accounting system should be expanded to allow them to conclude whether the controls over each significant part of the accounting system provide reasonable assurance that the system is free of material weaknesses.
- Management should publish a report on the condition of the controls over the accounting system as well as its response to the auditors' suggestions for the correction of the weaknesses.

The auditors should report on whether they agree with management's description of the company's controls and should describe any material uncorrected weaknesses not disclosed by management.

The Auditor's Communication with Users. The Cohen Commission found the present auditor's standard report unsatisfactory and in need of a thorough revision. The

Commission's examples of yesterday's auditors' report and today's auditors'. Both reports are deemed ideal for revision to clarify the present intended measuring, and to add important aspects of the audit function that are not covered explicitly at present. On that basis, the Commission suggested the preparation of an "illustrative".

The Education, Training, and Development of Auditors.

The Commission deplored the schism that has developed between academic and practicing accountants. It also suggested that formal accounting education does not provide students with a sense of professional identity. The solution recommended was an educational programme similar to that for the legal profession, which would consist of a four-year undergraduate and a three-year graduate programme in a professional school of accountancy.

The Process of Establishing Auditing Standards.

The Commission recommended that the present Auditing Standards Executive Committee be replaced by an Auditing Standards Board within the AICPA. The auditing standards would then incorporate a statement of the independent auditor's role and include the recommendations made by the Commission.

Regulating the Profession to Maintain the Quality of Audit Practice.

The system of regulation of the public accountant profession involves practitioners, the development and promulgation of technical and ethical standards, the design and implementation of quality control policies and procedures, and the establishment of an effective disciplinary system to penalize departures from standards established by the law, Securities and Exchange Commission (SEC) regulation, or the profession. The Commission found that the present regulatory structure of the profession was adequate. It felt, however, that an improvement might result if the following recommen dations were implemented:

- Secrecy should be removed from disciplinary actions and from the penalties imposed.
- Action on alleged violations of professional ethics should not be deferred pending the outcome of litigation, except when the accused demonstrates that the litigation is directly related to the changes.
- To reduce nuisance suits against auditors, courts should be given greater discretionary authority to assess costs against unsuccessful plaintiffs.

The contents of the *Adams Report* focus on the following technical issues: the independent auditor's role, enterprises subject to audit, the detection of fraud, illegal and questionable acts, the auditor's standard report, independence of auditors, and regulation of the profession.

The Independent Auditor's Role

The Adams Commission viewed adding credibility to financial information as the primary function of auditors. Their legal liabilities extend to a wider audience, although there seems to be a gap between what the public expects and what the auditors are doing. Servicing all these new users has created a challenge when it is not clear which group's views and information needs are permanent.

Given this new climate, the Commission recommended an extension of "qualified privilege" and its codification into statute, and defined "qualified privilege" as the provision of legal frankness by auditors as long as it is not maliciously inspired. The Commission also recommended a study of what responsibilities audit committees should be required or encouraged to assume.

However, the Commission was careful to test the extension of the auditor's role in costbenefit considerations. The audit committee should review the entire annual report, and the board of directors should consider the audit committee's recommendation and be responsible for the approval of the complete annual report. Unlike the Cohen Report, the Adams Report recommended an extension of the audit of nonprofit corporations to include the economy, efficiency, and effectiveness of the enterprise operations, referred to as the "value-for-money audit."

Enterprises Subject to Audit.

The Adams Commission recommended that all enterprises with public accountability be audited. Public accountability exists when a firm has widely held securities, significant social and economic impact, and/or the use of significant amounts of funds from the general public.

The Detection of Fraud.

The Adams Commission emphasized that it is the auditor's responsibility to make a reasonable search to discover material misstatement that can arise from errors or fraud and recommended attention to the following areas:

- The establishment of an effective client-investigation programme.
- The importance of having an adequate understanding of the client's business.
- Alertness for conditions that may suggest an increased likelihood of management fraud.
- Standards with respect to auditor's reliance on opinions and work of experts, whether outside parties or within the enterprise; this should include consideration of whether there are circumstances in which a report by the experts should accompany the financial statements.
- The accounting treatment and disclosure of related party transactions and the responsibility of auditors with respect to them.

Illegal and Questionable Acts.

The Commission recommended that any enterprise required to have an audit also set forth a code of corporate conduct in its bylaws. The enterprise's lawyers would advise the audit committee of any breaches in the law or the enterprise's code of conduct that might come to their attention. The duty of the accounting profession would be to establish the auditor's role and responsibilities concerning illegal and questionable acts by clients.

The Auditor's Standard Report.

The Commission recommended that the auditor's standard report be changed to more clearly express the auditor's message. Users of financial statements would have to be educated concerning the function of auditors and the meaning of their report. Similarly, attention to the following matters was recommended:

- Auditors may have to state whether proper accounting records have not been or were not kept.
- Auditors may have the responsibility of commenting on whether or not the accounting principles applied by management are the most appropriate.
- Reporting on uncertainties is a management responsibility; it may require a note disclosing all material uncertainties and their impact on earnings and the financial position.
- "Subject to" opinion should be eliminated.

Independence of Auditors

The Commission considered the fundamental objectives of independence rules to be:

- Protecting the substance of the auditor's independence;
- Ensuring that a reasonable observer would consider such independence to have been protected;
- Ensuring that auditors are not permitted to use their inside knowledge of client affairs for their own personal advantage.With regard to audit fees, the Adams Commission did not believe that audit fees from clients were a serious threat to auditor independence.

However, the Commission did recommend that an amendment to the rules of professional conduct be developed, requiring that when fees from one client exceeded a given percentage of an auditor's gross fee, the auditor should take the necessary steps to remove the apparent threat to audit objectivity. With regard to sources of strain on independence and pressures on staff to reduce time and costs, the Commission made the following recommendations:

- To encourage enterprises to move their fiscal year end to the natural year end.
- To include public accounting firms' bidding practices in the process of professional-practice review.
- To include an explicit statement in companies' press releases (or other releases) of preliminary earnings, warning that results are subject to revision on examination by independent auditors.
- To review with the audit committee the audit deadlines, especially in view of the reliability of internal control.

With regard to management advisory services, the Commission made two recommendations:

- To require auditors providing other services to clients to act in a consulting and not a decision-making role.
- To require auditors to inform the audit committee of the nature of fees and other services provided by the auditors.

Regulation of the Profession.

The Adams Commission acknowledged the importance of protecting the public interest by requiring a consistently high standard in the services provided by public accountants. To ensure this high standard, the Commission made several recommendations:

- To develop a single set of standards of qualification, performance, and discipline of practitioners.
- To establish or expend lay representations on professional standard-setting bodies and their committees.

- To consider the need for a class of paraprofessionals to perform, under supervision, the less demanding important tasks at present included in the work performed by students.

Accountants and Organizational Politics

Both financial and managerial accountants, as members of organizations, compete over resources, energy, information, and influence, either as individuals or as members of a coalition. Any conflict over means or ends calls for the use of power. The use may be nonpolitical or political. It is nonpolitical if it involves sanctioned means for sanctioned ends. Political use of power involves moving outside the formal authority, established procedures, and role descriptions. Political use of power is intended to influence other organizational members and defeat policy changes that can affect their own interests.

Not only is the traditional authority/responsibility linkage broken with the use of political power, but Machiavellian techniques may emerge such as "situational manipulation," "dirty tricks," and "backstabbing." According to Cavanagh et al., "there is, then, a need for a normative theory of organizational politics that addresses ethical issues directly and from the standpoint of the exercise of discretion."

They developed a model that integrates three kinds of ethical theories: utilitarianism (which evaluates behaviour in terms of its consequences), theories of moral rights (which emphasize the entitlements of individuals), and theories of justice (which emphasize the distributional effects of actions or policies).

It is very much applicable for an ethical analysis of the political behaviour of accountants within organization in those cases not covered by the code of ethics. The model is not necessarily unique. For example, instead of utilitarian ethics, deontological ethics could have been used. Similarly, a specific theory of justice could be used as the best norm of justice and fairness: justice according to Rawls, Nozick, or Gerwith.

Accountants find themselves performing tasks daily in an

environment governed by a complex set of rules, principles, and practices. In performing their tasks they are asked to take a certain role. A role is best described as follows:

The concept of a role is... one which enters in the sociologist's account of a social interaction. It is needed in describing the repeatable patterns of social relations which are not mere physical facts and which are structured partly by the rules of acceptable behaviour in the society in question.

In performing their roles, accountants face formal or legal rules of behaviour but also moral elements created by specific situations.

By accepting certain roles, accountants accept at the same time the resulting obligations and moral responsibilities of roles, or as F. H. Bradley puts it: "There is nothing better than my station and its duties, nor anything higher or more truly beautiful."

It implies that there are ethics behind "my station and duties" that need to be accounted for. By ethics, it is meant the concern with the moral judgments involved in making moral decisions about what is morally wrong and right or morally good and bad. This assumes the existence of moral standards that affect our human well being, are not established or changed by decisions of authoritative bodies, are intended to override the self-interest, and are based on impartial considerations.,

Various categories of ethical perspectives or modes of ethical thinking are applicable to accounting. They are reviewed next before a discussion of the implementation, teaching, and research of ethics in accounting.

ETHICAL PERSPECTIVES

Utilitarian Ethics

Utilitarian ethics or utilitarianism as an approach to resolving moral issues is also known as consequentialism. The approach considers an action as being morally right or wrong based solely on the consequences that result from performing it. The right action is the one that brings the best consequences, or the greatest amount of utility. The implicit assumption is that the costs and benefits of an action are measurable on a common numerical scale and can be added and subtracted from each other. The interests to consider when choosing an action are the nonegoist and altruistic approaches that consider the most utility for all the persons affected by the action. The advantages of utilitarian ethics are related to:

- The goal of morality: "It asserts that morality is important because the performance of right actions leads to the general satisfaction of human desires."
- The process of moral reasoning: "The consequentialist at least offers a relatively clear procedure for finding out what is the right thing to do: list the alternatives, ascertain their probable consequences, and evaluate the consequences in light of their implications for everyone affected."
- Flexibility and exceptions: "We simply need to recognize the special cases in which there is good reason to believe that the consequences of following the traditional moral rule are worse than the consequences of making an exception."
- Avoiding rule conflict: "From the consequentialist perspective, the existence of a conflict in rules is a signal that we are dealing with one of those exceptional circumstances in which we cannot simply follow even the soundest of rules."

The difficulties with utilitarianism relate to:

- The objection from special obligations. "It fails to take into account our special moral obligations to people with whom we have a special relation."
- The objection from rights: "(It) does not take into account the existence of individual rights in deciding on moral issues."
- The objection from justice: "By only paying attention to one factor, the consequentialist has left out other important moral factors, such as justice, that need to be weighed."

In addition, there are serious problems of measurement

in the sense that some benefits and costs are interactable to measurement, many benefits and costs of an action cannot be reliably predicted and measured, and there is a lack of clarity on what is to count as a benefit and what as a Cost.,

Deontological Ethics

Deontological ethics as an approach to resolving moral issues is also known as rule-based morality. The approach considers an action as morally right if it conforms with a proper moral rule. An action that violates the rule but results in beneficial actions is still considered wrong. The sources of the rule could be either theological in the sense that the actions are stipulated as moral by a religion, or societal in the sense that they are the result of a social consensus as to whether they are right or wrong.

Because of the limitations of these two sources, criteria have been adopted based on either the consequences of adopting a particular set of moral rules, or our supposed faculty of moral intuition. First, this rule consequentialism differs from the act consequentialism adopted by utilitarianism because it states that, in effect, "the rightness of a particular action lies in its conformity with the proper moral rule; the properness of the moral rule, in turn is based on the value of the consequences of it being followed."

Second, the intuitionist approach holds that our special faculty of moral intuition tells us which actions have the inherent properties of being morally right. Rule-based moralists can accommodate most of the weaknesses of utilitarianism. The weaknesses correspond to the strengths of utilitarianism.

The Notion of Fittingness

Because of the strengths and limitations of both utilitarianism and deontological ethics, a suitable compromise would be ideal. One compromise suggested by W. W. May is to use aspects of both approaches. An alternative to both utilitarianism and deontological ethics is offered by the notion of fittingness.

Fittingness, from the ancient Greek concept of *kathokonda,* may be used to evaluate the morality of actions by a reference to whether they are appropriate and proper with the *ethos* shared by the individual and the society. Martin Heidegger speaks of ethos as comprised of "freely accepted obligations and traditions," of "that which concerns free behaviour and attitudes," and of "the shaping of man's historical being.

" The ethos defines the fitting response, the arena for moral discourse and action. Compared to the other views of ethics the notion of fittingness proposes a dramatic shift. As Calvin Schrag states:

This shift is a shift away from the primacy of theological inquiry (what is the end of man in terms of his nature-conferred essence?), the primacy of deontological inquiry (what is the unconditional duty of man?) and the primacy of utilitarian inquiry (what is the greatest good for the greatest number?).

The question "How does one perform a fitting response?" is, we submit, more originative than inquiry about ends, duties and the good. It is only by addressing this question that ends duties, and the good achieve a context for definition.

The notion of fittingness places the individual in a context of responsibility and responsiveness to the ethos in which are gathered the social and political concerns of the society around him or her. To Reinhold Niebuhr, the fitting action is part of the ethics of responsibility. How others reacted to a previous act and how they will react to a similar act determines a responsible act. The responsible act must interpret the old reactions and fit itself in the new reactions. Fittingness becomes the criteria for evaluating moral choice. As stated again by Schrag: "The language of morality is the language of responsiveness and responsibility and if there is to be talk of 'an ethics' in all this it will need to be an ethics of the fitting response."

MORAL DEVELOPMENT

To uncover the general interpretive framework that a person brings to moral problems, moral judgment research attempts to examine the reasons individuals give for their decisions when faced with a variety of moral dilemma situations.

The approach rests on L. Kohlberg's research in cognitive development. The thesis is that individuals progress from lower stages of development to higher stages unless deprivations for opportunities for social interaction are used to retard their development.

Accordingly, Kohlberg's identified three general levels of moral thought, with each level consisting of two stages. Each stage of moral development constitutes a unique way of defining a given moral dilemma and of evaluating critical issues related to the moral situation under consideration. Each stage of moral development explicates how judgments are made and why a particular judgment was made. The six stages identified by Kohlberg are as follows.

Preconventional level

Stage 1: Internal Compulsion and Power. The physical consequences of actions determine their goodness or badness. Avoidance of punishment and unquestioning deference to power are valued in their own right. Basically punishment and obedience constitute the basis of moral order.

Stage 2: Simple Interpersonal Exchange and Need Satisfaction. Right actions satisfy one's own needs, and occasionally the needs of others, when reciprocity is present. Basically, instrumentalism and relativism constitute the basis of moral order.

Conventional Level

Stage 3: Maintaining Positive Interpersonal Relationships. Good behaviour is what pleases or helps others and is approved by them. Conformity to stereotypical images of what is common or natural behaviour wins approval by others. Basically, interpersonal concordance constitutes the basis of moral order.

Stage 4: Maintaining Social Order. Right behaviour consists of doing one's duty, showing respect for authority, and maintaining the social order for its own sake. Basically law and order constitute the basis of moral order.

Postconventional level

Stage 5: Intuitive Individualism and Humanism. Right actions are defined by general individual rights and standards agreed upon by society. Outside what is agreed upon by society, the right is a matter of personal values and opinions. Basically, the social contract constitutes the basis of moral order.

Stage 6: Individual Conscience. Right is defined by the decision of conscience in accord with self-chosen ethical principles of justice, equality, and dignity of human beings. Basically, ethics and principles constitute the basis of moral order.

J. R. Rest developed the Defining Issues Test (DIT) to gauge moral judgment development and determine the subject's stage of moral reasoning. The DIT is an objective measure composed of six moral dilemmas, each one describing a situation with competing social claims. The output of the test is a "P" (for principled) score. It is "interpreted as the relative importance a subject gives to principled moral considerations in making a decision about moral dilemmas." It indicates what percent of a subject's thinking is at a principled level (i.e., levels 5 and 6 in Kohlberg's model).

The accounting studies relied on the DIT to assess the moral reasoning of accounting subjects. The first study by M. B. Armstrong compared accounting practitioners (CPAS) to a broad section of college students, college graduate students, and adults. The practitioners' "P" score was lower than those of college students, college graduate students, and adults. These results are indeed disturbing:

"These results initiate that the CPA respondents appear to have reached the moral maturation level of adults in general, instead of maturing even to the level of college students, much less to the level of college graduates. In other words, their college education may not have fostered continued moral growth."

The second study by St. Pierre et al. examined the ethical development of seniors in ten different disciplines representing business and nonbusiness majors. Accounting majors and the other business disciplines scored lower than the students in the three nonbusiness majors. The results also raise disturbing questions:

Given that the majors outside the College of Business performed better in the DIT (statistically higher, except for Finance) and that the norm groups for college seniors in general performed better than the College of Business seniors, what can we say about the efforts of the profession in the ethics area? Does the moral atmosphere of the business school affect our majors' ethical development?

Are the nonbusiness majors exposed to an educational atmosphere or socialization process that is conducive to ethical development? A question that is even more basic focuses on the type of individual selecting business as a field study. Is it possible that, due to self-selection, those entering the business discipline are Stage 4 personality types and will function at that level regardless of the socialization process?

A more important question is whether or not students entering the accounting field are Stage 4 and will stay at that stage given the absence of teaching ethics in the accounting curriculum, and the absence of moral socialization process in the practice of accounting. It may also explain the findings that accounting students showed strong adherence to social norms and values. That is very characteristic of Stage 4 personality types. These results argue for major changes in the accounting curriculum and practice to instill higher moral principles in those choosing the accounting discipline.

THE TEACHING AND RESEARCH OF ACCOUNTING ETHICS

The call for accounting ethics was strongly made by the Report of the National Commission on Fraudulent Financial Reporting (the Treadway Commission). The Commission argued that "the independent public accountant's responsibility and accountability to the public requires a much broader exposure to ethics. Business schools should include ethics discussions in every accounting course." It also recommends that "business and accounting curricula should emphasize ethical values by integrating their development with the acquisition of knowledge and skills to help prevent, detect, and deter fraudulent financial reporting." The American Accounting Association Committee on the Future Structure, Content, and Scope of Accounting Education notes that "professional accounting education... must... instill the ethical standards and the commitment of a professional."

The teaching of ethics courses in business schools is on the increase. Auditing appears to be the only accounting course where there is a significant integration of ethics and accounting. Various reasons may explain this situ-ation:

- The textbook coverage of ethical and fraudulent financial reporting is minimal and focuses largely on reviewing the Code of Professional Ethics of the AICPA, forcing the accounting educators to devote a lot of resources to cover ethics in their courses;
- Business schools foster a climate where there is not a good understanding of ethics, business school professors rely heavily on the economic concept of Pareto optimality, and ethics issues are considered "soft" and unscientific;
- There is a belief that accounting faculty cannot solve the moral and ethical problems of the accounting profession. Cheryl Lehman warns, however, about four possible misinterpretations in the advocacy for accounting ethics:

First, we do not suggest that ethics are desirable because they will ensure survival of the system. There is a danger that educators will justify ethical practices as a public relations strategy (i.e., a practice to be followed because it increases goodwill and profits).

This would clearly distort the fundamental meaning of ethics and would perpetuate accounting ethics as an oxymoron — a self-contradiction — because an accounting culture reifying ethics for profits does not harmonize with the concept of ethics.

Second, we do not purport that the problematic consequences of unethical behaviour are the detriments to business referred to earlier (e.g., increased competition for clients in the securities market). Rather, we wish to highlight the broad deleterious effects on the environment, the sacrifice of human lives, the suffering of employees as the outcomes of unethical behaviour (e.g., Hooker Chemical's waste disposal in Love Canal, Nestlé's international promotion of powdered milk, the use of asbestos by Manville's employees).

A third misinterpretation would be to conclude that the task of educators is merely to prompt individuals to be more ethical. Education in ethics must go beyond the study of good deeds versus rapacious acts of individuals — a redefinition of inquiry into the subject is needed. Educators and students should be questioning the institutionalization of inequalities that empower some groups over others; they need to explore political constraints regarding ethics and challenge accepted hierarchies of power and control, and they should investigate the role of accounting in social conflicts.

The fourth possible misreading, related to the preceding points, concerns the political and regulatory arena. We do not view regulation as captured and beneficial only to some interest: rather, regulatory mechanisms are potentially useful for promoting moral values. We fail to usurp their potential by continuing to teach accounting and business (i.e., economic issues) as if they were separate from sociopolitical issues; this is neither desirable or possible.

Index

A

B

C

D

E

F

G

H

I

Q

R

S

T

U

V